THE PERFORMING ARTS MAJOR'S COLLEGE GUIDE

ARCO

THE PERFORMING ARTS MAJOR'S COLLEGE GUIDE

CAROLE J. EVERETT
Director of Admissions, The Juilliard School

Prentice Hall
New York • London • Toronto • Sydney • Tokyo • Singapore

First Edition

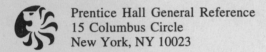

Prentice Hall General Reference
15 Columbus Circle
New York, NY 10023

An Arco Book

ARCO and PRENTICE HALL are registered trademarks
of Prentice-Hall, Inc.
Colophon is a trademark of Prentice-Hall, Inc.

Library of Congress Cataloging-in-Publication Data

Everett, Carole J.
   The performing arts major's college guide / Carole J. Everett.
      p. cm.
   ISBN 0-13-086679-2
   1. Performing arts—Study and teaching (Higher)—
United States—Directories. I. Title.
PN1577.E94   1992
791'.071'173—dc20   92-5355
                                        CIP

Manufactured in the United States of America

2 3 4 5 6 7 8 9 10

Designed by Cynthia Mortt Lamb

Contents

Introduction

At the annual convention of the National Association of College Admissions Counselors (NACAC) a few years ago, I served as moderator of a panel discussion titled "Counseling Students Gifted in the Performing Arts: Dance, Drama, Music." The session was well attended by college admissions professionals, high school guidance counselors, and independent counselors. The panelists included a college counselor from a New England boarding school, a headmaster of an arts magnet school, and another director of admissions from a university with programs in dance, drama, and music. During the question-and-answer period after the presentations, there was unanimous agreement that there must be a book written about this topic. I told the audience that I would write it.

Later that year I attended the conference of The Network of Visual and Performing Arts Schools, an organization of arts magnet and other specialized schools, both secondary and postsecondary. During one of the meetings a conversation took place about conservatory requirements and the difficulty teachers and counselors have in giving up-to-date and comprehensive advice to students who wish to go on in music, dance, or drama. Once again there was the request that "someone should write a book," and I mentioned that I was working on just such a reference guide.

This past year, James Gandre, director of admissions at The Manhattan School of Music, moderated a panel discussion about counseling students gifted in the performing arts. This time the panelists included William Banchs, president of the National Foundation for the Advancement of the Arts; Jamie Kirkpatrick, director of college counseling, Duke Ellington High School, Washington, D.C.; and me. Once again, it was clear that there is a great need for specialized information for performing arts majors. This book addresses the issues every performing arts major faces:

□ finding the best programs in dance, drama, and music;

□ choosing between college or conservatory;

□ preparing for the all-important audition; and

□ fulfilling entry requirements for performing arts programs nationwide.

Acknowledgments

Family, friends, colleagues, and acquaintances have all been instrumental in this project, providing information, guidance, and emotional support, as well as beautiful places to write. My sincere gratitude goes to the following:

Carolyn Adams, Stephen Albert, Joseph Alessi, Nancy Allen, Tracey Andersen, Toby Appel, Milton Babbitt, Buster Bailey, Bill Banchs, Jill Beck, Linda Bernbach, Edith Bers, Liz Chryst Bert, Carter Brey, Leonard and Janet Brown, Jr., Louis Jean Brunelli, Stephen Burns, Martin Canin, Colin Carr, Brian Cassier, Nico and Carol Castel, Alice Chalifoux, Cal Chaney, Linda Chesis, Stephen Clapp, Judy Clurman, Larry Combs, Roberta Cooper, Conrad Cummings, Harold Danko, Immanuel Davis, Warren Deck, Dorothy DeLay, Glenn Dicterow, Eugene Drucker, Mikael Eliasen, Patrick and Debby Everett, Mr. and Mrs. C. J. Everett, Jr., Gary Fagin, Jonathan Feldman, Daniel Ferro, Joseph Flummerfelt, Albert Fuller, Jim Gandre, Margo Garrett, Jon Gillock, Gordon Gottlieb, Jane Gottlieb, Mark Gould, Bill Graham, Maria Grandy, Shirley Greitzer, Don Harwood, Stanley Hastey, David Heid, Jane Hewes, Cynthia Hoffman, Linda Hohenfeld, Ed Houser, Sharon Isbin, Usman and Kathleen Ismail, Amy Kaiser, Lewis Kaplan, Ann and Morgan Keefe, Richard Kilmer, Jamie Kirkpatrick, Jeannette Kreston, Michelle Krisel, Julie Landsman, Alecia Lawyer, Frank Leana, Judith LeClair, Eugene Levinson, Jeanne Lewin, Steven Lipman, Yunsha Liu, Larry Loesser, Jerome Lowenthal, Bruce MacCombie, John Mack, Marlena Kleinman Malas, Ray Mase, Stephen Maxym, Homer Mensch, Richard Moll, Charles Neidich, Richard O'Meara, Ted O'Neill, Vincent Panzarelli, Lionel Party, Maitland Peters, Jackson Phippin, Joseph W. Polisi, William Purvis, Michael Recchiuti, Andrea Redcay, Ronald Roseman, Ronnie Rubin, Samuel Sanders, Peter Serkin, Fred Sherry, Renee Siebert, Jeanne Siegal, Leonard Slatkin, Joel Smirnoff, Tom Stacy, Herbert Stessin, Richard Stoltzman, David Stull, Sally Thomas, Muriel Topaz, Karen Tuttle, Keith Underwood, Ben Verdery, Karen Wagner, David Wakefield, David Walter, Steve Walton, John Weaver, Carol Wincenc, Ethel Winter, Melora Wolff, John Wustman, Andrew Yarosh, and Philip Yee.

Special thanks go to my mother, Phyllis Drew Mahoney, and eternal appreciation for his loving encouragement and wisdom goes to my husband, C. J. Everett.

1
The College Admissions Process

Choosing Your Educational Future

Self-Assessment

Choosing a college is a great challenge for every student. When you have special talent in the performing arts, the choice is even more critical and you must make some personal assessments at a rather early stage about priorities, goals, professional commitment, and direction for your future. It is important that you take the time to be brutally honest with yourself as you examine your values, strengths, weaknesses, and dreams. It is also essential that you find the college program that will be best for you. As a performing artist, you must begin this process early enough to prepare for any auditions required. While most students start the college admissions process in the spring of their junior year, performing arts majors should begin to explore colleges and programs in their sophomore year.

Start your personal assessment by answering the questions that follow:

☐ How do I like to spend my time? What makes me happiest? What bores me to tears?

☐ What am I good at? Where do my academic strengths lie? What do I never want to have to study again?

☐ Why do I want to go to college? What do I expect to gain? What am I looking forward to?

☐ Do I want to stay close to home or go away? How often do I expect to come home during the course of a year?

☐ What kind of surroundings make me happiest? City? Country? Suburbia? Am I sensitive to weather—do I hate the cold or heat?

☐ What kind of people do I like to be around?

☐ What values are most important to me? What do I care most about?

☐ What kind of person do I want to become?

☐ What has been the best decision I've made in the past three years? Why?

☐ What has been the worst decision I've made in the past three years? Why? What did I learn from that experience?

☐ What decisions have I let others (parents, teachers, friends, etc.) make for me? Why? What was the outcome?

☐ How free do I feel to make my own college decisions? Do my parents generally agree with my plans for college? How important to me are the opinions of family? Friends? Teachers?

☐ Is there anything preventing me from enrolling in a postsecondary program (college, conservatory, etc.) right out of high school?

☐ What do I think about general education (liberal arts) versus specialization (conservatory training)? How does this relate to the way I want to spend my time?

☐ What is my favorite postsecondary program now? What characteristics make this program my favorite?

☐ How do I feel about the size of an institution? Do I work best in small groups? With lots of individual attention? Do I like larger settings?

☐ How do I respond to competition? Do I thrive on pressure or need a more nurturing environment? Do I want a program in which I must work hard constantly, or would I prefer one in which I can obtain respectable grades without knocking myself out? How would I feel if I were in the middle or at the bottom of my class? Is it important to me to be near the top of the class?

☐ How do I learn best? What teachers and methods of teaching have worked best for me?

☐ How would I feel about a program in which there are few requirements? How much structure is best for me?

☐ How have I done in high school? Where are my academic strengths? What are my standardized test scores (on PSATs, SATs, ACTs, or achievement tests)? Is my academic record an accurate measure of my ability? What do I consider the best measures of my potential for college work?

Once you have answered these questions and ones that you, your parents, your guidance counselor, and your teachers will also pose, you can begin your search for the best program for you. Guard against choosing the "designer-label" school of the year. Look, instead, for an institution where you will be able to learn, grow, have fun, make friends, and cultivate your special talents. This is an exciting time. It is also a time when you have more control over your choices than you probably imagine. Colleges and conservatories all compete for students. If you choose five to eight appropriate schools and if you do your best in the application, interview, and audition process, you may find yourself with multiple acceptances. You are the consumer and schools need you. So, you see, you control your future.

Assessing Your Talent

Sometimes it's difficult to know how you measure up in terms of talent. Many of you have starred in a high school musical, sung solos with a glee club, and perhaps even attended a district or all-state band or chorus. Everyone in the community raves about your talent and you think you want to develop it still further at college. But how do you really know if you've got what it takes? Your answers to the following questions may help you clarify just how dedicated you are to the development of your talent.

Dancers

- ☐ Are you taking classes regularly? In ballet? In modern dance?

- ☐ Do you enjoy taking classes?

- ☐ What is the background of your teacher(s)? What feedback have you received?

- ☐ How many public performances have you done? How did you feel during the rehearsal stage? During the performance? Afterwards?

- ☐ Have you auditioned for any competitive summer programs? For regional productions? What was the outcome?

- ☐ Do you have the body type suitable for further study in dance? Have you ever had a weight problem?

- ☐ What books about dance have you read?

- ☐ What performances have you seen?

- ☐ Do you feel that you are musical or musically sensitive?

- ☐ Do you enjoy the physicality of dance?

- ☐ Are you self-motivated regarding dance?

- ☐ Do you remember the sequences of dance steps well?

- ☐ Are you self-disciplined?

- ☐ Do you eat, drink, breathe, and dream dance? Are you prepared to make the sacrifices necessary to make your passion to study dance a reality?

- ☐ Is there anything else you could pursue that would make you happy? (If you answer "yes" to this, you probably should decide not to follow a full-time dance program of study.)

Actors

- ☐ Have you participated in theater productions in your school? How did you feel during the rehearsal stage? During the production? Afterwards?

- ☐ Have you taken any acting classes? Singing? Movement? Improvisation?

- ☐ Are you prepared to meet both the physical and emotional demands of acting?

- ☐ What is the background of your principle acting teacher? Director? What feedback have you received?

- ☐ Do you know your "type"?

- ☐ Do you memorize well? Quickly?

- ☐ What kind of acting are you interested in? Film? TV? Theater?

- ☐ Do you have the patience for the hours of memorizing and sometimes tedious rehearsals required of actors?

- ☐ Do you have the emotional fortitude to deal with the inevitable rejection that accompanies life in the theater?

- ☐ Are you aware that show business is really just that: a business? How will you feel about dealing with the business side of the entertainment industry?

- ☐ Is there anything else you could pursue that would make you happy? (If you answer "yes" to this, you should probably decide not to follow a full-time drama program of study.)

Musicians

- ☐ How many years of study have you had on your major instrument?

- ☐ Have you studied intensively with a private teacher? What is that teacher's background? What feedback does your teacher give you?

- ☐ Do you listen to music regularly? To recordings? To the radio? Do you attend classical concerts as well as alternative performance events?

- ☐ Have you prepared the repertoire required for any auditions?

- ☐ Have you participated in musical events in your school? How did you feel during the rehearsals? During the performances? Afterwards?

- ☐ Have you auditioned for and been accepted at any competitive programs? All-state programs? District programs? Youth symphonies or community choruses? Bands? Summer programs?

- ☐ Have you been a soloist? How often?

- ☐ Have you studied any music theory? Sight reading? Music history?

- ☐ How many hours a day do you practice?

- ☐ Do you have the emotional fortitude to deal with the inevitable rejection that accompanies the audition process?

- ☐ Are you realistic about the business nature of the music industry?

- ☐ Is there anything else you could pursue that would make you happy? (If you answer "yes" to this, you should probably decide not to follow a full-time music program of study.)

Getting Objective Opinions about Your Talent

It is sometimes possible to arrange an "advisory" audition to help you determine your level of expertise. In dance, you might call your regional ballet company for a referral to a teacher who can provide an objective evaluation of your ability. Does that teacher think that you are ready to audition for a regional company or a conservatory program? Or, should you consider dance only as an avocation?

In drama, it is virtually impossible to do an advisory audition for a selective school program. You might call a casting director or ask a working actor for some advice. It is not wise to send an unsolicited videotape of your monologues to programs in which you are interested. The admissions committee wants to see you in person or at a regional audition. Your best bet is to participate in your school and community theater group and in summer drama programs. Investigate taking private classes, too, if they are offered in your area. For your further education, the best recommendation is to follow a liberal arts program of study with specific training in drama after two to four years of more general education.

In classical instrumental music, it is common for well-known teachers to give advisory auditions or consultations. If you live near a conservatory or plan to visit one, write to a teacher in advance and request a consultation or lesson. (Be prepared to pay for this, however. See the section on researching teachers in the Music Auditions chapter in Part Four.) If you do not live in the vicinity of a conservatory, try calling the nearest regional orchestra and asking if the principal player on your instrument is willing to hear you and give an opinion. For popular music, you might ask about sitting in with some "name" players and seeking their opinion and advice. Or you might ask if they would be willing to listen to a live or taped performance and give you an evaluation.

For singers, it is a bit more difficult to get an objective opinion. At 17 or 18, very few singers have the physical development to reveal the true quality of their voice. While there may seem to be potential, it is usually very raw talent. Unfortunately, some voice teachers are happy to string students along as long as they are paying for regular lessons. Choir directors or directors of musical theater are usually very encouraging of young singers. However, before young singers become deluded with the sense of having a major career in opera, they should seek some objective assessment of their talent. Some colleges and conservatories are now requiring videotapes for first-time college applicants as a way of pre-screening. As with drama majors, young singers should plan on at least two years of liberal arts, studying foreign languages (especially French, Italian, and German), literature, history, and economics, as well as music theory, music history, ear training, and, especially, sight singing. Because of everything from basic physical development to hormonal changes in the body, the voice is slower to develop and so there is time for general study.

Composers and conductors have an even more difficult time obtaining an early assessment. Composers might write in advance to ask a faculty member to evaluate copies of scores. Conductors might inquire about sending videotapes of performances.

Educational Choices

Once you have done some self-evaluation, you will probably find that you fall into one of the following groups:

A. You are sure that you want to focus on your performing art now and will apply only to conservatory or preprofessional programs or audition for companies.

B. You are not quite sure that you want to be totally focused on your performing art. You want to keep your options open and plan to apply to conservatories, joint programs, and liberal arts colleges with strong performing arts programs. You will explore Bachelor of Arts (BA), Bachelor of Fine Arts (BFA), and/or Bachelor of Music (BM) degree programs.

C. You are not clear about the level of your talent, or you may think that you have talent in more than one area and want to expand your background before focusing. You think that applying to liberal arts colleges or universities is best for you at this time.

Many students do end up changing their majors; therefore, if you are the least bit uncertain about pursuing an area within performing arts, you should keep your options open by choosing an institution that has a good department in the area of your main interest but also has general distribution requirements. If you end up changing your major, chances are that it is because another department within the college or university offered courses that inspired you.

Whichever category best describes you, there are certain procedures in the college admissions process that are common to all programs. The next chapters will discuss various aspects of the entire admissions process and then focus specifically on the unique requirements for dance, drama, and music auditions and applications.

Beginning the College Search

Obtaining Catalogs

Start your college search by calling or writing to the schools that interest you for catalogs and admissions information. If you call, be prepared to give your name, address, area of concentration, birth date, and social security number. (If you do not have a social security number, now would be a good time to get one; you'll need it for computer identification.) If you write, follow the style of the sample letter on page 7.

Once you have made initial contact with a school, whether by telephone or by letter, most schools will set up a computer file on you. They will send you materials and may even deluge you with propaganda. Now it is your job to assess this information critically and systematically.

Sally Smith
1 Main Street
Anywhere, ST
April 9, 1992

Dear Director of Admissions:

I am currently a sophomore at Anywhere High School and am interested in learning more about (name of school). Could you please send me your most recent course catalog, an application, and any other admissions information. I am interested in studying dance (or drama or music—and specify instrument) further in college, so any specific information about your program in (your performing art) would be very helpful. I would also like to learn about any financial aid or other scholarship information.

Thank you for your attention to this request.

Sincerely,

Sally Smith
(Social Security Number)

Organizing Your College Notebook

The best way to organize your college information is to set up your own college notebook. You can use it to keep track of your mailings, to make checklists for yourself, and to record your impressions of each school. Start with an entry like the one on page 8.

Set up a page in your college notebook to keep track of your impressions of each school you contact. Use a list like the one on page 9 or one of your own design.

My Criteria for Postsecondary Education

Type of School
- ❏ Liberal Arts College
- ❏ University
- ❏ Conservatory
- ❏ Joint Program

Student Body
- ❏ Single-Sex
- ❏ Co-ed
- ❏ Historically Black

Setting
- ❏ Rural
- ❏ Small Town
- ❏ Small City
- ❏ Large City

Size of School
- ❏ Very Small (under 1,000 students)
- ❏ Small (1,000 – 3,000 students)
- ❏ Medium (3,000 – 8,000 students)
- ❏ Large (8,000 – 20,000 students)
- ❏ Very Large (over 20,000 students)

Special Programs
- ❏ Dance
- ❏ Drama
- ❏ Music
- ❏ Other: _____

_____

_____

_____

The College Catalog

Much of the information about each school can be gleaned from the college catalog. This publication contains a wealth of material about the size, location, history, philosophy, calendar, costs, admissions policies, financial aid availability, faculty, and degree requirements of a school. Reading it carefully and critically will help illuminate the differences among schools. For instance, if you want to be a drama major at a liberal arts college but hate to write papers, a college that requires a written senior thesis may not be appropriate. Or, if you are a dancer and never want to take another foreign language course, a program that requires you to show proficiency in at least one foreign language may not be the one for you. Reading the catalog will help you narrow your list, come up with intelligent questions to ask your interviewer, and give you the most objective information on the policies, procedures, and climate of a campus.

Viewbooks and Videos

Because there is great competition among schools for qualified students, many colleges have produced glossy viewbooks and professional videos to send to prospective students. These are often written and produced by public relations or marketing specialists and include glamorous photos of the campus at its best, with the most photogenic students and the perfect view of buildings. While viewbooks and videos can give you some flavor of a campus, they should not replace your own research with a careful reading of the course catalog and a campus visit if possible.

School Impressions

Name of school:
  Address: Phone:

Date information requested:

Tests required:

Audition required:
  Dates and locations of auditions: Tapes or videotapes accepted?

Interview required:
  Date of interview appointment:
  Name of interviewer:
  Date thank-you note sent:

Date letter sent to faculty member you want as teacher:

Financial aid available:

Impressions of campus visit:
  Weather

  Architecture (Gothic, Modern, Colonial, etc.)

  Students (preppy, artsy, friendly, etc.)

  Social life (active, dull, wild parties, etc.)

  Housing (on-campus, off-campus, dorms, apartments)

  Food

  Overall facilities (practice rooms, library, theaters, etc.)

Recreation and activities:

Student services (psychological support, tutoring, health care):

Community environment (big city, small town, rural, etc.):

Academics (degrees granted, majors offered):

Faculty (big names?):

Special programs:

Things I liked most:

Things I liked least:

Decision:
  Think I'll apply
  Cross this one off the list because:

Narrowing the List

After you have read the college catalogs (some students send for 25 to 50 catalogs at first), you should be able to narrow your list of schools to 12 to 18 that seriously interest you. This list should reflect a range of selectivity, including some "reaches," "possibles," and "safeties." Other means of gathering more information about these schools before deciding to visit include:

☐ speaking to your guidance counselor and reviewing the entire list;

☐ speaking with any students in your area who attend the college and are home on vacation;

☐ obtaining names of alumni in your area and speaking with them;

☐ talking to your current teachers about colleges and conservatories;

☐ attending college fairs and speaking with admissions representatives; and

☐ attending meetings where college and conservatory admissions representatives are available to answer your questions.

A Word about Decision Plans

Colleges and conservatories have many different policies for applying. In narrowing your list, you should also consider whether you want to play a strategy game and juggle application deadlines and decision plans. For instance, if you have decided to apply to liberal arts colleges or universities and have fallen in love with one particular college, you might consider applying by an Early Decision plan, if the college has one. This plan means that you apply early to that one school and if you are admitted, you must attend. Other plans include Early Action (you apply early and get an early reply, but do not have to make the commitment to attend right away) and Rolling Decision plans (decisions are made on a first-come, first-served basis). There are strategy games that you can play with deadlines and decision plans. Be a smart applicant and see if any will work for you.

If you are applying to conservatories, the traditional time to apply is in January for auditions in February or March, when most conservatories have their main auditions. Since some conservatories also have later auditions, you might juggle the audition process, applying to your first choice and auditioning in March and, if admitted, attending, but if not, doing further auditions in May. You do gamble when taking this approach, as some departments may close, but more about this in the music chapter.

Campus Visits

Once you have narrowed your list further, you may want to visit a campus. There is really no substitute for seeing a campus yourself, experiencing the atmosphere, meeting students, sitting in on classes, and picturing yourself in the environment. If a school requires an interview and you are ready, you can combine the campus visit with the interview. "Drop-ins" at an admissions office are not necessarily welcome. It's worthwhile to call ahead and schedule an appointment.

When to Visit

There are advantages and disadvantages to the timing of the visit.

Spring of Junior Year

Many students try to visit three or four colleges during spring break of their junior year. The problem with this is that many college admissions offices are at their busiest at this time, holding auditions or finalizing decisions on students who have applied. While you may be able to take a campus tour and speak to some students, this may not be a good time for your college interview.

Summer between Junior and Senior Year

The advantage of a summer visit is that the admissions office is more relaxed and you may be given more time and personal attention. You can go on a campus tour and see the facilities, but, unless there is a summer session, you cannot get the flavor of the campus in action. Your family may want to include a few summer visits to colleges as part of a vacation trip, or you may plan to visit before your summer program starts or after your summer job ends.

Fall of Senior Year

This is probably the best time to visit the colleges in which you are interested. Just be careful not to miss so much of your own school that you fall behind in your classes. First-semester senior-year grades are extremely important. Some high schools set aside college visiting days and there are also the traditional fall holidays (Columbus Day, Jewish High Holy Days) when many colleges are open and may have classes in session. Be sure to make appointments for these times well in advance of your visit.

When Not to Visit

It is not a good idea to visit a campus when the admissions office is closed or on major holiday breaks, such as Thanksgiving, Christmas, or New Year's. Other dates to avoid include pre-exam, exam, and jury weeks. While some colleges have Saturday morning interviews during the busy fall, there are seldom classes you can sit in on over the weekend.

The Ideal Visit

It is best to arrive on a weekday afternoon. Take an admissions-sponsored guided tour of the campus, stay over in a dormitory with an admissions host or with a friend who attends the school, eat in the cafeteria, and observe and talk to as many students as possible. Try to attend a concert or production that evening. In the morning sit in on some classes, watch a rehearsal or coaching, and speak to faculty members. (Arrange for this in advance.) If an interview is recommended or required, have your interview, preferably after lunch.

What to Look for When You Visit

You want to gather as much information as possible during your visit. Pick up a copy of the campus newspaper, read bulletin boards to see the variety of activities announced, and look at the ride board. Are students going away every weekend? Get the calendar of events for the week or month during which you are visiting. Does it represent a variety of activities? Look through a yearbook if possible. Observe the people around you. Are they "your kind of people"? Sit in on a rehearsal. What is the level of expertise? Explore the surrounding neighborhood. Do you feel safe? Does it provide the kind of environment which makes you feel comfortable?

Questions to Ask Your Tour Guide

Here are some general questions that you might ask your tour guide or student host. (Specific questions about your area in the performing arts are covered in later chapters.)

- ☐ How diverse is the student body? Where are students from? Do they represent different racial, ethnic, and economic backgrounds?

- ☐ What percentage of the student body is from abroad? Which countries are represented by the most students?

- ☐ What do students like most about College X? What are the most frequent complaints?

- ☐ How would you describe the overall tone (attitude, morale) of the campus?

- ☐ What have been the issues or tensions on the campus this year?

- ☐ What do students do for fun?

- ☐ What do students typically do on a weekend?

- ☐ What is the role of fraternities and sororities?

- ☐ What sports are available?

- ☐ What extracurricular activities are strongly supported by the administration?

- ☐ Are faculty generally accessible?

- ☐ What is the workload like? How would you describe competition among students?

- ☐ What were the cultural highlights of last year? The social highlights?

- ☐ What are the housing options for freshmen? For transfers? Are there single-sex floors? Nonsmoking dorms? Quiet study facilities?

- ☐ How are roommates chosen?

- ☐ What kind of meal plans are offered? Is there vegetarian or kosher food? Must I subscribe to the meal plan if I live in college housing?

- ☐ Are student health services provided? Is a doctor, nurse, or psychologist provided at no additional charge?

☐ How is the library? The media center? Are there any student complaints about these facilities?

☐ What is the relationship between the college and the surrounding town or city?

☐ How are the academics? Are there any outstanding faculty members I should know about?

☐ When you register for classes, what percentage of courses that you want to take are you able to enroll in?

☐ Is the campus safe? What are the crime statistics? (Colleges are now required to make crime statistics available to the public.)

☐ Are there problems with drugs or alcohol?

☐ How are racial relations on the campus?

☐ Is there career counseling? What do most graduates do?

If you have questions that your tour guide cannot answer, ask your interviewer or speak to an admissions counselor.

Follow-up to Your Visit

After your visit, it is appropriate to write a thank-you note to your interviewer. It may be just a simple, handwritten note saying that you enjoyed the conversation and look forward to applying to College X, or you may want to add something to the conversation you had. Often this note becomes part of your file, and admissions officers tend to react favorably to finding a thoughtful note among all the other information there. You should also write a note of thanks to your host, if you stayed over.

Record your impressions in your college notebook as soon as possible after your visit. Be careful not to be overly influenced by personalities on a campus. Although admissions representatives tend to be positive and perky types, anyone can have a bad day. If someone is abrupt or less than friendly, you should not let this color your view of the entire campus. Also, beware of thinking that a school seen on a perfect, sunny, crisp fall day is more appealing than another school seen on a gloomy, rainy day. Be honest with yourself, too. A prestigious school visited under ideal conditions may be seductive, but is it the right match for you?

If You Are Unable to Visit

If financial restrictions, time restrictions, or other reasons make it impossible to visit a campus, you should call the admissions office and find out about alumni, current students, and admissions representatives living or traveling in your area. Try to schedule an interview with one of these individuals for firsthand information—and request the college video if one exits.

College Interviews

When you read the catalog, note whether an interview is optional or required. (Let's keep this topic separate from auditions, which are quite another matter and discussed in later chapters.) Because of staff restrictions, travel difficulties, and financial constraints, very few colleges make the interview mandatory. If you do decide to have an interview, never drop in—be sure to make the arrangements well in advance.

What to Expect from a College Interview

This is your opportunity to be more than just a stack of papers in the admissions office; it's a chance to personalize the process. Interviews do not usually make or break admissions decisions, but you should try to have an interview at those schools that are of real interest to you and are realistic choices.

Timing of Interviews

If you are prepared, plan your interviews as part of your campus visit. Don't schedule your first interview at your first-choice school; you'll do better after you've had some experience in an interview situation. Try to avoid making your first-choice school your last interview, also, as you want to remain fresh and spontaneous in your responses.

Practice interviews are helpful to some students. Ask your guidance counselor to conduct a mock interview with you or have a family friend role-play with you.

Schedule all interviews well in advance. And, if you cannot attend an interview appointment, be sure to call and cancel. A cancellation will not be held against you, but a missed appointment probably will be.

What to Wear

Just as there are costumes for performances, there are interview "costumes." For women, a nice skirt (not too short) and a blouse, possibly with a blazer, or a simple dress is recommended, worn with low to medium heels. Men should wear nice pants with a shirt, jacket, and tie or with a turtleneck or shirt and sweater.

Before Your Interview

Preparing for an interview is important. Be sure to read the catalog and write down a list of questions that you want to ask. Take time to think about your strengths and weaknesses, and be prepared to speak about them in a positive way. College interviews are not the time for modesty and monosyllabic answers. At the same time, you do not want to appear boastful and arrogant.

Take stock of the extracurricular activities in which you have participated, your hobbies, volunteer work, and other ways that you spend your time. If there are special circumstances in your life that have affected your academic record, you may want to bring them up at an interview. For instance, if you missed a great deal of school because you had a heavy performance schedule but were able to make up the work, or if your family went through a particularly grueling year, with divorce, unemployment, or sickness, you may want to talk about it with your interviewer. Take care not to sound as though you are making excuses for yourself, but rather adding to the college's understanding of who you are.

What Not to Do at Your Interview

Here are some things you should NOT do at an interview:

- ☐ smoke;

- ☐ chew gum;

- ☐ complain or make excuses;

- ☐ swear or use language that is too colloquial;

- ☐ exhibit a negative attitude (bored, arrogant, etc.);

- ☐ answer in monosyllables or one-sentence answers;

- ☐ ask questions if you have no interest in the response;

- ☐ ask for an evaluation of another school you are considering;

- ☐ bring your scrapbook of programs, reviews, articles, or term papers for the interviewer to read;

- ☐ twitch, fidget, or slump in your seat; or

- ☐ pretend to be someone you are not. BE YOURSELF!

Typical Interview Questions

Every interviewer has his or her favorite questions, but there are some common areas that are covered in most interviews. These include:

- ☐ your high school experience;

- ☐ your personal traits, relationships with others, and your family background;

- ☐ your interests outside the classroom—hobbies, extracurricular activities, summer vacations, movies you've seen, etc.;

- ☐ your values and goals, and how you view the world around you;

- ☐ your impressions of the college you are visiting;

- ☐ answering your questions.

You might anticipate questions like these:

Tell me about your high school. How long have you attended? What are the students like? Do you like your high school? What would you preserve or change about it?

Which courses have you liked most? Which least? Which have been the most challenging?

How well do you think your school has prepared you for your future study?

How would you describe yourself as a student?

Do you know what you want to major in?

What has been your most stimulating intellectual experience?

What extracurricular activity have you been most involved in? How much time do you devote to it?

Do you have hobbies or special interests?

After a long, hard day, what do you enjoy doing most? What do you do for fun? For relaxation?

How have you spent your summer vacations? Why did you decide to spend them that way?

How would you describe yourself in five adjectives?

What is your family like? Describe your upbringing. How has your environment influenced your way of thinking?

How would your friends describe you?

Which relationships are most important to you? Why?

Have you ever encountered people who thought and acted differently from you? What viewpoints or actions challenged you the most? How did you respond? What did you learn about yourself?

If you had a year to go anywhere and do whatever you wanted, how would you spend that year?

What magazines or newspapers do you read regularly?

What books have you read recently? Are there any authors you particularly like?

What movie have you seen recently and what did you think of it?

What play, concert, recital, or dance performance have you seen recently? What did you think of it?

Who are your favorite dancers or dance companies? Why?

Who are your favorite actors? Why?

Who are your favorite musicians? Why?

Who are your favorite performers?

How did you choose your particular area in the performing arts? Why do you want to pursue this art form?

What has been your most memorable performance to date? Why?

Have you worked with a director, choreographer, or conductor who was particularly challenging or inspirational? Describe the experience.

Who has been your most memorable teacher? Why?

Why do you want to go to college?

Why have you chosen this college to investigate? What first brought us to your attention?

What do you picture yourself doing 10 years from now?

What do you think of the National Endowment for the Arts (or some current affair in the arts)?

What distresses you most about the world around you? If you had the opportunity to change the world, where would you start?

What more do you want to know about us?

This last question is your opening to ask about the school. Do not be shy about taking out your list; no one expects you to memorize a list of questions, and you want to be sure that you are learning everything you need to know about a school. Here are some general questions you may want to ask. (Specific questions about your area in dance, drama, or music are covered in later chapters.)

Sample Questions to Ask Your Interviewer

Who teaches freshmen? Transfers?

How does registration work? Is it easy to get the classes I want to take?

What is the advising system like? What are its strengths and weaknesses?

Are any changes anticipated in the curriculum?

Are there any departments that might be cut or discontinued? What departments have been discontinued in the past two years?

Are there any planned cutbacks in faculty? Any new appointments scheduled?

Are there any new programs being contemplated? What are they?

What percentage of students receive financial aid?

Are there jobs on campus for students? What is a typical work/study job? Are there jobs in the community?

Are there any opportunities for internships? For study abroad?

Are financial aid decisions made separately from admissions decisions? Will applying for financial aid influence admissions decisions?

Do you have any merit-based scholarships?

What is your policy on fee waivers, if I cannot afford the application fee?

What is the overall financial security of the school? Is tuition increased annually? What additional fees might I anticipate?

What is most important in admissions decisions?

After the Interview

Be sure to write your impression of the interview in your college notebook. And, most importantly, write the interviewer a quick thank-you note. Mention something specific that came up in the conversation. Three lines on nice stationery or even a postcard should be sufficient.

The Application

When you have finally narrowed your list to the five to eight schools to which you have decided to apply, it is time to approach the application. Application forms have several components. When you decide to apply to a school, do *not* sit down with the application and start to fill it out. First, read the entire document carefully.

Then make a photocopy of the application and fill it out as your draft. It is important that applications be neat and legible, either typed or printed in black or blue ink. Fill out the informational section first and then think about the essay questions, if required.

Academic Profile

Colleges will require a copy of your high school transcript(s). Be sure that you have checked your transcript for accuracy before it is sent by your high school. Many schools will also require college entrance examination scores. Some schools use standardized test scores for placement, and some use them as another indicator in the academic profile. As a performing artist, if you plan to apply to schools that require SATs, Achievement Tests, or ACTs and have not received the scores you think are truly representative of your ability, you should consider doing some test preparation and retaking the test to raise your score.

In analyzing your scholastic record, colleges are trying to decide whether you will be able to withstand the academic rigor of their environment. Taking a full complement of challenging courses in high school is important to demonstrate your academic ability. If you are applying to a conservatory, your academic profile is secondary to your demonstrated talent, but at liberal arts colleges and for joint programs, the academic profile is more important in establishing the match. If you want to leave all your options open for college, the best approach is to take a challenging assortment of academic courses, including math, science, and foreign-language electives. However, if you absolutely know that you are applying to a conservatory, taking an extra year of difficult courses is probably not going to have any effect on an admissions decision.

Personal Profile

The personal profile that a college gathers on you consists largely of information that is entirely in your control. This includes your list of extracurricular activities, your recommendations, essays, and any appropriate supplementary materials you send. Let's consider each of these.

Extracurricular Activities

This term refers to any activity outside of the classroom. Many colleges will ask you to put this information in a table, showing the activity, any position of leadership, hours spent in the activity, etc.

As a performing artist, you may not have joined any clubs in your high school, focusing all your time on one activity. That's great! Do not hesitate to acknowledge such dedication. If you have participated in many activities, draft a list including school activities, any jobs you've held, hobbies, community or volunteer activities, church groups, summer camp, honors, and awards. The point is to make the list comprehensive, but not exhaustive. Depth in one activity is important, so don't try to pad the list. Do not include anything that sounds like a cult.

Recommendations

Many colleges request teacher recommendations as well as the guidance counselor report. You should choose teachers who know you well as a student and as a person, who like you, and who write well. When you ask a teacher to write a letter of recommendation, remember to:

- ask politely;
- give the teacher the forms, with the top part filled out with your name, etc. well before the deadline;

- ◻ provide the teacher with stamped envelopes addressed to the colleges; and

- ◻ include a cover letter to the teacher that gives the deadlines for each school, a list of your extracurricular activities, or anything else that might be helpful to the teacher in writing your recommendation.

Guidance counselors are often also asked to fill out a counselor recommendation form, which may include a checklist and narrative. If you attend a large school where the counselors have many responsibilities, you would do well to establish a relationship with your guidance counselor. Schedule meetings, stop by the office to ask quick questions, and, in general, make yourself known to your guidance counselor.

Essays

While most admissions representatives say that an essay will not make or break an application, there have been applicants who essentially "wrote" themselves into acceptance. The essay is another opportunity for the admissions committee to get to know you better. Even if the essay is optional, it's a good idea to provide one. A well-written essay will make your application more memorable and distinctive.

Perhaps the hardest thing about the essay is getting started. One method which has worked well, especially with students in the performing arts, is to set your cassette recorder beside you and start talking. Then play back the cassette and transcribe what you said. Usually this technique will allow you to capture your personal voice and help you over any obstacle that you have about putting your thoughts on paper.

The best essays resonate with the personal voice of the applicant, describing ideas in very specific, reflective ways which may reveal fears, fantasies, or insecurities, but are always thoughtful, fresh, and spontaneous. The worst essays present a factual, often chronological version of an experience—the orchestra's tour to Europe, for example, or a recent performance—in a way that is totally lacking in creativity or individuality. The orchestra tour to Europe essay that simply describes arriving in Paris, playing at a concert hall, and then taking a bus to the next place, is hardly rivetting. The same essay telling how you got lost and could not find the stage door, and how you dealt with that situation, becomes specific and says something about you.

There is no "right" essay, but there are several approaches which you should avoid. For example, do not submit a poem as an essay. If you have talent as a poet, consider submitting samples of your poetry as supplementary material. Also, do not use the essay to make excuses for something in your background. If you have a special situation, consider writing about it in a separate letter or asking a teacher or your guidance counselor to mention it in his or her letter of recommendation. Do not repeat information from other parts of your application, and stay away from trendy topics like nuclear war or recycling, drugs, sex or alcohol, or the importance of a college education. Do not try to impress the admissions committee with your vocabulary, revealing that you have thumbed through the thesaurus. Rather, write simply about something you really care about in a personally specific manner.

Try to limit yourself to the space provided, or type your essay on separate sheets and write, "See essay attached." In general, it is the quality not the quantity that counts.

Supplementary Materials

Because you are a performing artist, you will want to document your special talent with additional materials, but you must choose extra materials carefully. A letter of recommendation from your dance, drama, or music teacher would be appropriate. Here are some items you should *not* send:

☐ additional letters of recommendation from people who do not know you well: congressmen, mayors, the neighbor's uncle who attended your college choice, but whom you've never met, etc. Such letters do not usually add to an understanding of who you are.

☐ copies of awards or honors. No scrapbooks!

☐ copies of lengthy reports or term papers. If a college wants a graded paper, they will specify this in the application directions.

☐ a pile of newspaper clippings. If you have received many positive reviews, select two or three, but do not send the entire stack and never send original copies.

☐ copies of programs in which you have participated. Your list of extracurricular activities or résumé should reflect this.

☐ lots of photographs of yourself. One or two good ones, especially if you are a dancer, would be appropriate; an entire portfolio is not.

☐ every article you've ever written. If you write for the school newspaper, you might send a copy of one or two articles—not every issue of the paper in which one of your articles has appeared.

Deadlines

You can do yourself and the admissions office a favor by submitting your application before it is actually due. This may help you to get the better audition times, if auditions are required, as some schools schedule on a first-come–first-served basis. Drama programs, in particular, but some other programs, too, use the deadline as one way to eliminate applicants. Remember to proofread your application before you mail it and to keep a photocopy of it for your files. It's a good idea to include a postcard saying, "College X has received the application from Mary Jones. Signed by admissions: Date." Also watch for your cancelled check to be returned. Things do get lost in the mail, and you want to be sure that your application does not go astray.

The College Admissions Timetable on pages 22–23 can serve as a guideline for the admissions process, whatever your chosen major.

Admissions Outcomes

After the application review and audition, if required, admissions committees will meet to determine whether to admit you, reject you, or place your name on a waiting list.

If you are admitted to more than one school, weigh the pros and cons of each institution, perhaps visit again, ask lots of questions, and try to respond to the Office of Admission in plenty of time, before their deadline. Most institutions comply with the guidelines established by the National Association of College Admissions Counselors (NACAC) and the College Board, which set the Candidate's Reply Deadline (CRD) as May 1. If a school requires you to make a decision before that deadline or before you have heard from all of your schools, you have every right to question that institution. If, in order to make an informed decision about your college choice, you need more information or your financial aid package has not arrived in time to meet the deadline, call the college and request an extension on the deadline. If you do not contact the college at all by May 1, the admissions staff may assume that you have decided to attend another institution and offer your place to someone on the waiting list. Be certain to contact your colleges by the deadline stipulated.

If you are rejected, do not become despondent. See if you can get any feedback about ways in which you might improve before auditioning or applying again. You may want to think about applying another year as a transfer student. Speak to your guidance counselor or college advisor about what you might do differently.

The Waiting List, sometimes called "Alternates," is a positive place to be. It means that a college realized your strengths, but due to a limited number of openings, was not able to offer you admission at this time. Your initial response will probably be disappointment and irritation, but wait a few days before you do anything. Then you will be more able to make a rational decision about whether to remain active on a waiting list or to accept the offer of a college which admitted you right away.

If you want to be considered from the waiting list, write to the college to say so and include any new information about yourself since the review of your application. If it is true, let a college know that, if taken off the waiting list, you will enroll. Talk to your guidance counselor about any further steps you should take, and then be patient. You should probably submit a deposit to your second-choice school to protect yourself, in the event that the first choice does not take anyone from the waiting list. If you are admitted from the waiting list, however, and intend to accept the offer of admission and enroll, be sure to contact the school where you gave your deposit so that they can offer your place to someone else.

Financial Aid

The majority of students considering postsecondary education need some form of financial aid. Do not eliminate a school from your list just because of the school's cost. Often the most expensive schools have the highest endowments and are able to be particularly generous in financial aid. In order to qualify for financial aid, you must apply for it. Many middle-income families, in particular, assume that financial assistance is not available to them; this may not be true. Read the catalog and any financial aid information very carefully, and be sure to speak to a financial aid officer at the colleges to which you are applying. Ask questions about the financial aid process and find out exactly what forms you will need. It is essential that you submit all the required forms and documents,

College Admissions Timetable

SOPHOMORE YEAR

SEPTEMBER & OCTOBER
- ❏ Take the Preliminary Scholastic Aptitude Test (PSAT) — This is good practice for junior year, when PSAT scores count toward National Merit Scholarships.

DECEMBER
- ❏ Obtain your PSAT results — Review the answer sheet. Talk to your guidance counselor about the advisability of taking a test preparation course.

JANUARY to APRIL
- ❏ Write for college catalogs — Read them, noting repertoire and audition requirements.
- ❏ Start your college notebook.
- ❏ Obtain a social security card if you don't already have one.
- ❏ Investigate the National Foundation for Advancement in Arts (NFAA or ARTS) scholarship.
- ❏ Meet with your guidance counselor — Discuss course plans: APs, honors, arts classes.
- ❏ Research financial aid and scholarship opportunities — Talk to your parents about submitting the Early Financial Planning Service application.
- ❏ Keep a file of your performances — Keep reviews, programs, and videotapes of your performances as well as papers, articles, or stories you have written.
- ❏ Attend college fairs — Find out all you can about schools you are considering.

JULY & AUGUST
- ❏ Consider taking Achievement Tests in courses in which you have done well.
- ❏ Plan your summer to expand your experience in the arts — Participate in a summer dance, drama, or music program. Remember to ask for recommendations.

JUNIOR YEAR

SEPTEMBER
- ❏ Meet with your guidance counselor or college advisor — Review plans, register for the PSAT, and renew or establish your acquaintance.
- ❏ Get good grades — Do well in your classes this year.

OCTOBER
- ❏ Take PSATs (again) — This time they count for National Merit Scholarships.
- ❏ Obtain applications — Get catalogs and applications from all schools you are considering.
- ❏ Continue to investigate financial aid opportunities.
- ❏ Keep your college notebook up-to-date.

DECEMBER
- ❏ Review PSAT results — PSAT scores indicate what areas you need to strengthen for the SAT.
- ❏ Register for SATs or ACTs — Also consider Achievement Tests and TOEFL if appropriate. Prepare on your own or take a review course.

MARCH to JUNE
- ❏ Meet with your college advisor and parents/guardian to discuss college plans.
- ❏ Take the SATs, ACTs, TOEFL, and Achievement Tests, if necessary.
- ❏ Attend college fairs — Ask questions and pick up current catalogs.

JULY & AUGUST
- ❏ Start your college visits.
- ❏ Plan another enriching summer — Continue to send for applications, visit colleges, and interview. Join a drama, dance, or music program. Work on your repertoire.

College Admissions Timetable

SENIOR YEAR

**SEPTEMBER &
OCTOBER**

- ❑ Continue your college visits — Record your reactions in your college notebook.
- ❑ Meet with your guidance counselor or college advisor — Discuss your college list and try to narrow it down.
- ❑ Consider applying for Early Decision — Check deadlines. November 1 and November 15 are common dates.
- ❑ Get letters of recommendation — Ask teachers and former employers.
- ❑ Apply for the ARTS recognition scholarship through NFAA.
- ❑ Be sure you have all application forms — Start drafting college application essays.
- ❑ Do a run-through of your audition material.

NOVEMBER

- ❑ Many Early Decision applications due.
- ❑ Fill out college application forms — Continue to revise and perfect your essays.
- ❑ Take any additional tests — SATs, ACTs, TOEFL, or Achievements.
- ❑ Send out your test results — Request that ETS or ACT send your test results to the colleges that require them.
- ❑ Continue practicing for your audition.

**DECEMBER &
JANUARY**

- ❑ Early Decision results are mailed — Celebrate if you were admitted and meet deadlines for enrollment deposits. If you were deferred or rejected, submit other applications and move on.
- ❑ Complete and submit your applications — Proofread them carefully and photocopy before mailing.
- ❑ Obtain the FAF — Start filling out financial aid forms and be aware of deadlines.
- ❑ Perfect your audition material. Do another run-through.
- ❑ Forward transcripts/test scores — Be sure to have your guidance counselor or college advisor send transcripts and test scores to schools you've chosen.
- ❑ Last chance to take the SAT or ACT.

**FEBRUARY &
MARCH**

- ❑ Attend scheduled auditions.
- ❑ Check to make sure all financial aid documents are in order.

APRIL

- ❑ Make your decision — Consider with your parents and guidance counselor the pros and cons of each institution at which you were accepted.
- ❑ Revisit any college if your decision to attend is not crystal clear.
- ❑ Notify colleges of your decision by May 1 — If a school asks for a decision before May 1, you have a right to request an extension until the May 1 CDR.

MAY

- ❑ Be sure to notify all colleges by May 1 — even if you are on the waiting list.
- ❑ Take AP exams, if applicable.
- ❑ Take additional auditions, if necessary.

and meet deadlines in applying for financial aid. For safety's sake, keep photocopies of every form you send.

Aside from scholarships, there are a variety of grants, loans, and work-study opportunities to help you finance your education. The Foundation Center, 79 5th Ave., New York, NY 10003 (212-620-4230), is an excellent resource and also has regional branches in the United States. There are also many helpful financial aid guides at libraries and in guidance offices. Do not overlook religious organizations, community and civic organizations, or state programs in your quest for funding.

Here are some questions you may want to ask about financial aid:

☐ Are scholarships based on merit? On need? On a combination of both?

☐ Are financial aid decisions made separately from admissions decisions?

☐ What are the most common mistakes people make in filling out financial aid forms?

☐ Should I assume that if my parents make (some dollar amount) as their income, that I would not be eligible for any aid?

☐ Do you have deferred payment plans?

☐ What happens if I do not meet deadlines in filing forms for financial aid?

☐ Do you give financial aid to applicants admitted from the waiting list?

☐ Do I have a better chance of obtaining financial aid if I audition during the main auditions (usually February or March), than if I audition in May or later?

Deadlines are very important when applying for financial aid. It is critical that the FAF be completed and mailed to the College Scholarship Service (CSS) as early as possible, but not before January 1. Many colleges have January and February deadlines for submission of this form. If parents have not completed their income tax returns by February, estimate income as accurately as possible, and submit corrections later in the process.

If the financial aid package you are offered is not adequate, or if your first-choice school offers less than a second or third choice, call the admissions or financial aid office of your first-choice school and discuss this with them. Schools may reconsider their original financial aid offer. In general, there is a great deal more comparative shopping in financial aid these days.

Checklist for International Students

Any student who is not a citizen or permanent resident of the United States is usually considered an "international" or "foreign" student (the term varies at schools). Many schools recruit abroad and most schools welcome international students. The admissions procedures at most schools are the same for foreign students as for U.S. applicants. However, there are a few additional aspects foreign students should take into account.

☐ Begin your search extra early. International mail takes additional time and catalogs cannot be FAX-ed at this point.

College Admissions Checklist

Use this convenient checklist to remind yourself of individual college admissions requirements and to record the progress of your application procedures.

College Name								
College Address								
Application Deadline								
Application Fee								
Required Tests:	Registration Deadline	Testing Date	Registration Deadline	Testing Date	Registration Deadline	Testing Date	Registration Deadline	Testing Date
PSAT/NMSQT								
SAT								
ACT								
Others								
Course Requirements Fulfilled								
Personal Interview Required								
Interview Date								
Audition Required								
Audition Date								
Applications Requested								
References Required								
Names/Addresses of References								
References Completed								
Application Filed								
Transcript Forwarded								
College Reply Date								
Financial Aid Deadline								
Financial Interview Required								
Required Financial Forms:								
CSS Financial Statement								
ACT Financial Statement								
Others								
Housing Deadline								
Housing Fee								
Housing Application Mailed								

☐ Determine whether you must take the TOEFL (Test of English as a Foreign Language), if English is not your native language. Arrange to take the test, if necessary, so that your scores can be submitted at the required time.

☐ Be sure to study English intensively. There are many good English as a Second Language programs both in the United States and abroad. The Language Institute for English (LIFE) is a Berlitz affiliate and runs its program at Juilliard in the summer. Information about other programs may be obtained through the USIA (United States Information Agency), with offices throughout the world, or through the Institute of International Education (IIE), U.N. Plaza, New York, NY 10017.

☐ Investigate the visa process early. If you must travel to the United States for an audition, many conservatories or colleges will issue a letter you can present to a consulate to obtain a "B-2 Prospective Student Visa." An I-20 will be issued to admitted students only. Everything regarding visas does take time, however, so plan ahead.

☐ Determine a school's policy on financial aid for foreign students. Government or state loans are not available to students from abroad and many schools reserve their limited scholarship funds for domestic students. Some schools will not admit a qualified international student who has applied for financial aid. Be sure to ask for the current policy, and do not hesitate to ask for clarification of the policy if you are in doubt.

☐ Find out whether the school requires a guarantee of financial support in advance.

☐ Ask about tape or application pre-screening or regional auditions in your country.

☐ Complete your application on your own, especially the essays. If your English is not good enough to write an acceptable essay, you probably won't be able to understand the lectures or complete the assignments at a U.S. school.

☐ Be sure that schools know about your academic history in terms of the overall educational system in your country. For instance, if no one from your high school has ever applied to a United States school before, you should send a prospectus or profile of your school.

☐ Find out whether it is possible for foreign (international) students to work while attending the program.

☐ Ask whether there are quotas on the number of students from a certain country or on foreign students in general.

☐ Find out about advisors and other support services for foreign students.

2
For Dance Majors

Advanced Study in Dance

Age

Age is more of a factor in the dance world than it is in the other performing arts. If you are now a sophomore in high school, one question that you may want to ask yourself is whether it is important for you to finish your high school program. If you do decide to spend all four years in high school be sure that you are taking regular dance classes and performing as often as possible. If you decide to finish or leave high school at the end of three years, there are other options for you.

Early Admission

Early Admission policies apply to students who want to be admitted to college before the end of their senior year of high school. (This is not to be confused with Early Decision policies, which apply to your senior year.) You should think about Early Admission ideally in your sophomore year but no later than fall semester of junior year so that you will have time to plan ahead. You may approach this in one of two ways: either plan to finish the requirements for high school and graduate early, at the end of your junior year, or leave high school at the end of junior year, enroll at a college, and see if your high school will grant your diploma, pending the successful completion of your freshman year.

You may also decide that a high school diploma is not important to you and enroll at the college which admits you as an Early Admission candidate.

If you plan to finish high school early, you may have to take a summer course or two and take additional courses during the regular school year, too. Work carefully with your guidance counselor to see if this is feasible. It is usually an English or history requirement which you will need to fulfill in order to graduate.

If you decide to leave high school and have your diploma awarded after your freshman year, be sure to get all the terms *in writing*. Does your high school require that you not only successfully complete your freshman year, but require you to take certain courses and achieve a certain grade? If your high school does not put the terms in writing, be sure that you or your parents write a letter stating your understanding and keep a copy of this letter for your files.

Choosing Your Teachers

It is important that you study with someone who will inculcate the best habits in your early development and teach you a solid technique. As you investigate teachers in your area, here are some questions you might want to ask:

- Where did the teacher go to school?

- Did the teacher dance professionally? With what company?

- Does the teacher talk about placement?

- Does the teacher explain how to do an exercise as well as what to do?

- Does the teacher give corrections?

- Does the teacher save stretching for after you are warmed up?

- Does the teacher stress turnout from the hips rather than from the knees or feet?

- Is there any discussion about musicality?

- Are the dance classes focused towards learning a routine for a dance concert or recital, or is technique taught regularly?

Application Photographs

Often you will be asked to submit a photograph of yourself in dance attire along with your application. Unlike drama applicants trying to find the most appealing headshot, you need not go to the trouble of expensive professional photos. You should have someone take a full-length photograph of you in either color or black and white. It should show you in a flattering pose or dance position, in appropriate dance clothing. If you have a photograph that was taken of you in a performance this would be fine, also. These photos are used for reference to remember you and should show you at your best. No provocative poses or outrageous attire should be chosen.

Dance Auditions

What to Expect

When you arrive at a dance audition, check in and then go to the dressing room to change. (Never leave valuables in any dressing room.) At the beginning of the audition, you will be put in lines based on the order in which you arrived or in alphabetical order. Often you will be required to wear a number or your name. While you may feel that this is dehumanizing, it helps the audition panel recognize you, and you do not want to be confused with another applicant. You should also be aware that more and more dance auditions are being videotaped for reference, and you should ignore the camera. Adjudicators may have your file and photos with them and compare to see that you really do look like your photograph.

During the audition, be sure to listen carefully and follow instructions. Perform the material as it is asked for, even if it is unfamiliar, and be sure to apply any corrections given to the class in general to yourself.

Timing of Auditions

Most major auditions for dance programs are held in February or March, with possible late auditions in May. If you have a choice, try not to do your first audition at your first-choice school. Make sure that you have done plenty of preparation.

What to Wear

Schools and programs usually specify what they would like you to wear at your audition. The norm seems to be:

For a ballet class: black leotard, pink tights, and ballet shoes for women; white T-shirt, black tights, white socks, and ballet shoes for men.

For a modern class: You can be a little more creative here, wearing a different color leotard, if you want, but usually you must be barefoot.

You should be neat and comfortable. Because dance is physical and your body is your instrument, it is important to wear proper attire and not try to hide your body. No big T-shirts or sweats. Your hair should be out of your face and nicely groomed.

Before You Audition

Whether it is for a company, a conservatory, or for a dance department at a liberal arts college or university, you should be prepared well in advance of your audition time.

Be sure to read carefully and thoroughly the catalog or any audition information which is sent to you.

Bring with you what you will need:

☐ your attire for a ballet class;

☐ your attire for a modern class;

☐ any other change of clothing or shoes;

☐ cassette tape of the music for your solo or piano accompaniment;

☐ another copy of your résumé and photographs, in case they are requested; and

☐ any health form which is requested.

If admission is based primarily on your performance in a class or two, be sure that you arrive in plenty of time to do a complete warm-up and to get a good spot in the room. If they arrange you alphabetically for the class, you have no control, but if they arrange you according to the order in which you arrived, you may be in the front if you arrive early enough.

If you are asked to perform a solo which you have choreographed or someone has choreographed for you, be sure to choose audition material which accentuates your strengths as a performer. Stay within stipulated time regulations, as well.

Be prepared to know how to speak about your material: the title of the piece, the choreographer, and the composer.

If for some reason you are injured before your audition, it is best to call and try to postpone your audition. Going to an audition and saying, "I'm not allowed to jump, due to an injury," is not going to win you favor with the audition panel.

Practice Auditions

Practice ahead of time. Rehearse everything: how you will enter the room, how you will introduce yourself and your solo piece, and what you need to tell the pianist (including the tempo). Go over your solo many times so that you can perform it under almost any circumstance, even with a severe case of nerves. Frequently, the students who become nervous in auditions are the ones who have not rehearsed a piece long enough and so have some element of insecurity based on lack of preparation. Since being well prepared can help you relax, Dr. Beth Rom-Rymer, a psychologist in Chicago, says that it sometimes helps if you pretend the audition is two weeks earlier than it is to get the feeling of having gained some extra time. Try to arrange to perform for a group of your peers and for your teacher several months before the audition and videotape yourself; critique your performance and then do it again, at least a month before the audition. About a week before, try to get a group together and set up a mock audition situation for yourself.

Music for Your Auditions

You may be asked to perform, with music, a solo which you have choreographed or someone else has choreographed for you. It is safest for you to have your music on a cassette tape. If you bring a tape, be sure that it contains only musical accompaniment for your solo and is cued to play.

If you do not bring a tape, most auditions will have a pianist who accompanies the class and is available to play for your solo. If your piece is standard and not too difficult, bring the sheet music for the pianist. Be certain that it is legible, that it is assembled so that it is easy for the pianist to turn pages, and that any cuts or repeats are clearly marked. You may want to talk to the pianist ahead of time or send a copy of the music in advance. Be sure that you and the pianist communicate about the tempo before you begin your solo.

Regional Auditions

Many colleges will hold auditions in a number of different cities and sometimes in other countries as well. While doing the audition on campus gives you an opportunity to see the facilities and probably meet with more faculty, if you are unable to get to the campus for any reason, take the regional audition. Ask about who will conduct the auditions, which faculty members will teach classes and evaluate the audition, and if a videotape will be made of the audition for other faculty to review.

Videotaped versus Live Auditions

Some programs will accept a videotape of your dancing in lieu of a personal audition. The best advice is to use a videotape only as a last resort. Faculty members like to see applicants in person, whether at a regional audition or on campus. A videotape is never as good as a live audition, and you may diminish your chances of admission by submitting your audition on tape.

Nerves

While a college interview may make you nervous, an audition may induce a real anxiety attack. The best defense is to be sure that you are so well prepared that you can almost function on automatic pilot. Arrive early and do a careful warm-up, including deep breathing exercises. Also, if you make yourself think of the audition as a *performance*, you may actually be able to develop the positive energy that you bring to the stage. It seems that the word "audition" with the connotation of judgment makes even seasoned performers nervous. Remember that the panel watching the audition really wants you to do well; so, do your best and keep your focus on performing with confidence.

Audition Evaluation Criteria

When you audition, the faculty and administrators in attendance will evaluate your performance in terms of certain criteria established by the school. Forms vary from school to school, but as you will note from the samples that follow, many similar criteria are reviewed. Some programs may give you copies of the evaluation or notes on how you might improve; other programs consider this information confidential. (See Dance Audition forms on pages 32–34.)

What NOT to Do at a Dance Audition

☐ Do not run away after you have finished. Take your appropriate bows and then wait until you are dismissed. Many times the adjudicators may want to ask you something. If you disappear, an opportunity may be lost.

☐ Do not wear inappropriate attire. Leave the big T-shirts, sweats, and tights with holes at home.

☐ Do not "play" to the judges. It is best to look a little over their heads.

☐ Do not choose a solo which you think the audition panel wants to see. Choose something which you love to dance and which is appropriate for your level of development.

☐ Do not perform a solo which is longer than the time stipulated in the guidelines.

Dealing with Injuries

If you have had an injury in the past, be honest about it. Many colleges will require that you submit a health form or have an orthopedic evaluation prior to being allowed to take the audition. If you are not honest and a doctor finds out about a past problem, however small, it is not a good reflection on you.

In looking at your future in dance, you must consider how injuries will influence your choices. All serious dancers are bound to incur some injuries. You must be brutally

Modern Dance Audition Sheet
NCSA School of Dance

Date _____

Auditioning for:

_____ regular school only

_____ summer school only

_____ both summer school and regular school

Audition No. _____

Accept _____

Reject _____

Summer school to re-audition

NAME _____ SEX: M F _____ N.C. RESIDENT_____

DATE OF BIRTH _____ AGE _____ HEIGHT_____ WEIGHT _____

PAST STUDY: Years _____ Classes/wk _____ Studios _____

APPEARANCE

	good	fair	poor		good	fair	poor
Body tone				Turnout			
Carriage of torso				Feet			
Placement (static)				Hamstring flexibility			
Abdominal support				Hip flexibility			
Shape of leg				Lower back strength			

Comments:

TECHNIQUE

	good	fair	poor		good	fair	poor
Basic dance vocabulary				Coordination			
Torso flexibility, strength				Placement in space			
Use of upper back, arms				Learning ability			
Use of legs and feet							

Comments:

PERFORMANCE

	good	fair	poor		good	fair	poor
Use of space				Musicality			
Motivation				Projection			
Phrasing				Technical degree of difficulty			
Dynamics				Type of music used			

Comments:

Auditioner _____

BALLET AUDITIONING SHEET
NCSA School of Dance

AUDITIONING FOR:
_____ regular school year only
_____ summer school only
_____ both summer school &
regular school year

Audition date   N.C. resident   Audition number

Name		Sex	Age	Height	Weight	Entering grade level

Past study (years)   classes per week   Studios

	Good	Fair	Poor	
Height				too tall/too short
Weight				overweight/underweight
Head				small/average/large
Neck				long/medium/short
Shoulders				sloping/straight/high/narrow/broad
Torso				short/medium/long
Spine				straight/curved (upper/middle/lower)
Hips (pelvis)				small/medium/wide
Legs				long/average/short
Shape of legs				(stand candidate straight with feet toward en face) straight/bowed top to bottom/bowed between knees and ankles
Knees				flat/sway back at knee joints/knees do not straighten/knock-kneed
Feet				small/large/flat/no arch/no points/no coupe de pied/stiff in ankle joints
Turnout				loose/tight/not from hips
Flexibility				
Placement (static)				shoulders up/shoulders back/lower back swayed/abdomen dropped/chest dropped/not centered
Plié demi				
Plié grand				
Extension				
Adage				good épaulé/poor épaulé/good extension/poor extension/no center
Turns en dehors				
Turns en dedens				
Turns diagonal				
Petite allegro				no speed/no turnout/no use of feet
Grand allegro				no elevation/no line/no turnout/no use of feet
Port de bras				placement of arms/correct position/incorrect positions
Quality of movement				coordination/fluidity/carriage/expression
Musicality				ahead/behind/cannot count
Schooling				correct for age/behind for age/ahead for age
Placement (in space)				
Presentation				outgoing/withdrawn/unfocused/blank/sullen
Energy				

Outstanding talent   _____   COMMENTS:
Scholarship material   _____
Accept   _____
Further discussion   _____
Reject   _____   AUDITIONER

THE JUILLIARD SCHOOL

ENTRANCE AUDITION EVALUATION--FORM FOR DANCE DIVISION

Student Information	**For Dance Office Use Only**
(Computer Label)	Admit _____ Waiting List _____ Reject _____ Re-audition _____ Scholarship Decision: _____ Audition Rating: _____ Scholarship Rating: _____ Combined Rating: _____

	Exceptional	Superior	Very Good	Good	Adequate	Possible	Unacceptable
Ballet Technique							
Modern Technique							
Performance							
Body Proportions							
Musicality							

Piece Performed: _____

Remarks:

Overall Rating (circle one):

E   S   VG   G   A   P   U

Accept _____

Possible _____

Reject _____

The student should be encouraged to re-audition.   ❏ Yes   ❏ No

Why ?

Signed: _____

Date: _____

FORM AUD89-C1

Scholarship Recommendations

Definitely   ❏

Probably   ❏

Possibly   ❏

No   ❏

honest with yourself about when an injury will have to be taken into account in determining your future training. You should also be sure that you educate yourself about basic health issues, including good nutrition, basic injury prevention, and strengthening exercises, and you should read about how posture and psychology can contribute to injuries. Learn about strapping and padding techniques that support injuries, and become aware of the range of therapies available.

Although some great dancers have survived knee surgery and other injuries, every young dancer must decide whether personal injuries or physical restrictions are severe enough to interfere with career goals. The following books address the topic of dancers and health. All are published by the Princeton Book Company/Dance Horizons Series, P.O. Box 57, Pennington, New Jersey 08534—609-737-8177. (They also have a Dance Book Club which has videos as well as books on dance.)

Arnheim, Daniel, D. *Dance Injuries: Their Prevention and Care,* 3d edition, 1991.

Spilken, Terry L., M.D. *The Dancer's Foot Book,* 1989.

Vincent, L. M., M.D. *The Dancer's Book of Health,* 1978.

Watkins, Andrea, and Priscilla M. Clarkson. *Dancing Longer, Dancing Stronger: A Dancer's Guide to Improving Technique and Preventing Injuries,* 1989.

A Dance Company versus College

If you are a junior or senior in high school and have the opportunity to audition for some companies, by all means take the auditions. You can learn a great deal about yourself and about a company just by auditioning. If you are admitted into the company, you must do some serious thinking about what you want to do. Review your contract very carefully. Some of the concerns you should evaluate include:

- ☐ How good is this company? How long do the dancers seem to stay with it? Where do they go from here?

- ☐ Are there any reviews of the company that you could read?

- ☐ What is the daily routine? How many classes? How many hours of rehearsal? How many performances a week?

- ☐ Will you be cast? What are the casting policies? Or are you corps de ballet?

- ☐ What do people like most about the company? What are the most common complaints?

- ☐ What is the financial profile of the company? Is payroll met regularly? Any problems?

- ☐ What are the plans for the near future? Any tours? What are the long-range plans?

- ☐ Where do most company members live?

Some companies that admit young dancers include: New York City Ballet, Pennsylvania Ballet, Pittsburgh Ballet, and Cleveland Ballet.

Some experienced dancers suggest that the company route is right for only a small number of dancers. These dancers pointed out that while dancers who join a company and those who follow a college curriculum may end up with the same acquired knowledge, the college route telescopes the learning time while the performing route leaves the dancer to learn by trial and error over a span of many years. These dancers also said that life after your years as a performer can be much more difficult if you do not have a college education, and most directors and choreographers have attended college.

Be sure that you distinguish whether you are admitted to the *school* for a company, or to the company itself.

If you are admitted to a company, and your parents object because they want you to go to college, you should point out to your parents that most colleges do not have an age limit but a dance career does. If you are ready now, you might want to "leap" at the opportunity if the company meets your standards. It should be noted, however, that most modern dancers do have college degrees. In ballet, if you have no company options by age 17, college is a good choice. You might try taking a year off after high school and doing a lot of auditions, or you could try to graduate from high school early and complete college in three years. By then, you would be 19 or 20 and still young enough to begin a dance career.

If you are admitted to the school of a company, the decision about whether to enroll at a degree-granting conservatory or at the company school becomes even more difficult. Some of the company schools that you might investigate include the School of American Ballet, Dance Theater of Harlem, Alvin Ailey School, Joffrey, Cleveland Ballet School, Pennsylvania Ballet School, San Francisco Ballet School, Boston Ballet School, Atlanta School, Graham School, Nikolais School, and Merce Cunningham School. (The *Stern's Performing Arts Directory* is a good reference for these programs. See Bibliography.) Here are some of the questions you should ask.

Sample Dance Questions to Ask

What is a typical schedule for a freshman? Are there any electives?

What is the policy on casting?

How many dance performances are there? Fully produced concerts? Workshops?

What kind of flooring is there in the studios?

How many studios are there? What are the facilities available to students? (If you have not seen them on your campus tour.)

Who have been the recent choreographers?

Who has taught any recent master classes?

What kind of technique is taught?

What kind of repertory is studied?

How will the audition be run?

Who evaluates the audition?

Is it possible to focus on ballet (or modern) or do I have to be proficient in both?

What do most graduates go on to do?

What companies now employ graduates from your program?

Do you help with job placement?

What is the enrollment in the dance department? How many males? How many females? Has this been steady? Is it growing? Diminishing? How many graduate students? How many undergraduates?

How many technical classes are required per week? In ballet? Modern? Jazz? Ethnic? Pas de deux? Pointe? Other?

Do you accept videotapes in lieu of a personal audition? If so, what special instructions should I know about? Format? Length? Do you accept videotapes for prescreening, to let me know if it is worthwhile to come for a personal audition? Any special directions for these?

Adding to Your College Notebook

You might add a page to your personal college notebook with a chart like this one listing the areas of dance you are interested in studying.

Areas of Dance Taught

❏ **Classical Ballet**
❏ **Modern Dance**
  __ Graham-based technique
  __ Limón-based technique
  __ Nikolais-based technique
  __ Cunningham-based technique
  __ Other:
❏ **Repertory**
❏ **Jazz**
❏ **Tap**
❏ **Historical Dance**
❏ **Ethnic forms:**
  __ African   __ Spanish
  __ Indian   __ Other: _____
  __ Middle Eastern

❏ **Movement Techniques**
  __ Alexander
  __ Feldenkreis
  __ Laban Movement studies
  __ Other:
❏ **Dance Composition/Choreography**
❏ **Pedagogy** (any teacher certification?)
❏ **Labanotation**
❏ **Anatomy**
❏ **Music**
❏ **Stagecraft**
❏ **Other:** _____

_____

_____

Dance Admissions Checklist

Here are some questions to ask yourself at various points in the admissions process:

Have I...

❏ requested catalogs and read them carefully?

❏ requested applications and made photocopies of those in which I am most interested?

❏ started a college notebook to record impressions of colleges, audition and repertoire requirements, and deadlines?

❏ obtained a social security number?

❏ registered for the PSATs?

❏ obtained information about the ARTs scholarships? (National Foundation for Advancement in the Arts, 3915 Biscayne Boulevard, Miami, Florida 33137 (305) 573-0490.)

❏ made an appointment with my guidance counselor or college advisor to discuss future plans?

❏ looked into working with an independent counselor, if appropriate?

❏ talked with my current dance teacher about my future plans?

❏ participated regularly in school, community, or professional productions?

❏ made plans to continue my dance classes?

❏ discussed my future high school curriculum with my guidance counselor?

❏ discussed standardized test choices with my guidance counselor?

❏ investigated summer programs/jobs and applied as necessary?

❏ investigated sources of financial aid?

❏ kept a file of performance programs, videotaped shows, good term papers, articles, etc.?

❏ attended college fairs and met with college representatives?

❏ registered for standardized tests (SAT, ACT, TOEFL, Achievement Tests)?

❏ arranged my college visits?

❏ scheduled interview appointments?

❏ sent thank-you notes to admissions counselors after interviews?

❏ chosen my audition material?

❏ narrowed my list of colleges?

Have I...

❏ considered applying for Early Decision? (Deadlines generally are in early to mid-November.)

❏ asked for letters of recommendation from teachers/former employers?

❏ drafted my college application essays?

❏ finished my essays and applications and photocopied everything before mailing?

❏ practiced my audition material regularly?

❏ applied for financial aid?

❏ requested that ETS, ACT, or TOEFL send official score reports to the colleges that require them?

❏ videotaped practice auditions to be critiqued?

❏ submitted videotapes for prescreening, if necessary?

❏ had necessary photographs taken to submit with applications?

❏ prepared a résumé?

❏ requested that a copy of my transcript be sent to colleges, as required?

❏ communicated regularly with my guidance counselor or college advisor about my progress in school and in college admission?

❏ kept up with schoolwork?

❏ perfected audition material?

❏ prepared a list of extracurricular activities in which I've participated?

❏ completed all financial aid documentation?

❏ read carefully all audition and schedule information sent to me?

❏ arranged for an accompanist for my audition, if necessary?

❏ taped music for my solo piece and photocopied sheet music, if necessary?

❏ responded to colleges about acceptance offers?

❏ requested an extension beyond the May 1 Candidates Reply Deadline, if necessary?

❏ continued with my regular dance classes?

3
For Drama Majors

Advanced Study in Drama

"All the world's a stage" and so many young people aspire to be in the spotlight. Unlike dance and music, where you must have had years of previous training even to consider auditioning, drama auditions require only that you be able to memorize and recite a monologue. High school and college thesbians who have visions of stardom should be sure to take auditions to avoid living with regrets or the nagging, "What if…."

There is a debate among actors about the best training. Some believe that years of training provide a distinct advantage. Others suggest relying on natural talent and instincts. There is a school of thought that says that taking too many classes in acting develops a dependency wherein you become a professional student, rather than a professional actor, and another that says you can never take too many classes in voice, acting, and movement, and should never stop studying. For a young actor, there are many available options.

Bachelor of Arts versus Bachelor of Fine Arts

The essential difference in these two programs involves proportion in course work. In a Bachelor of Arts (B.A.) degree program, you will be expected to study a broad range of courses in the liberal arts and sciences and at some schools to fulfill distribution requirements. You major in drama (called a theater major at some schools) and take a certain number of credit hours in this as your major, but the proportion of liberal arts to drama courses is tilted in the direction of the liberal arts. A Bachelor of Fine Arts (B.F.A.) program is more heavily weighted on the drama side.

For certain people there is a distinct advantage to attending a liberal arts college and majoring in drama. For one thing, the number of students who change their major after freshman year is extremely high. If you are locked into a B.F.A. program, you may have more trouble changing to another major than you would in a B.A. program, where changing majors is common. Another reason to attend a liberal arts college to obtain a B.A. is just for the very breadth of learning in a wide range of subjects. When you create a role, you can bring more to it if you have a background in literature and history, than if you know only the theater. Finally, you are likely to encounter a more diverse student body at a liberal arts college than you would at a specialized school. This very diversity might influence you in creating a role someday. If you choose the liberal arts route, you must look very carefully at the strength of the drama department. In some liberal arts colleges, drama courses are taught through the English department. What is the curriculum? A liberal arts college offering a drama major that teaches only theater history, dramatic literature, and a basic acting course probably is not the strongest department. How many faculty members are there? Do they also work in conjunction with a Dance and/or Music department? A Drama department with fewer than four faculty members may not be considered a priority by the administration and may not present to you enough variety in your learning. Investigate carefully!

The B.F.A. program is for students who want to focus immediately on specific theater skills. If you know, without a doubt, that you want to pursue your major in drama and that you want the focus, then a good B.F.A. program may be for you.

Most B.F.A. programs, either at conservatories or at universities, do require an audition, even if you have been admitted into the main school. Prepare thoroughly for the audition.

Note for International Students: If English is not your native language and you speak with any accent, quite bluntly, your chances for admission in a drama program in a competitive U.S. conservatory or B.F.A. program are not strong. A B.A. program will be more flexible.

Résumés for Drama Students

Most drama programs ask for a copy of your résumé. If you have had a great deal of experience, putting your résumé together will not be a problem. Just get used to keeping it up to date. If your experience has been limited to high school productions and classes, this is absolutely fine. Present your background and qualifications honestly. Knowing about your previous experience may be useful to the admissions committee, but how you handle the audition will count the most.

There is no one prescribed format for drama résumés. There is certain standard background information which should appear, however, including your name, address, phone (days and evenings), height, weight, eye and hair color, and voice range, if you sing. Experience may be broken down into categories including: theater or stage, musicals, summer stock, film, television, etc. A high school student might list high school productions, summer work, worshops, and master classes. Include names of your teachers, and mention any specialized training, such as on a musical instrument, gymnastics, stage combat, fencing, etc. (If you have not had any lessons in these areas, do not be intimidated. These should become part of your postsecondary training and prior experience is not required.)

A good résumé should be on 8½ x 11 paper, word-processed (easy for regular updating), and certainly no longer than two pages; a one-page résumé for drama is best. This résumé should be attached to your head shot. Following on pages 43–45 are three typical résumés: one for a freshman applicant, one for a transfer student, and one for a graduate student.

Head Shots

Many programs will request that you submit a head shot with your résumé and application. If you do not have a professional photo, do not allow this to stop you from applying or delay you in sending in your application. Instead, submit the application with a note saying that you are having a head shot done and will submit it as soon as possible.

Freshman Résumé

John A. Doe
123 Main Street
Anytown, U.S.A.
(123) 456-7890

EDUCATION

A. I. Du Pont High School   Senior, 1990–91

EXPERIENCE

1991	This Is A Test (Pat)		One-act play
			A. I. Du Pont High School
1990	Renaissance Faire		
	St. George and the Dragon (Reginald Brown)	Delaware Theater Company
1990	Cinderella, Cinderella. . . (Prince Charming)	Wilmington Drama League
1990	To Kill A Mockingbird (Townsperson)	Delaware Theater Company
1990	Baby (Father)		One-act play
			A. I. Du Pont High School
1990	Zombie Army (Orderly)		Film
			Cheapshot Productions, Inc.
1989	Get Smart (Professor Dante)	Senior play
			A. I. Du Pont High School

TRAINING AND EXTRA ACTIVITIES

Two years drama/acting class   A. I. Du Pont High School
One year public speaking   Carson Long Military Institute
Senior Literary Society   Carson Long Military Institute
The Art of Acting   Delaware Technical &
                                                       Community College

Drama Club   A. I. Du Pont High School
The International Thespian Society

TECHNICAL WORK

1989   Get Smart   Play

One-Act Plays

1991   This Is A Test   A. I. Du Pont High School
1990   Pink Lemonade
1990   Drive-In

AWARDS AND COMPETITION

Third Place, Declamation Contest   Carson Long Military Institute
   Julius Caesar (Marcus Antonius)

REFERENCES AND RECOMMENDATIONS

Will be available upon request.

Transfer Student Résumé

MARCIA SMITH

123 4th Avenue   Height: 5'4"
New York, New York 10003   Weight: 120
212-123-4567—home   Hair: Brown
                                                             Eyes: Brown

THEATER

THANK YOU AMY	Amy	Theater in the Square
THE DINING ROOM	Ensemble	Tisch School of the Arts
NO COMMENT CABARET	Sandy	Tisch School of the Arts
VESTLESS ATTIRE	Ensemble	The Gas Station
CINDERELLA	Cinderella	Boston Children's Theater
LUDLOW FAIR	Rachel	Directing Project—
		Williamstown Theater Festival
PARLOUR GAMES	Ensemble	Massachusetts College of Art
THIRD RAIL	Cathy	Emerson College

TELEVISION AND FILM

RAP AROUND	Jessica	WBZ TV
(Four Segments)		
PUBLIC SERVICE ANNOUNCEMENT	Girl	WBZ TV
CHILDREN AND DIVORCE		WNEV TV
SIDEWALK	Girl	Tisch School of the Arts/N.Y.U.

SUMMER

Institute Member	1989	National Shakespeare Conservatory
Apprentice	1988	Williamstown Theater Festival
Young Critic's Institute	1987	Huntington Theater

TRAINING

Classes: Lyric Stage, Wheelock Family Theater, Boston Children's Theater
Participant: Oberlin Theater Institute
              Circle in the Square Theater School
Currently attending B.F.A. program Tisch School of the Arts/New York University

AWARDS

National Endowment for the Advancement in the Arts:
Arts Recognition and Talent Search Awardee 1989

National Endowment for the Humanities Scholar:
Young Critics Institute—Huntington Theater

Presidential Scholar in the Arts:
Semifinalist 1989

Graduate Student Résumé

SARA GREEN

Height: 5'6"   service: **212 . 666 . 1111**
Age Range: 18-24   home: **212 . 345 . 6789**

SAG/AFTRA
AEA (Eligible)

---

theatre

BLACK ICE	Lady Die	Kampo Cultural Center/*Dean Mitchell*
CRIMES OF THE HEART	Lenny	Herald Square Players/*Bob Byrd*

films

NEW JACK CITY	Crack Addict	Jac/Mac Prods./*Mario Van Peebles*
IDENTITY CRISIS	Gang Member	Block & Chip Prods./*Melvin Van Peebles*

television

AMAZING UNSOLVED MYSTERIES	Angelica	WWOR-TV
COSBY SHOW	Church Attendant	NBC
CHEERS	Karen (Bar Patron)	NBC
L.A. LAW	Court Stenographer	NBC
HARD BALL	Sara B (Homeless Woman)	NBC
THE LAKER GIRLS	Laker Cheerleader	CBS (Pilot)

commercials/voice overs   List Available Upon Request

training

Commercial: Reed-Sweeny-Reed—Pat Sweeney ... *On-Camera Technique*
SAG & AFTRA Conservatory—Affiliated Instructors ... *On-Camera Commercial Tech. & Improv.*
Hyde Hamlet Casting—Sara Hamlet ... *On-Camera Technique*

Acting: Video Perspectives—Bob Byrd ... *Sitcom Workshop*
Herbert Berghof Studios—Michael Beckett ... *Scene Study & Technique I, II*

Dance: Broadway Dance Center—Sue Samuels ... *Jazz Technique I*
Broadway Dance Center—Farnsworth ... *Ballet Technique I*
Ruth Williams Dance Studios—Ruth Williams ... *Modern Dance/Ballet*

Voice: NY School of Commercial Music—Ruth DeBrow ... *Mezzo-Soprano*

Education: B.A., Architecture—Syracuse University
Member of Black Filmmakers Foundation

special skills

Jamaican, Southern & New York Dialects, Syracuse University Cheerleader (3 years), Aerobics/Weight Training, Roller Skating, Double-Dutch Jumping, Scuba Diving (certified), Licensed Driver, Excellent with Children and Pets. Own Evening Gowns, Nurse Uniform and selection of 10 Wigs and Hairpieces.

You really should have a head shot, however, and there are some inexpensive ways to go about getting one. Your application head shot should look like you and present a pleasant impression.

Just as you should go for a somewhat conventional look in your dress for a college interview, you should choose a pose and overall look for your head shot that calls attention to your eyes and your face. Don't wear outrageous jewelry, pose in a provocative way, or choose a hairstyle that focuses attention on your hair rather than on you. Selective schools claim never to have admitted candidates who submitted head shots that were either in bad taste or particularly weird or inappropriate.

Finding a good photographer to take your head shot can be a challenge. If you do not live in a city, you might ask the photography teacher at your high school for recommendations. Bring along some head shots you like from programs or newspapers as samples. Yearbook photographers who are experienced in photographing in black and white are also a possibility for you. You don't have to spend an exorbitant amount of money on your head shot. Go for quality with economy, if that is possible. The *Back Stage Handbook for Performing Artists* (Sherry Eaker, editor) has a helpful article about head shots. It suggests that you ask a prospective photographer some of the following questions:

- Have you taken head shots before? Could I see your portfolio? (When reviewing the portfolio, look at the expression in the subject's eyes. Is the look engaging or vacant? Is the smile genuine or tense? Does the pose capture the "best side" of the person, or just look staged? Does the skin texture look real? Does the photograph have the look of a real person or of someone who has been retouched and airbrushed into a homogenized glamorous look? How is the lighting in the shots?

- Do you take Polaroids first? Could I see some before and after shots?

- What do you charge for head shots? (Prices seem to range from $75 to $750.) What is included in this fee?

- How many rolls of film do you shoot? What format do you use? Do you give your clients the negatives or charge for them? Do you charge for airbrushing or retouching? Do you do the blowups and reprints yourself or will you recommend where I can get them done?

- How long will it be before I get to see the contact sheets?

- How far in advance do I need to book a sitting? How long is a typical sitting?

- Do you require a deposit? Will you refund the deposit or reshoot if I don't like the results?

- Are hair and makeup included in the price? Will you recommend a stylist?

It is very important that you feel a rapport with the photographer. When you feel comfortable during a photo session, the photographs themselves reflect this. If the chemistry just is not right between you and the photographer, find someone else.

Here are some things you should bring to your photo session:

- changes of clothing, with particular attention to your waist-up look;

☐ additional makeup;

☐ hairbrush, comb, hairspray, mousse, or gel;

☐ extra shaving equipment for men;

☐ a favorite photo of yourself done in the past;

☐ anything which will help you to relax such as tapes. (I've even known people to bring a favorite stuffed animal or herbal tea.);

☐ any props that you discuss in advance with your photographer, such as glasses, a book, or a musical instrument; and

☐ additional jewelry, such as a change of earrings.

Once you have the contact sheets, show them to a variety of people—parents, teachers, friends, and an agent (if you have one)—and seek opinions. Keep track of these opinions on a separate piece of paper. The photographer will probably indicate his or her two favorite choices. Remember that this is a photograph you will have to live with for a time, so choose carefully. Be sure that your photo has your name either on the front or the back, so that if it becomes separated from your résumé, the photograph can still be identified.

Drama Auditions

What to Expect

Most drama auditions consist of you presenting monologues of your choice from memory. Some programs may assign required monologues or ask you to improvise, sing *a cappella* (unaccompanied), participate in a movement class, possibly do a dance combination audition, or a cold reading. Some may also ask you to write an essay while you are there for the audition.

When you attend an audition, there may be a group warm-up. If so, use this time to make sure that your voice is working and your body is relaxed. Once you enter the audition room, be prepared to answer a few short questions from the audition panel. Questions like, "Where are you from?" or "How did you get here today?" are intended to help you relax. If the audition panel suggests that you "take a few minutes to gather yourself before you present your first monologue," do not use the time to go through your whole warm-up in front of them. Just take a few deep breaths and think about getting into character for the part you will play.

Timing of Auditions

It is very important for drama students to submit applications well in advance of any deadlines. Because there are usually many more applicants to drama programs than can be accepted, one means of elimination is to observe the deadline strictly. Do not procrastinate in sending your application! And, if possible, schedule your first-choice school as your second or third audition, not your first.

Choosing Monologues

Some programs will give you a list of suggested monologues. The list is just that: suggestions. You need not choose something from the list, but consider it as a guideline for the type of material the audition panel considers appropriate. Be sure to observe the time limit suggested: usually two monologues not to exceed a total length of four minutes. Most often you are asked to present one monologue from the classical repertoire and one contemporary monologue of a contrasting nature. While looking through a book of monologues may be helpful, you should also know the whole play and the monologue in context. Jocelyn Beard has edited a number of books of monologues, which may be obtained from Smith and Kraus Publishers, Inc., Main Street, P.O. Box 10, Newbury, Vermont 05051 (802-866-5423).

In choosing your monologues give some thought to your "type." Are you an ingenue? A character actor? What age range are you most comfortable playing? Some people will work from a process of elimination: "I'm not a (fill in the blank)." The best advice is to choose a monologue you are comfortable performing and that you can present with conviction. Remember, an audition is a performance.

Suggested Monologues for Auditions

In surveying various Theater/Drama departments, the following seemed to be commonly suggested monologues.

Sample Audition Scenes for Women

CLASSICAL

Aeschylus	*AGAMEMNON*	Clytemnestra (telling how she killed Agamemnon)
Beaumont/ Fletcher	*THE MAID'S TRAGEDY*	Aspatia, Act II, Scene 1 (line 5)
Euripides	*TROJAN WOMEN*	Andromache (giving up son to be killed by Greeks)
	IPHIGENIA AT AULOS	Iphigenia
Middleton	*THE CHANGELING*	Beatrice Joanna
Shakespeare	*THE MERCHANT OF VENICE*	Portia, Act III, Scene 2 (line 149)
	ALL'S WELL THAT ENDS WELL	Helena, Act I, Scene 3 (line 197)
	KING JOHN	Constance, Act III, Scene 1 (line 43)
	RICHARD III	Anne, Act I, Scene 2, (line 1)
	HENRY IV, PART 1	Lady Percy, Act II, Scene 3 (line 40)
	HENRY IV, PART 2	Lady Percy, Act II, Scene 3 (line 9)
	HAMLET	Ophelia, Act III, Scene 1 (line 158)
	OTHELLO	Desdemona, Act I, Scene 3 (line 249)
	COMEDY OF ERRORS	Adriana, Act II, Scene 2 (line 111)
	MIDSUMMER NIGHT'S DREAM	Helena, Act III, Scene 2 (line 195)
	THE WINTER'S TALE	Hermione, Act III, Scene 2, (line 90)
	THE WINTER'S TALE	Paulina, Act III, Scene 2 (line 173)
	CYMBELINE	Imogen, Act III, Scene 6 (line 1)
	HENRY VI, PART 3	Queen Margaret, Act I, Scene 1 (line 230)
Sophocles	*ANTIGONE*	Antigone (answering Creon, daring his law)
Webster	*THE WHITE DEVIL*	Vittoria (Trial Scene)

CONTEMPORARY

Anouilh	*THE LARK*	Joan
Chekhov	*THREE SISTERS*	Irina
	UNCLE VANYA	Sonya
Elder	*CEREMONIES IN DARK OLD MEN*	Adelaide
Giradoux	*APOLLO OF BELLAC*	Agnes
Hansberry	*A RAISIN IN THE SUN*	Beneatha
Martin	*TALKING WITH...*	
McNally	*NOON*	Allegra
Medoff	*WHEN YOU COMING BACK, RED RYDER*	Angel
O'Neill	*BEYOND THE HORIZON*	Ruth
	MOURNING BECOMES ELECTRA	Levomoa
Patrick	*KENNEDY'S CHILDREN*	Carla
Rabe	*IN THE BOOM BOOM ROOM*	Chrissie
Shange	*FOR COLORED GIRLS...*	
Shaw	*HEARTBREAK HOUSE*	Ellie
	MAJOR BARBARA	Barbara
Shepard	*TOOTH OF CRIME*	Becky
	ANGEL CITY	Miss Scoom
	BURIED CHILD	Shellie
Williams	*SUMMER AND SMOKE*	Alma
	TALK TO ME LIKE THE RAIN	Girl
	CAT ON A HOT TIN ROOF	Maggie
	ORPHEUS DESCENDING	Carol

Sample Audition Scenes for Men

CLASSICAL

Euripides	*HIPPOLYTUS*	Hippolytus (speech against women, after learning of Phaedra's love)
Jonson	*THE ALCHEMIST*	Sir Epicure, Act II, Scene 1
		Subtle, Act II, Scene 2
Middleton	*THE CHANGELING*	Deflores
Shakespeare	*TAMING OF THE SHREW*	Petruchio, Act IV, Scene 1 (line 191)
	TWO GENTLEMEN OF VERONA	Proteus, Act II, Scene 6 (line 1)
		Val, Act III, Scene 1 (line 170)
	MUCH ADO ABOUT NOTHING	Benedick, Act II, Scene 3 (line 7)
	TWELFTH NIGHT	Sebastian, Act IV, Scene 3 (line 1)
	TROILUS AND CRESSIDA	Ulysses, Act III, Scene 3 (line 145)
	HENRY VI, PART 3	Richard of Gloucester, Act III, Scene 2 (line 124)
		Richard, Duke of York, Act I, Scene 4 (line 111)
	HENRY V	Henry, Act III, Scene 1 (line 1)
		Henry, Act I , Scene 1 (line 259)

	JULIUS CAESAR	Brutus, Act III, Scene 2 (line 13)
	OTHELLO	Iago, Act I, Scene 3 (line 338)
		Othello, Act III, Scene 3 (line 258)
	RICHARD II	Mowbray, Act I, Scene 3 (line 154)
	KING LEAR	Edgar, Act III, Scene 6 (line 102)
	MEASURE FOR MEASURE	Claudio, Act III, Scene 1 (line 117)
	THE TEMPEST	Ferdinand, Act III, Scene 1 (line 1)
	HENRY IV, PART 2	Prince Hal, Act IV, Scene 5 (line 20 or 138)
	PERICLES	Pericles, Act I, Scene 1 (line 121)
	TITUS ANDRONICUS	Aaron the Moor, Act IV, Scene 2 (line 88)
Sheridan	*THE RIVALS*	Jack Absolute
Sophocles	*ANTIGONE*	Messenger's Final Speech
Webster	*THE DUCHESS OF MALFI*	Ferdinand, Act III, Scene 2 (line 120)
		Basola, Act V, Scene 2 (line 328)

CONTEMPORARY

Babe	*KID CHAMPION*	Kid
Bullins	*IN THE WINE TIME*	Cliff Dawson
Chekov	*THE THREE SISTERS*	Andrey
	THE SEAGULL	Treplev
Davis	*MASS APPEAL*	Mark Dolson
Elder	*CEREMONIES IN DARK OLD MEN*	Mr. Bluehaven
Gordone	*NO PLACE TO BE SOMEBODY*	Johnny Williams
Horowitz	*THE INDIAN WANTS THE BRONX*	
Ibsen	*GHOSTS*	Oswald
Inge	*PICNIC*	Hal
O'Neill	*BEYOND THE HORIZON*	Rob
	AH! WILDERNESS	Richard
Peterson, D.	*DOES THE TIGER WEAR A NECKTIE*	Bickell
Peterson, L.	*TAKE A GIANT STEP*	Spencer
Rabe	*THE BASIC TRAINING OF PAVLO HUMMEL*	Pavlo
	STREAMERS	Billy
Shepard	*TOOTH OF CRIME*	Hoss
	BURIED CHILD	Vince or Tilden
	CURSE OF THE STARVING CLASS	Wesley
Wilder	*OUR TOWN*	George
	THE MATCHMAKER	Cornelius
Williams	*SWEET BIRD OF YOUTH*	Chance
	CAT ON A HOT TIN ROOF	Brick
	THE GLASS MENAGERIE	Tom
Wilson, L.	*BURN THIS*	Pale

What to Wear

Black seems to be the color for drama auditions: women in black dresses or leotards with a skirt or black pants and a black turtleneck, and men in black pants and turtlenecks. If this is your color, that's fine. The bottom line for your audition is to dress comfortably so that you can move freely and yet nicely to indicate respect for the situation. Dress for drama auditions does seem to be more casual than for classical music auditions. For the basic monologue part of the audition women should wear a skirt (not too short) and blouse or a simple dress or pants with a sweater or blouse, and shoes with low to medium heels. Men should choose a turtleneck and pants or a shirt and pants. Suits, or jackets and ties, are not recommended—and neither are sweat suits! Since an actor's body is his or her instrument, it is important to wear something that gives some indication of what shape you are in. You should inquire if there is a required movement class also, and bring appropriate attire for that.

Before You Audition

It is important that you know exactly what will be expected of you at the audition. Will you have to write an essay while you are there for the audition, to show that you can write in English? Does the audition schedule involve callbacks? How much time should you realistically set aside for this audition? Be sure to ask enough questions so that you know exactly what to bring with you and what to expect, without making a pest of yourself.

Practice Auditions

The best way to prepare for an audition is to practice often in a mock audition situation. Videotape your mock audition and ask members of your audition audience to critique your performance as you watch the tape. Do this often, up to a week before the audition, so that you feel totally comfortable about your presentation. Prepare yourself mentally so that you go to every audition with the most positive mental attitude, anticipating success.

Regional Auditions

Drama programs will sometimes hold auditions in chosen cities as well as on campus. Because regional auditions are very popular, it is important that you submit your application early, before all audition openings are booked.

Videotaped versus Live Auditions

A live audition is always better than a videotape. If you absolutely must submit a video as your only possible way of auditioning, do not go for a glitzy professionally produced video which will cost you a fortune. A well-done (hold the camera steady and have the picture in focus!) home video is fine for this, but remember you are not helping your chances for admission by not attending in person! Do not send an unsolicited videotape as it will probably end up in a pile—unwatched.

Nerves

What do you do if you walk into the audition room and your knees are shaking, you cannot get a good breath, and your voice is quaking? It helps to remember that everyone else is in the same boat, and an attack of nerves is totally normal. Try deep breathing:

breathing in on a count of four and out on eight. Do not be ashamed to say, "I'm so nervous," but do not let that be an excuse for yourself. Use the beginning of the audition to relax as best you can, and then to get into the character of the first monologue. If you think of the audition panel as an audience at your performance, you may get past the nerves.

Audition Evaluation Criteria

When an audition panel watches you, they are evaluating several things. The audition sheets on pages 54–56 indicate the kinds of things they are looking for.

What NOT to Do at a Drama Audition

☐ Do not try to play something other than the core of the part. Play the character and do not get caught up in the language.

☐ Do not just learn the monologue. Read the entire play and know the context for the monologue.

☐ Never leave the room during an audition. There are some humorous yet sad stories about applicants who either wanted to make an entrance or exit, in character, for their monologue and walked out of the room, only to discover that the door would not open again. Applicants who think they may need water should bring a plastic cup in with them to the audition, so as not to need to leave the room. Also, at the end of the audition, do not leave until the faculty panel invites you to go.

☐ Do not drag in props or set pieces. A piece of paper for a letter scene may be fine, but anything beyond that is not appropriate. Most places will have a chair or two and a table to use as props if you need them.

☐ Do not even think of changing costumes between monologues!

☐ Do not stand too close to the audition panel.

☐ Do not get up on the audition table.

☐ Do not use the audition panel as your scene partners. It is better to play slightly above their heads.

☐ Do not tell the audition panel your life story if you are asked a simple question.

☐ Do not cry before your scene.

☐ Do not do your warm-up in the audition room. Walk in prepared.

☐ Do not take forever with your "actor focus moment" before you start your scene.

☐ Do not throw things around the room.

Sample Drama Questions to Ask

What is the enrollment in the drama department? Males? Females? Undergraduates? Graduates?

How many faculty members are there? Full-time? Part-time?

How many faculty members are working professionals? How many have more of an academic background and approach?

Do you require an audition? If so, what is required?

What does the basic curriculum entail? What acting technique is taught?

What is the philosophy of the program?

Who are your resident directors?

Who have been recent directors of your productions?

Do you have a program of master classes with guest speakers? Who have been the guest speakers in the past two years? Did students have an opportunity to get to know the guests?

What repertoire is performed?

How and when do you evaluate a student's progress? Do you have a "cut" after one or two years?

How often do the students perform each semester? Which of the following types of performing opportunities are available and how frequently? Fully produced productions? Informal workshops? Workshops? In-school performances (at high schools, etc.), off-campus performances?

Are student-initiated projects encouraged? Is there a budget for these? What are examples of such projects in the past two years?

What performing facilities are available for students (if you have not seen them on your campus tour)?

How many productions are presented by your drama program each year?

What is the casting policy? (Ask a student, "Is the casting policy fair?")

(At a liberal arts college): Is there a drama club? What is the relationship between the extracurricular drama activities and the drama department?

Does the college have any relationship with a professional theater company or summer stock theater? If so, which one and what is the relationship?

Does the college help students to obtain an Equity card?

Are there any restrictions on first-year (freshman) activities in the department? In casting?

What are the strengths and weaknesses of this program?

(Ask a student): If you had it all to do over again, would you choose this program?

Who are some famous alumni?

What do the majority of alumni go on to do?

Do you teach auditioning skills?

Is there any sort of alumni network?

Is there a technical requirement? If so, what is it?

Does the school recruit at any thespian societies? Which ones? Are there any scholarships available through these?

Does the school participate in any of the regional events of the American College Theater Festivals?

YALE DRAMA   CONFIDENTIAL

1992 AUDITION NOTES

Auditioner: _____

Date: _____

NAME: _____   Program: M.F.A.   CERTIFICATE

CONTEMPORARY: _____

   Is talking immediate:

   Are actions used:

   Is there a purpose/arc:

   Is it spontaneous:

   Is there an organic character:

   Is it personalized:

   Are there clear transitions:

   Sense of humor:

   Trainable:

CLASSICAL: _____

   Vocal quality:

   Speech:

   Physically alive:

   Phrasing:

   Sensitivity to language:

   Use of actions:

   Use of self in the circumstances:

   Spontaneity:

_____	_____	_____	_____
TAKE	POSSIBLE	LOW POSSIBLE	NO

COMMENTS:

Carnegie Mellon
Department of Drama — Audition Form

Audition City _____ Audition Date _____
Option: Acting _____   Music Theater _____

_____
Last Name   First Name   Initial

_____
Street   City   State   ZIP
( )
Phone   Age   Height   Weight
Can you: read music? _____ sing? _____
    play an instrument? _____ ... If yes, what? _____
Music Theater Option ONLY: _____
            Language studied   Years studied

_____
High School or College Name   City   State

Is there any reason why you can NOT participate in a strenuous program of physical development?

_____

_____

Polaroid picture

TRAINING...outside of high school   Acting   Singing   Dancing
  Years Studied   _____   _____   _____
  Teacher's Name   _____   _____   _____
EXPERIENCE...list representative roles; If you have a résumé, please attach.
  Play   _____   _____   _____   _____
  Role   _____   _____   _____   _____
  Date Performed   _____   _____   _____   _____
  Place Performed   _____   _____   _____   _____
AUDITION   Acting (two pieces REQUIRED)   Singing (Music Theater ONLY...two pieces REQUIRED)
  Play/Song   _____   _____   _____   _____
  Character   _____   _____   _____   _____

_____ DO NOT WRITE BELOW THIS LINE _____

0 1 2   3 4 5   6 7 8   9

_____ signed   _____ date

Juilliard Drama

CITY _____   DATE _____

NAME _____   YES _____

AGE _____   NO _____

POSSIBLE _____

	CLASSICAL	CONTEMPORARY	COLD READING	ADDITIONAL
SCENE				
VOICE				
SPEECH				
BODY				
PERFORMANCE				

General Impressions:

APPEARANCE:

TRAINING:

ATTITUDE:

POTENTIAL:

OTHER REMARKS:

Signed_____

Adding to Your College Notebook

You might want to keep a page of impressions about your drama department visit and include some of the information provided on the Drama Program Rating Sheet below.

Drama Program Rating Sheet

Size of department: (Too large, you won't be cast; too small, no variety)

❑ Small ❑ Medium ❑ Large

Faculty: ❑ Professional Actors ❑ Academics ❑ Combination

Specific Acting Technique:

Courses Offered:

❑ Alexander technique
❑ Dramatic verse/literature
❑ Drama history
❑ Masks
❑ Commedia del'Arte
❑ Movement
❑ Music studies
❑ Liberal arts courses
❑ Physical comedy
❑ Singing
❑ Speech
❑ Stage combat
❑ Stage makeup
❑ Tap dance
❑ Voice

❑ Text analysis
❑ Monologue class
❑ Audition workshop
❑ Period styles
❑ Mime
❑ Improvisation
❑ Scene studies
❑ Acrobatics
❑ Jazz dance
❑ Technical theater (scene shop)
❑ Design (scene, costume, lighting)
❑ Directing
❑ Stage management
❑ Arts management
❑ Other: _____

Facilities: ❑ State-of-the-art ❑ Bare bones ❑ Anything in between (describe)

Productions: Number, quality, diversity

Current students' opinions:

Famous alumni:

Job placement record:

My Personal Reaction:

Drama Admissions Checklist

Here are some questions to ask yourself at various points in the admissions process:

Have I...

❏ requested catalogs and read them carefully?

❏ requested applications and made photocopies of those in which I am most interested?

❏ started a college notebook to record impressions of colleges, audition and repertoire requirements, and deadlines?

❏ obtained a social security number?

❏ registered for the PSATs?

❏ obtained information about the ARTs scholarships? (National Foundation for Advancement in the Arts, 3915 Biscayne Boulevard, Miami, Florida 33137 (305) 573-0490.)

❏ made an appointment with my guidance counselor or college advisor to discuss future plans?

❏ looked into working with an independent counselor, if appropriate?

❏ talked with my current drama or acting teacher about my future plans?

❏ participated regularly in school, community, or professional productions?

❏ made arrangements to continue my involvement in drama activities?

❏ discussed my future high school curriculum with my guidance counselor?

❏ discussed standardized test choices with my guidance counselor?

❏ investigated summer programs/jobs and applied as necessary?

❏ investigated sources of financial aid?

❏ kept a file of performance programs, videotaped shows, good term papers, articles, etc.?

❏ attended college fairs and met with college representatives?

❏ registered for standardized tests (SAT, ACT, TOEFL, Achievement Tests)?

❏ arranged my college visits?

❏ scheduled interview appointments?

❏ sent thank-you notes to admissions counselors after interviews?

Have I...

- ❏ chosen my audition material?

- ❏ narrowed my list of colleges?

- ❏ considered applying for Early Decision? (Deadlines generally are in early to mid-November.)

- ❏ asked for letters of recommendation from teachers/former employers?

- ❏ drafted my college application essays?

- ❏ finished my essays and applications and photocopied everything before mailing?

- ❏ practiced my audition material regularly?

- ❏ applied for financial aid?

- ❏ requested that ETS, ACT, or TOEFL send official score reports to the colleges which require them?

- ❏ videotaped practice auditions to be critiqued?

- ❏ submitted videotapes for prescreening, if necessary?

- ❏ had necessary photographs taken to submit with applications?

- ❏ prepared a résumé?

- ❏ requested that a copy of my transcript be sent to colleges, as required?

- ❏ communicated regularly with my guidance counselor or college advisor about my progress in school and in college admission?

- ❏ kept up with schoolwork?

- ❏ perfected audition material?

- ❏ prepared a list of extracurricular activities in which I've participated?

- ❏ completed all financial aid documentation?

- ❏ read carefully all audition and schedule information sent to me?

- ❏ responded to colleges about acceptance offers?

- ❏ requested an extension beyond the May 1 Candidates Reply Deadline, if necessary?

4
For Music Majors

Advanced Study in Music

Bachelor of Arts (B.A.) versus Bachelor of Music (B.M.)

Unlike drama students choosing between a B.A. and a B.F.A., music students will find more differences between a B.A. and a B.M. than just proportion of courses taken in the liberal arts and in applied music. Often students choosing the route of the B.A. do not want to major in music, but do want to take some music courses and continue private lessons. If you want to apply to graduate school on the master's level, it is important that at the bachelor's level you do continue your musical study, otherwise you will fall behind in both your major area of study (instrument or voice) and in music history, ear training, and music theory.

The instrument you play has some bearing on your choice of a program. For instance, singers can pursue liberal arts studies for at least two years before turning to more concentrated voice study. If you are a violinist or pianist, however, age seems to be more important and if you are serious about a performing career, you may want to focus on a Bachelor of Music degree program. Age seems to matter slightly less for cellists and little for violists and double bass players, in the string family. Most wind, brass, and percussion players can also wait to pursue focused musical studies in a B.M. degree, but flutists are advised to go directly into the B.M. program. Because of the intensely competitive nature of the flute, age does matter more than on other wind instruments.

Popular music, musical theater, and jazz do seem a bit more flexible in admissions and the age factor, so whether to pursue focused musical studies at the undergraduate level or to get a more general education seems to be a matter of personal choice.

There are many well-known musicians whose choices may serve as examples. Some which come immediately to mind are cellist Yo-Yo Ma, who did his undergraduate work at Harvard, while continuing his cello studies and participating in music programs during the summers; he then went on to Juilliard for graduate school. Pianist Emanuel Ax went to Columbia. Flutist Eugenia Zukerman attended Barnard College for two years, and then transferred to Juilliard. Guitarists Eliot Fisk and Sharon Isbin did their undergraduate work at Yale. And then there are the legions of musicians who went directly to conservatories. Obviously this is a highly personal decision, and you must do what feels right to you.

Music Auditions

What to Expect

When you read the catalog, take careful note of whether an audition is optional or required. All major conservatories and joint programs require auditions, as do many college music departments.

Music auditions have been portrayed in a variety of movies and plays, sometimes very accurately. *Fame, A Chorus Line*, and more recently *Running on Empty* all have that hollow, disembodied voice calling out in a hall, "Thank you," often right before that fiendishly difficult passage that you have practiced so carefully and are so sure will reveal your true musical potential. To be honest, very few musical auditions are pleasant experiences. It is generally conceded that music auditions are an experience unto themselves, neither a performance, nor a lesson, nor a rehearsal, nor a "woodshedding" session. After having prepared for years, you are usually given 10 to 15 minutes to demonstrate your level of achievement, talent, and potential, often in a dry, stuffy room, for a group of faculty members who are known worldwide. Sometimes the faculty members whisper among themselves, pass notes, argue about what repertoire to request next from you, or indulge in other activities which do not relate to your performance. It can truly be an intimidating experience. If you know what to expect, however, you will be better prepared to handle even the worst situation.

Remember that you have paid for the audition and this is your time, so make every moment count and take some control of the situation yourself. Also remember that even the most jaded, tired person on the audition panel will respond to excellence, so psyche yourself up to do your best, performing music that you love.

Timing of Auditions

If possible, plan to take your audition during the main audition period for a school, usually in February or March. This is when the school will be filling the greatest number of openings; any further auditions will be held to fill a limited number of vacancies that might exist after the newly admitted applicants from the main audition period have responded to the offer of admission. So, if you wait until May, some departments may already be closed and others may have only a few openings.

Schools usually set audition weeks and then contact the faculty to see which day within that week is best for them to hear auditions. To be safe, block off the entire audition week listed in a school's catalog. You are not able to choose the day that you would like to audition; the school determines this. If you run into a major conflict, call the admissions office and see if there is any way to resolve it.

By submitting your application early, you may possibly secure a better audition time. If you know of a conflict in advance, you might request that your audition be on a certain day, but whether or not your request is honored will depend upon faculty availability. Never try to contact faculty directly to reschedule an audition; this must go through the admissions office.

Should you need to cancel your audition or postpone it to the later audition period, be sure to call and then follow up with a letter. Many admissions offices will take note of your phone call, but only consider your communication official when put in writing. If you must cancel on the day of the audition or if you are somehow delayed, be sure to call as soon as possible. Nothing is more frustrating to an audition committee than wasting time waiting for a no-show.

Try to arrive at least one hour ahead of your audition time, but be sure to read any schedule letter sent to you by the school very carefully. Some schools have group activities or speeches you are expected to attend before the auditions start. In any event, you do want to have time to locate the audition room, check in, and find a practice room for a good warm-up. It is a good idea to do a preliminary warm-up before you leave for your audition. Practice rooms or warm-up space may be at a premium, and you may not be altogether comfortable going through your entire warm-up routine surrounded by other applicants.

What to Wear

What you wear to an audition is important. Just as for an interview, you should have an "audition costume." Singers tend to be dressier than instrumentalists. Neatness, cleanliness, and comfort are all important, but so is the fact that you are appearing in a performance. You want to convey to the faculty that you take this audition seriously and have dressed for it appropriately. Recommendations:

Women instrumentalists: a nice skirt (not too short or too long), blouse, and a blazer, if comfortable; or a simple dress (not too frilly, flouncy, or provocative). Low to medium heels.

Women singers: a simple dress, neither too short nor too long. Silk, or a silklike fabric, seems to be the most popular. No glitter, evening gowns or fancy recital dresses, plunging necklines, or outrageous stockings. If you want to make a "statement," let it be with the color, not the style. (Brown and beige are not good stage colors.) Be sure that the dress fits well so that you have plenty of room to breathe, without bursting any seams, buttons, or zippers. (This happens more often than you would imagine!) Shoes should be low to medium heels—no spike heels.

Men (including singers):   a nice pair of pants, a shirt, jacket and tie, and loafers or shoes. (The traditional look of gray trousers, white shirt, tie, and navy blue blazer is very popular and appropriate.) If you want to make a "statement," let it be with your tie! No tuxes, tails, fancy suits, jeans, or sneakers. For singers and wind players, be sure that the shirt is large enough so that you do not have to leave the top button open or loosen your tie.

Before You Audition

The importance of preparation for your audition cannot be stressed enough. Classical musicians should start with the repertoire. Check your catalogs in your sophomore year and start planning your repertoire accordingly. Usually you must perform from memory. You need to live with your selections long enough to know that you can perform them with total security technically and emotionally. By choosing your repertoire early, you also allow yourself time to make a switch if you want to.

Popular musicans should also start early with repertoire preparation. If you are required to perform standards, get them in your blood so that you will be able to improvise easily. And, if you plan to perform any original compositions, preparing early will allow you to try out the compositions in a variety of settings and get some feedback from teachers, colleagues, and audiences.

As you read the catalog, note whether you will be required to take any additional examinations, such as an ear training, sight reading, or a music theory test. If so, be sure to do some review and familiarize yourself with the test as best you can. The most common texts for study seem to be:

Music Theory

Piston, Walter. *Harmony,* 4th edition.

Jeppesen, Knud. *Counterpoint: The Polyphonic Vocal Style of the 16th Century.*

Fux, J. J. *Gradus ad Parnassum.*

Kennan, Kent. *Counterpoint.*

Music History

Grout, Donald. *The History of Western Music,* 4th edition.

Salzman, Eric. *Twentieth Century Music: An Introduction.*

Piano Literature

Hinson, Maurice. *Guide to the Pianist's Literature.*

Matthews, Dinis, ed. *Keyboard Music.*

Keyboard Studies

Morris, R. O. *Preparatory Exercises in Score Reading and Figured Harmony at the Keyboard, Book I.*

Once your repertoire is under control, you must begin your mental and emotional preparation for the audition. There are many parallels between music performance and sports. Just as an athlete must have tremendous powers of concentration, so should a musician. You must not allow distractions from the audition panel to interfere with your performance. Learn to focus your concentration on the music and your performance of it. Walk into the audition with confidence and a positive attitude. Know your music inside and out but when you play, play from the heart.

Types of Auditions

Auditions are run in different ways from school to school, but there do seem to be some common types of auditions.

On-campus for a Representative Group of the Faculty

This seems to be the most common type of audition. You arrive at the campus and are told that the auditions for your major field of study (instrument, voice, musical theater, etc.) are being held in a certain room. You locate the room, check in with a monitor, meet your accompanist, have a few minutes to warm up and check tempi, and then are told that the faculty are ready to hear you. You walk into the room and are confronted with from three to sixteen distinguished faculty members. (Piano, violin, and voice seem to have the largest number of audition panel members.) One of these people will usually act as coordinator of the audition. Take your lead from this person. You might say, "Hi, my name is Sally Smith," and proceed to sit down (or stand) and wait for the panel to acknowledge you. If you are playing with an accompanist, the pianist should already have your music in order. Do not start until the coordinator of the audition tells you to. In some auditions, you may be asked some simple questions to help you relax before you play. In other auditions, the coordinator may simply say something like, "With what would you like to start today?"

Most schools let you start your audition with a piece of your choosing. You should select that piece very carefully. It need not be the most difficult piece in your repertoire, but it should be a piece that you really love and one that shows you off to your best. The audition panel may cut you off while you are in the midst of this piece, but do not start off expecting to be stopped; this will leave your concentration unfocused. Rather, keep focused and enjoy yourself as best you can, getting "into" the music.

Usually the audition committee will ask you to perform something else from your repertoire. Before you start that selection, be sure to take a deep breath and focus your mental energy and concentration on this new piece. If you are asked for another selection following this one, follow the same procedure.

Before you start to play or sometimes before you leave an audition, faculty members may ask you a few simple questions, such as, "Where are you from?", "How long have you studied and where?", "How much do you practice each day?", "Do you make your own reeds?", "What kind of horn is that?", "What is the extent of your orchestral experience?", etc. You may or may not be asked to name your current teacher. Whatever you do, do not be thrown by these questions and be sure to answer honestly, thoughtfully, and completely. International students are not allowed to bring translators, so you might want to practice your responses to questions such as these prior to your audition. Your audition is over when the faculty indicates that you may go. The length of auditions varies, but tends to be 10 to 15 minutes on the average, depending on the instrument. Percussion, accompanying, and organ auditions are usually a little longer. You may feel that the faculty is being remote, detached, or unfriendly in an audition of this nature. In fact, they are trying to be objective and fair, and judge you on the quality of your music-making. You should also realize that sitting for many hours listening intently to auditions is hard work, and people do get tired and cantankerous. If you take control of your instrument and are as pleasant and confident as possible, the image that you project will help to warm up the room.

For a Single Faculty Member

Some schools will have you audition only for the faculty member you have indicated you want to study with, or the school will have a one-person department. These auditions may be run like the audition just described, or they may be more like a lesson or consultation, so that the faculty member can see how you work and decide whether or not you are responsive to the teaching methods he or she uses. These auditions may be longer, perhaps even 30 minutes. Be prepared to be flexible.

Regional Auditions

Regional auditions, sometimes called "external auditions," held in selected cities around the country and more frequently, internationally, are usually conducted by a member of the administration. Sometimes faculty representatives are present, but usually regional auditions are taped or videotaped and those tapes are then played for the faculty.

If you cannot go to the campus for a personal audition, a regional audition is a good alternative. Anticipate walking into the room, introducing yourself, choosing your first selection and then being asked to play something contrasting from your repertoire list. A third selection may be requested, and you may be asked a few questions before you are dismissed

Taped versus Live Auditions

Some schools are requesting that audiotapes or videotapes be submitted with applications for a pre-screening review to see who should be invited to audition in person. Be sure that you follow the format a school requires: if audiotape, is it a standard cassette? If video, must it be American-format VHS? The audio quality of the tape should be as high as possible, and if it is a video, be sure that the camera is in focus and that the background is not distracting. (Do not bother with an expensively produced video. A good home video with high quality audio is just fine.) You should label your tapes carefully with your name, address, instrument, and the repertoire presented, in the order in which you perform it on the tape. If you make it past this prescreening, you will be invited to perform in person.

Live auditions are always preferred to tapes, so you should make every effort to get to an on-campus or a regional audition. Sending an audiotape or videotape for your actual audition may slightly diminish your chances for admission. If you are a prize-winning performer, with many professional credits, then you may present yourself well on tape. Anyone else should really aim to perform in person.

Difficult Situations to Anticipate

No matter how well prepared you are, you may still encounter a situation which you could not possibly have anticipated. Some examples follow.

Faculty members who argue among themselves about your repertoire choices: You have just presented your first selection and now the coordinator asks for something else. Another faculty member does not want to hear that and speaks up. A debate ensues. You should just sit there patiently until this debate is resolved.

Lack of interest from the faculty: This may either be because you are scheduled right before lunch, when the focus is on food, or right after lunch, when panel members may be sleepy, or late in the day, when they are tired. The best way to handle this situation is to be as energetic and positive as possible, and totally dedicated to the music. If they do not ask you to play a second selection, it does get a little tricky. They may have really liked you and not needed to hear more. On the other hand, if you did not do your very best on that first piece, you might tactfully try suggesting, "Well, I do have my Paganini *Caprice* and it's really short. Since I've only had five minutes of your time, perhaps you'd let me start this." If you do not feel comfortable with this, then stop by the admissions office and let them know what happened.

Unfortunate remarks by faculty members: Sometimes you may say the name of your teacher, and there may be some history or politics involved, and someone on the audition panel may say something like, "Oh, is that person *still* teaching?" Do not let this throw you. You are being evaluated on the quality of your music-making, not on who your teacher is.

Faculty members who stand up and walk around, pass candies among themselves, or engage in some other distracting activity: Keep your concentration. Some people may move around because they cannot see your embouchure or fingerings from where they are sitting. This does not necessarily mean that they have lost interest or want you to stop. Some may have been sitting for quite a while and need to stand up and move around.

Anything out of the blue: Perhaps the hardest thing at an audition is being asked to do something you had not expected or prepared for. For example, you might be asked to improvise, to sight-read, or to answer questions about a piece you may have studied but are not prepared to play. Since this is your time, take control of the situation and present your strengths. If you have not had much practice at sight reading and did not anticipate this as part of your audition, you might say, "I'd be happy to give this a try, but I would love a minute or two to look it over, as I spent my time preparing the specified repertoire for this audition."

What if your accompanist plays poorly? Remember, the faculty is listening to you, not to the accompanist. Just keep going and do your best.

If an audition really goes poorly, you should stop at the admissions office and ask to speak with either the director or assistant director. Be very specific about what transpired. Perhaps another audition can be arranged.

Repertoire Choices

If you do not submit the required repertoire on your application, many schools will not allow you to audition and will reject your application outright, so be sure that you are conforming to the requirements. If you have any doubts, write a letter (not a phone call in this case) to the admissions office and ask if what you are planning meets with the faculty's standards. This is particularly true in piano, where the repertoire is vast and the interpretation of the word "substantial," used in several catalogs, is open to debate.

Be sure to choose music which you really love from within the repertoire requirements; this will make it much more pleasurable to perform under duress. Don't make the mistake of choosing an aria or sonata you think the audition panel *wants* to hear. You will do well only if you really like what you have chosen to perform.

Changing repertoire may be permitted, but be sure that whatever composition you are substituting conforms with the overall requirements. You should write to the admissions office with your change of repertoire, but also announce it at the beginning of your audition. Typing a new "Audition Repertoire List" and having enough copies to distribute to the faculty at the audition may be a good thing to do.

Practice Auditions

One of the best ways to prepare for the audition is to do it, under mock or concert circumstances many, many times. Videotape each mock audition and critique it yourself, as well as seeking the evaluation of others. One pianist from Texas who was admitted to several schools used her mock audition times as an opportunity for fund-raising. She would charge a modest admission, as though this were a mini-concert, and then play and discuss the performance with the audience afterwards.

When you set up these mock auditions, try out the clothing which you think that you will wear. Can you breathe? Can you walk in the shoes you have chosen? Also give yourself a number of sample rooms to audition in. While some audition rooms may be concert halls with wonderful acoustics, others are teaching studios with very dead acoustics. Get used to performing under a variety of circumstances and don't let anything distract you from doing your best.

What to Bring with You

Before you leave for your audition, look at the catalog one more time and reexamine the letter sent to you with your audition schedule. Do you need to bring manuscript paper and pencils? (Conductors and composers often do.) It may also be helpful to take a look at your photocopy of the application you sent in, just to refresh your memory about what you wrote. Here are some questions to ask yourself before you leave for the audition:

☐ Do I have copies of the music which I am prepared to perform?

☐ Do I have a copy of the schedule letter which was sent to me to glance at for reference?

☐ Do I have all my audition clothing? Shoes?

☐ Do I have all the equipment I need? These may include a music stand, sticks and brushes (percussionists), your instrument—including mouthpiece, mutes, bows, etc. (Believe it or not, a guitarist once showed up at Juilliard with his guitar case but no instrument inside!), any extra copies of your audition repertoire list just in case it is requested, tissues or handkerchiefs (for sweaty palms, to wipe the brow, or as a basic prop), or a cup for water, if you think you may need it.

Partners / Accompanists

Most schools require that classical instrumentalists play a sonata or concerto with piano accompaniment. If it is at all feasible, bring your own accompanist, with whom you have worked regularly. If this is not possible, call in advance (two weeks usually) and get the name of the school's accompanist assigned to your instrument. Call that person and ask if he or she would be willing to play for you. If at all possible, arrange to rehearse a day in advance. While this may cost you anywhere from $15 to $50, it is well worth the charge, as you will feel more at ease if you have done this extra preparation and worked out tempi in advance with the pianist. If the accompanist does not know something on your repertoire list, ask if he or she would like you to send a copy of the composition in advance or if there is someone else whom he or she might recommend.

Singers should follow essentially the same procedure as for classical instrumentalists. It is best to make repertoire selections from the standard repertoire of arias and art songs if you plan to use anyone other than your own accompanists.

In musical theater, an accompanist is usually provided. Plan in advance what you want to say to the pianist about tempi. You should plan on being cut off after a limited number of measures in your songs.

Popular musicians (jazz) are often invited to sit in with a "house band" for their audition. Have fun!

Accompanists are usually encouraged to bring their own "partners"—usually a violinist and a singer with whom they have worked in the past. If you are unable to bring your own partners, call the school at least two weeks in advance and get the names of the people the school has assigned for these auditions. See if you can schedule a rehearsal the day before the audition.

Whenever you use an accompanist, you must present the music in the best form possible. Arrange to have either the original score or very legible photocopies bound in a loose-leaf notebook or pasted onto cardboard. If you are taking any cuts in the music, be sure that they are marked clearly and that you point these out verbally before the audition. If your interpretation has particular nuances with tempi or dynamics, be certain to mention these verbally and have them clearly indicated in the score. An accompanist is a valuable collaborator and can really give you support during your audition. Make sure that you develop a good rapport with this person and prepare as much as possible. It is generally not advantageous to have your parent or teacher accompany you. Better to use the person assigned by the school and to rehearse in advance with this person.

Nerves

Being nervous for an audition in music is *de rigueur*. In general, the best prescription for nerves is preparation. If you love the compositions you have chosen, focus on the performance aspect of the audition, and cancel out of your mind any sense of judgment, you may have a good time and not be nervous at all. Remember, the people listening want to like you.

Dr. Beth Rom-Rymer, a psychologist in Chicago, did a workshop with members of the Chicago Youth Symphony Orchestra, who shared their feelings about a number of topics, including nerves. (*Upbeat*, Spring, 1991, Vol.6, No.2.)

> *"Many students related to a string player who had such bad stage fright that she had to give up after walking on stage three times, unable to play the piece she had perfected for a competition through many hours of practice. Many other students could empathize with another string player who said he sometimes gets so tense his fingers cramp up and won't move.*

> *"To avoid anxiety before a competition, Dr. Rom-Rymer suggested meditation/relaxation exercises, including cognitive rehearsal for the expected and unforeseen event, using positive and flexible cognitive imagery. You can use your inside as a refuge for relaxing and reverse the anxiety response.*

> *"When feeling tense muscles during long hours of practice, Dr. Rom-Rymer recommended taking time off to relax the body."*

Diane Nichols, head of Mental Health at the Miller Health Care Institute for Performing Artists in New York City, suggests strategies of quieting the physical and psychological symptoms of performance anxiety:

"Develop a pre-performance ritual. It doesn't matter what the ritual entails, as long as you do it regularly to give you a sense of comfort and security. One actor pushes against a wall before every show; a student breakfasts on cereal and bananas before taking an exam. A singer takes a shower. You could lift weights, call Mom, the choice is purely personal.

"Yawn. Yawning relaxes the jaw, neck, and shoulders, and releases tension. It tells the body there's no danger.

"Talk to yourself. When you're fearful you lose sight of your strengths. The next time images of hissing audiences cloud your vision, say out loud, 'I don't have to be perfect,' or some other verbal reminder to put the situation into perspective.

"Breathe. Before stepping into the spotlight, take two slow, deep breaths. It sounds simple, but once you're in control of your breathing patterns, you'll feel more in control of the situation.

"Finally, SMILE. Studies show that you can't smile and feel fear at the same time. In addition to relaxing your muscles, smiling engages the listener as your presentation begins."

Audition Evaluation Criteria

While you are playing or singing, the audition panel will usually be completing forms, evaluating you on a variety of factors. To demystify the process, copies of audition forms from a number of schools are on pages 71–78.

Additional Examinations

As part of some auditions, you will be asked to take additional examinations. These vary from school to school and are used differently: some for admissions purposes and some for placement. Be sure that you are clear about what is expected of you so that you can prepare appropriately. If you are asked to play a separate orchestral placement examination, which will include sight reading excerpts, speak with your teacher about common excerpts, so that you can look them over in advance. Music theory, music history, piano proficiency (for non-keyboard applicants), and ear training are all fairly common audition examinations. For applicants for whom English is not the native language, there may be an English examination. There may be a diction evaluation for singers or a foreign language proficiency examination for doctoral students. Help yourself by preparing as best you can in advance.

THE JUILLIARD SCHOOL

ENTRANCE AUDITION EVALUATION FORM

BACHELOR OF MUSIC OR CERTIFICATE

Student Information	Audition
(Computer Label)	❑ March ❑ Regional ❑ May ❑ Special

Audition Evaluation

Please evaluate the applicant using the categories indicated below:

	Exceptional	Very Good	Good	Fair	Poor	
Technique						
Tone						
Interpretation						
Intonation (Where applicable)						
Rhythm						
Potential						
Overall Rating						

Would you accept this applicant in your schedule?

❑ Yes   ❑ Possibly   ❑ No

Specific Comments: (Please note that this form is used for Admission Committee purposes only.)

Orchestral Instrumentalists:

If admitted, I recommend placement in   ❑ Juilliard Symphony   ❑ Juilliard Orchestra

Signed: _____   Please Print Your Name:

Date: _____   _____

FORM AUD89-A1

THE JUILLIARD SCHOOL

ENTRANCE AUDITION EVALUATION

PIANO

<u>*MASTER OF MUSIC OR ADVANCED CERTIFICATE*</u>

Student Information	**Audition**
(Computer Label)	❏ March ❏ Regional ❏ May ❏ Special

Audition Evaluation	**Bachauer Eligibility**

Performance Grade:

❏ Exceptional

❏ Very Good

❏ Good

❏ Fair

❏ Poor

(Please mark specific numbers)

_____ Exceptional (21-25)

_____ Very Good (16-20)

_____ Maybe (11-15)

_____ No (1-10)

Would you accept this applicant in your schedule?

❏ Yes   ❏ Possibly   ❏ No

Specific Comments: (Please note that this form is used for Admission Committee purposes only.)

Signed: _____

Date: _____

Please Print Your Name:

_____

FORM AUD89-83

THE JUILLIARD SCHOOL   *JUILLIARD OPERA CENTER*

ENTRANCE AUDITION EVALUATION FORM

Student Information	**Audition**
(Computer Label)	❑ December ❑ Regional ❑ Spring

Audition Evaluation

Please evaluate the applicant using the categories indicated below:

	Exceptional	Very Good	Good	Fair	Poor	
Voice						
Technique						
Operatic Personality						
Operatic Presentation (i.e. Dramatic Skills)						
Languages: Italian						
French						
German						
English						
Other						
Musicianship						

Does this applicant have the vocal equipment to succeed in a professional career? ❑ Yes ❑ No	Would you accept this applicant in your schedule? ❑ Yes ❑ Possibly ❑ No	❑ Admit JOC ❑ Admit Voice Dept. ❑ Reject

Specific Comments: (Please note that this form is used for Admission Committee purposes only.)

Signed: _____   Please Print Your Name:

Date: _____   _____

FORM AUD89-D1

SMU AUDITION EVALUATION

NAME _____ DATE _____ In Person _____ Tape _____

ADDRESS _____ PHONE _____

Instrument / Voice Part _____ SS # _____

MAJOR IN: ☐ Music Education   ☐ Music Therapy   ☐ Theory / Composition
☐ Piano Pedagogy   ☐ Performance   ☐ Sacred Music   ☐ Conducting
☐ Music Minor   with possible major in _____

☐ First Year   ☐ Graduate   ☐ Transfer from _____

Repertoire Performed _____

_____

CIRCLE each characteristic from low (1) to high (10).

		unacceptable		weak		adequate		very good		outstanding	
A.	TONE QUALITY	1	2	3	4	5	6	7	8	9	10
B.	TECHNIQUE (articulation, diction)	1	2	3	4	5	6	7	8	9	10
C.	INTONATION (except keyboard)	1	2	3	4	5	6	7	8	9	10
D.	RHYTHM	1	2	3	4	5	6	7	8	9	10
E.	STYLE—INTERPRETATION	1	2	3	4	5	6	7	8	9	10
F.	OVERALL MUSICIANSHIP	1	2	3	4	5	6	7	8	9	10
G.	MUSIC READING (if checked)	1	2	3	4	5	6	7	8	9	10

Performance Applicants must score 7 or higher.   **COMMITTEE**
Other majors and minors must score 5 or higher.   **RATING** [   ]
                                                              (1 – 10)

COMMITTEE EVALUATION _____

_____

_____

This student ranks SMU as choice number _____ among these other schools being considered:

_____

FACULTY RECOMMEND: ☐ High Award   ☐ Moderate   ☐ Possible   ☐ None

EVALUATORS: _____   _____

_____   _____

_____   _____

CONFIDENTIAL

FACULTY EVALUATION REPORT

NAME OF APPLICANT _____   DEGREE/MAJOR_____
                                                 freshman ____   transfer ____

☐ Audition Date _____   ☐ Self-prepared Tape #_____

☐ Regional Center Tape #_____   Technical quality of the recording

                                           _____

COMPOSITIONS PERFORMED:

Evaluation of performance relative to degree program   Overall Performance Rating:
indicated above:

____ Exceptional (consider immediate acceptance)   Grade: _____

____ Very Good   Use Roman Numeral   (composite)

____ Acceptable   Talent: _____

____ Borderline - barely acceptable   Use letter A to D   (composite)

____ Not Acceptable for this degree
                                                    A = Exceptional musical talent
                                                    B = Above-average musical talent
                                                    C = Average musical talent
                                                    D = Below-average musical talent

Technique _____   Stylistic Accuracy _____

Musicianship _____   Personality _____

1. This student should receive _____ HIGH _____ MEDIUM _____ LOW priority for assignment to my class.
2. Would you want us to accept this student if we can admit only _____ 3 _____ 6 _____ 10?
3. Is this applicant's performance worthy of EASTMAN MERIT SCHOLARSHIP consideration? _____
4. Does this applicant appear to be strongly motivated to complete the intended degree program? _____

Please comment below on this applicant's musical development in relation to his/her formal training, his/her natural musical talent, foreign languages and diction (singers), etc.

_____   _____
          date   signature of faculty member

Please keep the yellow copy for your records and return the white copy to the Admissions Office as soon as possible.

OBERLIN COLLEGE
Conservatory of Music – General

Name: _____   ID: _____

Address: _____   Instrument: _____

Telephone: _____   Audition Location: Tape
Application Date: _____
Wishes to Enter: _____   ASI: PLI:
Application Type: _____   HS Grad Date: Program:
High School: _____
    Major 1:   Major 2:
    Major 3:   Major 4:
Rank: SATV: SATM: ACT:

Teacher 1 _____

Teacher 2 _____

Teacher 3 _____

Teacher 4 _____

Composition 1 _____

Composition 2 _____

Composition 3 _____

Composition 4 _____

Composition 5 _____

Rate the candidate in the following areas
[5=Superior 4=Above Average 3=Average 2=Below Average 1=Poor]

                                                                        Comments

Musical Talent	5	4	3	2	1
Tone	5	4	3	2	1
Intonation	5	4	3	2	1
Technique	5	4	3	2	1
Control	5	4	3	2	1
Rhythmic Accuracy	5	4	3	2	1
Interpretation	5	4	3	2	1
Contrast and Balance	5	4	3	2	1
Articulation	5	4	3	2	1
Sight Reading	5	4	3	2	1
Memory	5	4	3	2	1

Rate the audition using the 5-1   On the basis of this audition do you recommend
scale above   that the applicant be admitted to the conservatory?
   5   4   3   2   1   ☐ Yes   ☐ No   ☐ ?

Do you recommend that the applicant receive special talent   ☐ Yes   ☐ No
scholarship consideration?

Faculty Examiner _____   Date _____

OBERLIN COLLEGE
Conservatory of Music – Jazz

Name: _____ ID: _____

Address: _____ Instrument: _____

_____

Telephone: _____ Audition Location: Tape

Application Date: _____

Wishes to Enter: _____ ASI: _____ PLI: _____

Application Type: _____ HS Grad Date: _____ Program: _____

High School: _____

    Major 1: _____ Major 2: _____

    Major 3: _____ Major 4: _____

Rank: _____ SATV: _____ SATM: _____ ACT: _____

Teacher 1 _____

Teacher 2 _____

Teacher 3 _____

Teacher 4 _____

Composition 1 _____

Composition 2 _____

Composition 3 _____

Composition 4 _____

Composition 5 _____

Rate the candidate in the following areas
[5=Superior 4=Above Average 3=Average 2=Below Average 1=Poor]

Audition / Interview Comments: Comments:

Rate the audition using the 5-1   On the basis of this audition do you recommend
scale above   that the applicant be admitted to the conservatory?
   5   4   3   2   1   ☐ Yes   ☐ No   ☐ ?

Do you recommend that the applicant receive special talent   ☐ Yes   ☐ No
scholarship consideration?

Faculty Examiner _____   Date _____

Oberlin Percussion

NAME _____   Address _____

Performance Medium _____   Probable Major _____

Length of Study   Years _____ Mos. _____   Present Teacher _____

Personal Audition   Date _____ Time _____   Examiner _____

Recorded Audition _____ Transfer _____   College _____

	Superior	Above Average	Average	Below Average	Poor
MARIMBA, XYLOPHONE: Composition					
Tone (touch, evenness of sound)					
Roll					
Technique and Hand Position					
Contrast and Balance (dynamics, phrasing)					
Sight Reading					
Rhythmic Accuracy					
Pitch Accuracy					
Interpretation					
SNARE DRUM: Composition					
Tone					
Rolls and Embellishments					
Technique and Hand Position					
Contrast and Balance					
Rhythmic Accuracy					
Sight Reading					
Interpretation					
TIMPANI: Composition					
Intonation					
Technique and Hand Position					
Roll					
Contrast and Balance					
Tone, Touch					
Interpretation					
Rhythmic Accuracy					
MULTIPLE PERCUSSION: Composition					
Interpretation					
Contrast and Balance					
Rhythmic Accuracy					
Pitch Accuracy					
Intonation					
MUSICAL TALENT					
SENSE OF METER					

In the space below please give your comments about the audition. Give special attention to the candidate's strengths and weaknesses. These comments are very helpful to the Admissions Office in making decisions and in counseling candidates who request specific criticisms.

On the basis of this audition, do you recommend that the applicant be admitted to the conservatory?

☐ Yes   ☐ No   ☐ ?   Comments: _____

Please check appropriate rating.   ☐ Superior ☐ Above Average ☐ Average ☐ Below Average ☐ Poor

FACULTY EXAMINER _____

What NOT to Do at a Music Audition

- ☐ Dress inappropriately

- ☐ Arrive late or forget to cancel

- ☐ Chew gum

- ☐ Forget to introduce yourself

- ☐ Start playing before you are asked to begin

- ☐ Make excuses for any slip you may have or curse out loud if this happens to you

- ☐ Tell your life story in answer to a simple question intended to help you relax

- ☐ Have to leave in the middle of the audition. If you have a tendency towards dryness, particularly as a singer or wind player, bring a plastic glass of water into the audition room with you, and be sure you have gone to the bathroom before the audition.

- ☐ Cry

Special Audition Advice

Woodwind and Brass Players

Many woodwind and brass players come from a background which has focused mainly on band music. This is tremendously valuable experience, providing players with a fundamental grasp of their instrument and helping them to develop a good musical sense and the ability to phrase, to be part of an ensemble, and to follow a conductor. However, it is recommended that this band training be augmented with an awareness of Western European orchestral tradition. Listen to recordings of the great orchestras, attend orchestra concerts, and learn some standard orchestral excerpts for your audition. If there is a youth symphony in your area, audition and try to join this organization or investigate the community orchestra. Lists of youth symphonies may be found in *Musical America*.

Some specific tips: Imitate your favorite recordings. Watch videos of your favorite soloists and orchestral players. Listen to a passage of a piece and imitate it—like a jazz musician learning a solo. Listen to articulation as well as tone. Take responsibility for teaching yourself. Your own style will come from what you want to hear. Your own point of view is important and you must know what you like.

Oboe and English Horn Players

Very few schools will let you major in English horn; most programs require that you major in oboe and play oboe d'amore and English horn as ancillary instruments on which you develop proficiency. Many double reed players complain that very few students develop any dynamic range on their instruments; they leap into playing concerti far too soon, before they have developed a basic technique. Work diligently on your etudes and learn how to stop and start a note attractively. Work on your breathing. Know also that music preparation involves studying scores, harmony, theory, having keyboard proficiency, and advanced listening skills. You should also know that the politics of the oboe/English horn world often focuses on an American versus European bias and discussions about vibrato. Be sure that whatever department you are joining represents your preference and that you are aware of both camps and have an idea about your future should you choose to play in one style over another. Ask questions about this.

Trombone and Tuba Players

Some books worth reading include *The Art of Trombone Playing*, Edward Kleinhammer (Evanston, IL, Summy-Binchard, 1963); *Art of Brass Playing*, Philip Farkas (Bloomington, IN, Brass Publications, 1962), an article on breathing by Arnold Jacobs, which appeared in *The Instrumentalists* (Brass Anthology), and a collection of memoirs of Jacobs' students entitled *Arnold Jacobs: Legacy of a Master*. Trombonists should be acquainted with the Rochut etude books (3 volumes), Max Schlossberg, *Daily Drills and Technical Studies*, the Arban book, and Blazevich Clef Studies. They should also look at the Bach cello suites, the David *Concerto*, Kopplash, *Book I and II*, and orchestral excerpts. Tuba players should learn to play both the little and big tuba. Standard orchestral excerpts include those from *Die Meistersinger*, *Die Walküre* (Ride of the Walküre), Vaughan Williams, *Solo;* and Berlioz, *Hungarian March*.

String Players

In discussing auditions, preparation for auditions, and playing in general, almost every string faculty member and player talked about two things: technical facility and musical intention. It seems tremendously important among string players that you pay special attention to your bow arm, left hand position, your basic sound production, vibrato, and having good intonation. It is also important that you think of the music musically and have definite feelings and thoughts about what you want to convey. Fast fingers without feeling, thought, and emotional involvement is vapid. You must work at all levels in order to prepare properly for an audition.

It is also important that string players perform on as good an instrument as possible. To present yourself positively, try to play on an instrument that will allow you to have a sound which is uniquely your own and will not stand in your way. This brings up the whole issue of instrument dealers. You should be aware that some teachers receive fees, sometimes very large ones, from instrument dealers for convincing students to buy certain instruments. While you may want your teacher to evaluate an instrument for you, and you would want to compensate the teacher for his or her time, buying an instrument just because a teacher suggests it, may not be wise. Stop and think about the instrument's suitability for you.

Harpists

It is helpful for harpists to have a background in piano. Because the harp is so expensive, some harpists will rent harps before they know that they are committed to the instrument, and then work to buy their own. (When you go for an audition, be sure to ask if you will be able to use the school's harp or if you need to transport your own—a rare occasion.)

It is important to get as much playing experience as possible. Often young harpists will offer their services to the local community orchestra in order to learn the basic orchestral excerpts and to get experience playing in an ensemble. Because harpists tend to work so much on their own, it is important to try to reach out and play in ensembles, learning how to relate in chamber groups and developing an ensemble sense of rhythm. The American Harp Society holds an annual conference and has competitions every three years for all levels. There are also regional events. It is a good idea to attend or compete in these American Harp Society gatherings so that you hear other harpists and get a sense of where your level of playing stands among your peers. It should also be noted that harpists have an easier time applying to conservatories at the undergraduate level and most professional harpists have chosen the route of conservatory training.

Organists

Within the world of organists there are some who are considered "antiquarians" and others who believe that the modern organ should be the vehicle for a vast repertoire. It is probably worth your while to investigate the philosophical point of view of any department or individual teacher to be sure that you will be in harmony. Be aware that some schools require that organ applicants also audition in piano. Ask questions about the repertoire required.

Pianists

One practical suggestion offered by many faculty members is that in playing your "mock auditions" you should play on a variety of instruments, so that you can play your repertoire no matter what the action or state of repair of the piano.

In speaking to piano faculty members at various institutions, the resounding piece of advice seems to be regarding the audition program. Faculty members stress that you should present what you play best and like to play, which falls within the guidelines required, and not try to play something too difficult just to be impressive. The audition program should fit together and demonstrate lyric qualities, fingers or "chops," and a full range of musical virtues: legato line, sensitivity, and technical solidity. The piano literature is vast and you should be making selections for yourself; however, the following selections are offered as a basic guideline of some repertoire which seems fairly common for auditions:

Babbitt: Three Compositions for Piano; Partitions
Bach: Well-tempered Clavier—Books I and II, Preludes and Fugues
Barber: Sonata
Bartok: Suite, op. 14, Sonata
Beethoven: Sonatas (excluding op. 14, op. 49, and op. 79)
Bolcom: Etudes
Brahms: Intermezzi, Variations on a Theme by Handel, E-flat Rhapsody, Sonatas, Variations on a Theme by Paganini
Chopin: Ballades, Etudes, Scherzi
Copland: Variations
Corigliano: Etude Fantasy
Debussy: Images, Estampe; L'isle joyeuse; Pour le Piano
Dello Joio: Sonata
Ginestera: Sonata
Lees: Sonatas
Liszt: Transcendental Etudes, Vallée d'Obermann, Après une lecture de Dante, 11th Rhapsody, Mephisto Waltz, Funérailles
Mendelssohn: Sonata
Messiaen: Vingt Regards sur l'Enfant Jésus or any of the Bird Pieces
Persichetti: Poems
Prokofiev: Sonata no. 3

Rachmaninoff: Preludes; Etude Tableaux, Moments Musicaux
Ravel: Jeux d'eau; Sonatine; Gaspard de la nuit
Rorem: Barcarolles; Etudes
Schubert: Moment Musicale, Impromtus; little A major Sonata
Schumann: 8th Novelette, Abegg Variations, G minor Sonata, Papillon
Takemitsu: Les yeux clos I & II

Accompanists

Many of the most famous accompanists stress that it is most important to get your "piano chops" together first, meaning that your level of technical ability should be developed and strong. Thus, very few schools have an undergraduate major in accompanying and most accompanists major in piano or attend a liberal arts college, keeping up their private piano lessons, and then attending a graduate program in accompanying.

It is important to note that some accompanying programs are only for vocal accompanying, while others are oriented towards instrumental accompanying. While there are a handful of truly accomplished accompanists who do well in both the vocal and instrumental worlds, most have made a choice about an area of specialization.

Be aware that if you choose to be a vocal accompanist/coach, you should have your foreign languages and English diction in order. Study French, Italian, German, and Spanish, emphasizing both language and diction. You should have dictionaries in all these languages as part of your library, also. Study the standard vocal literature, including the "hit parade" of arias for each voice category and the song repertoire including Brahms, Wolf, Schubert, Schumann, Fauré, Debussy, Chausson, Ravel, Italian art songs, works of Dowland and Purcell, and some of the standard American art songs, just to scratch the surface. Those wishing to pursue vocal accompanying should attend recitals and the opera often. They should listen to recordings of the great singers and try to make arrangements to accompany lessons for a good voice studio.

If you choose to specialize in instrumental accompanying you should attend master classes, learn as much as possible about the various instruments, attend solo and chamber music concerts and recitals, listen to recordings, and study the sonata and concerto repertoire. You should also know how to read an orchestral score and reduce it at the piano and be able to render an orchestral accompaniment with the proper inflection to do full justice to the orchestration. You should try to accompany lessons for various teachers, too.

There have been some wonderful books written about being an accompanist. Basic recommended reading includes Bob Spilman's *The Art of Accompanying* (New York: Schirmer Books, 1985) and Gerald Moore's many books, including *Am I Too Loud? Memoirs of an Accompanist* (London, Hamish Hamilton, 1962) and *Singer and Accompanist* (London, Methuen, 1953).

Singers

Do not prepare repertoire that is beyond your ability. For instance, young singers really should not sing the heavy verismo arias; Mozart is much more appropriate. Sample opera repertoire might include works of Mozart, Bellini, Donizetti, or Handel—no Verdi or Puccini! The point is not to dazzle your audition committee, but to demonstrate your ability with selections that do not overtax you but do allow you to show your personality and your languages. Lieder studies might include songs of Fauré, Schubert, Brahms, the

Italian Anthology, and Purcell or Dowland. If you are asked to prepare some twentieth-century repertoire, look at the songs of Ned Rorem, Richard Hundley, Benjamin Britten, Aaron Copland, Dominic Argento, or Samuel Barber, for example. Your lessons should include good vocalises, many of which will be special exercises that your teacher devises or classics such as the Nicola Vaccai's *Metodo Pratico di Canto* ("Practical Singing Method"), first published in 1832. Other good books on vocal technique include William Vennard, *Singing—The Mechanism and the Technic* (New York: Carl Fischer, Inc., 1967) and Johan Sundbert, *The Science of the Singing Voice* (Northern Illinois University Press, 1987).

Any teacher who says that you have a "big voice" and can handle the "large or heavy repertoire" may be hearing what your voice may become, but if you sing that heavy repertoire before you are physically, technically, or emotionally prepared, you will probably be doing damage to your vocal apparatus.

Most voice teachers say that it is a very rare 18-year-old who should even consider a conservatory. Most would do best studying at a liberal arts college, learning literature and foreign languages for at least two years, and taking private voice lessons with a reputable teacher on the side. It is important that singers be good sight-readers. It is suggested that young would-be soloists participate in choruses or choirs, to improve their sight-reading ability and explore a variety of musical styles. Some voice teachers also recommend that singers participate in a program such as the Experiment in International Living (VT) or the Middlebury College Intensive Summer Language Programs.

Choral Conductors

Most choral conductors seem to have a background as an organist or as a singer. Some have majored in music education, augmented by intensive piano studies. The best training for choral conductors seems to be in settings where there is a strong choral tradition, coupled with a good voice department, and opportunities with both opera and symphony chorus. In the United States right now, many choral programs are in a period of transition, as some of the well-known choral conductor/teachers are just retiring. Choral conductors should be as well-versed in score-reading, transpositions, languages, and other musical matters as any other conductor.

Orchestral Conductors

There seems to be much debate about the best training and background for conductors. Many working conductors feel that it is essential for an aspiring conductor to work at the undergraduate level on all of the following: becoming proficient on an instrument, including piano; studying composition and analysis; gaining a background in the humanities, with special attention to literature and art history; taking as much music theory and ear training as possible; attending rehearsals and concerts; and learning foreign languages.

A common belief is that it is good training to be an assistant to an established conductor, doing an apprenticeship of sorts. While the Exxon/Affiliate Artist program is the most established way of doing this, it is a highly competitive program. Concentration in conducting should come at the graduate level. Be sure to ask about how much time is spent in the classroom and how much time is spent actually conducting an orchestra. Are your rehearsals videotaped for your review? Will you ever have any opportunities to conduct in public? Are various art forms part of your training? Ballet orchestras? Opera? Twentieth-century ensembles?

In training to be a conductor, there seems to be no substitute for time. Since the development of the conductor's ear is critical, try to sit in on orchestra rehearsals, not just in the audience, but in various sections of the orchestra. It is also important to be aware of the politics of the business and to develop an appropriate presentation of yourself. Conductors must be extremely well organized, able to get along with everyone from the music director to the individual players in the orchestra to the members of the ladies' auxiliary committees. They must be prepared to conduct youth concerts, pops concerts, senior citizen preconcert lectures, and to be part of an organization's sense of civic pride.

Composers

While there is some consensus about what makes for good piano playing or singing, for instance, the scope of what is considered "good" or "bad" in the composition world is very broad. It is important, therefore, that you do careful research about composition departments. Are you comfortable with their philosophy? Do you understand and respect each other's musical idiom? Do you want your life as a composer to be more "academic," i.e., teaching and writing on the side, or do you intend to focus on having your music performed? What sort of facilities are available for your use? Computer publishing programs? How often will you be guaranteed that your music will be played? With what other composers will you have contact and in what forum?

One well-known composer suggested that composition majors look for a department which is strongly oriented towards synthesis and studio technique with a willingness to be on the cutting edge of new techniques in using computers and other technology. He suggested listening to National Public Radio (NPR), the noncommercial radio broadcast throughout the United States and parts of Canada, especially the "new sounds" of John Schaeffer's program and Tim Page's program. He also suggested that you hang out at your local music store, becoming acquainted with the new technology in instruments and getting to know the musicians in your neighborhood, and that you go to "alternative" concerts and talk to the performers afterwards.

Other composers stress the importance of having a strong background in music theory and music history, with careful attention to analyzing scores. They suggest learning everything from species counterpoint to the most complex analysis of music and listening to as much music as possible. One composer tells the story of a young person coming to an audition and being asked what composers he likes to listen to. The applicant responded, "Stravinsky." "What of his do you particularly like?" The applicant said, "The Rite of Spring." The professor said, "Oh, have you heard it live or do you have a favorite recording?" "No," said the applicant. "Then have you studied the score in depth?" "No, I've never looked at it," replied the applicant. Learn from this example: study scores, listen to music of all kinds, attend as many concerts as possible, talk to as many composers as you can. Look at scores with an eye toward figuring out orchestration, instrumentation, transpositions, clefs, and the basic layout of the score. Learn as much about computers as possible.

At your audition in composition, you will probably be asked to speak not only about your compositional choices and technique but also about the music of the "Masters," such as Bach and Beethoven, so prepare accordingly. (See recommended texts for review on page 64.) Also remember that when you send scores, you should not send the originals.

Popular Musicians

Popular musicians vary widely in their training, from the most sophisticated awareness of music theory and ear training to completely unschooled natural talent, enthusiasm, and ability. For jazz musicians, most programs require that you audition or send a tape. You are usually asked to perform three pieces. Be sure to offer standards and not present three of your own compositions. Play in the style with which you are most comfortable. (If you are not a bebopper, do not feel compelled to present a bebop solo.) You may be asked to improvise and even sit in with a house band. Listen well and be positive. Be aware that in many jazz programs at conservatories, you are expected to play at the same level as those auditioning for the classical program. Listen to the greats, including Charlie Parker, Duke Ellington, Thelonius Monk, and lots of others, study privately, and learn by doing—work with a band and get gigs.

Rock musicians have traditionally had about four years of private lessons and played in band situations. Many lack reading skills, but most rock musicians have great ears and if given a passage, can repeat it with little trouble. To make the leap ahead, rock musicians should study music theory and concentrate on chord/scale relationships along with their playing ability and ensemble experience. Rock musicians would do well to be acquainted with other musical styles, including jazz, R&B, the blues (people like Lightnin' Hopkins, John Lee Hooker, and Muddy Waters, for example), and country music. Also, because rock performances are almost athletic events, it is important for rock musicians to be in good physical shape.

Those who want to go on in commercial/pop music have also usually had at least three years of private lessons. Singers would do well to listen to Barbra Streisand, Ella Fitzgerald, Aretha Franklin, Frank Sinatra, Bing Crosby, Elvis Presley, and Sarah Vaughn, among others. It is also worthwhile to be exposed to a number of different styles: country music, big band, R&B, gospel, folk, the blues, and rock. Diction, rhythm, and good sight reading are very important skills to develop. Pop singers should also work at being as disciplined as the most focused classical musician. While there are a few good college programs for popular and commercial musicians, this is an area where you learn by doing, so performing as much as possible is vitally important, combined with good coaching and private instruction.

Musical Theater

The best preparation for musical theater is to study voice, dance, and acting. At many auditions you will be required to sing one or two selections from musical theater. In choosing these, look for contrasting styles—perhaps one up-tempo number and then another which has strong emotional content. At some schools you may be asked to discuss your choices and interpretation. You may also be required to take a dance class, where you may be taught a routine and then evaluated not only on how well you move, but also on how well you take direction and respond to corrections. Be sure to bring appropriate clothing for this: dance attire or gym shorts or sweats are common for this part of the audition. Read the school's material to see if anything is specified. For the drama segment of your audition, you may be asked to present a monologue or two or to do a reading. (See the Drama section about choosing monologues, page 48.) In preparation for this multi-level audition, be sure that you have rehearsed your song with a pianist and not just with the Broadway cast recording. You should have taken both dance classes and acting classes and have participated in school and community productions.

In evaluating any college-level musical theater programs, be sure that the training includes music, dance, and drama. Like singers, musical theater majors should consider acquiring a background in the liberal arts. Be sure that you spend your summers wisely, however, getting as much experience as possible in summer stock.

Researching Teachers for Consultations and Lessons

Choosing the teachers with whom you would like to study is a vitally important decision. Ask your current teacher for recommendations and then do lots of investigation on your own. Read the biography of the teacher in the catalog. Has the person studied with other people who uphold a tradition that you would like to follow? What is the teacher's performing background? Are they adjudicators for major competitions? Talk to students who currently work with the person you are thinking of. Are they pleased with their progress? Do they have regular lessons? During those lessons do they have the teacher's undivided attention?

Because so much of the relationship between teacher and student is personal, you must be sure that the chemistry between you works. This is difficult to determine unless you are able to speak to the teacher directly or, even better, to arrange a sample lesson, often called a consultation. You should be prepared to pay anywhere from $50 to $250 for such a meeting. At that time, you will play for the teacher, see if you can work together, and ask all the questions you want. Do not be afraid to ask questions about how this person works, where he or she sees your major weaknesses now and what direction your lessons may take. If a personal meeting is not possible, you might call the teacher or write and ask if you could send a cassette or videotape for his or her evaluation. Then follow up with a telephone conversation.

"Famous" or big-name teachers are not necessarily the best. You are looking for a teacher who will be best for *you* at this stage of your development as a performer. While "name" teachers may help at a certain time in your development, they may not give you the attention you need to progress in the early stages of your preparation. Will you receive a weekly lesson from that teacher, or be taught by an assistant? Is the "big name" still actively teaching?

If you have chosen a teacher and are admitted to a school and assigned to study with the person you have chosen and then discover that the relationship is not working out, do not fall into despair. A student–teacher relationship is a business agreement of sorts; the teacher is being paid to teach you. If you need to make a change, most conservatories and departments of music have a procedure to make a teacher change which will involve as little misery on either part as possible. You will have to have a conversation with the teacher, or perhaps write the teacher a letter, and this may be difficult, but better to make a change than to remain trapped in a situation which is not beneficial.

Sample Music Questions to Ask

What role does the audition play in my admission? Is it the major criterion, or does my high school or college record count also?

What role do exams such as ear training play in my admission?

Is a personal interview required? If so, who conducts the interview?

What is the Music Department enrollment?

What is the enrollment in my instrument? Is there a quota?

What general education courses are offered? Required? Any cross-registration with another school?

How many faculty members are there for my instrument? Will I have a wide enough variety of choice in case I want to make a teacher change?

How often do students have lessons? Am I guaranteed to have lessons with my major teacher? How often do assistants teach major lessons?

What is the policy on performance evaluations (juries)? How often are they held? Are students ever cut from the program based on a jury?

What are the facilities like? How many teaching studios? What equipment is in them? How many performing halls are there?

How many practice rooms are there? What is their availability? (Ask a student if there is ever a problem securing a practice room.)

In general, how often do students perform each semester? How many fully produced concerts? Informal concerts? Operas? In-school performances (e.g., at a high school)? Recitals? Contemporary music concerts? Other opportunities?

Is there a program of master classes? Who has taught them recently?

Who are some of the well-known alumni of the school?

What sort of job-placement service does the school provide?

What do most alumni do?

Is there an alumni network of any sort?

What is competition like at the school?

What ensembles will I be required to participate in?

How are orchestral assignments made? (Ask a student if the orchestral assignments are fair.) Is there a policy of rotation within the orchestra?

Do you have a program for engaging guest conductors? Who have been the recent conductors?

What is the policy for casting operas? Is the policy fair?

What chorus requirements are there for singers?

· Is there an opportunity to get certified in music education?

What other related courses are taught? Music engineering? Music criticism?

Is there any affiliation between the school and any other musical organization, such as the local symphony, opera, or jazz clubs?

Are any tours anticipated?

Are there exchange programs with any schools?

During the auditions, are teachers informed about who has applied for them?

Who evaluates the auditions? How are they run?

What chamber music opportunities are there? Any requirements for chamber music? Who coaches ensembles?

Do you hold any sessions on how to audition for orchestras, companies, etc., for after graduation?

What is the feeling at this school about regional auditions? Taped versus live auditions?

Do you ever defer admissions decisions?

Adding to Your College Notebook

You might want to add a specific music page to your college notebook to record the responses to the questions you ask. Use the sample Music Program Rating Sheet on page 89 or one of your own design.

Music Program Rating Sheet

Size of department:

Enrollment _____   Teachers _____

Lessons: How often?   With major teacher or assistants?

Facilities: Number of teaching studios, practice rooms

Performances: How often?   Type (concerts, operas, recitals, etc.)

Master classes: Availability?   Recent teachers?

Exchange Programs with other schools?

Affiliation between school and other musical organizations?

Curriculum: General education requirement?   Certificate in Music Ed?

Techniques taught:

Audition workshops:

Job placement record:

Famous alumni:

Current students' opinions:

My Personal Reaction:

Music Admissions Checklist

Here are some questions to ask yourself at various points in the admissions process:

Have I...

❏ requested catalogs and read them carefully?

❏ requested applications and made photocopies of those in which I am interested?

❏ started a college notebook to record impressions of colleges, audition and repertoire requirements, and deadlines?

❏ obtained a social security number?

❏ registered for the PSATs?

❏ obtained information about the ARTs scholarships? (National Foundation for Advancement in the Arts, 3915 Biscayne Boulevard, Miami, Florida 33137 (305) 573-0490.)

❏ made an appointment with my guidance counselor or college advisor to discuss future plans?

❏ looked into working with an independent counselor, if appropriate?

❏ talked with my private music teacher about my future plans?

❏ participated regularly in music programs at school or in the community?

❏ made plans to continue my music classes and private lessons?

❏ discussed my future high school curriculum with my guidance counselor?

❏ discussed standardized test choices with my guidance counselor?

❏ investigated summer programs/jobs and applied as necessary?

❏ investigated sources of financial aid?

❏ kept a file of performance programs, videotaped shows, good term papers, articles, etc.?

❏ attended college fairs and met with college representatives?

❏ registered for standardized tests (SAT, ACT, TOEFL, Achievement Tests)?

❏ arranged my college visits?

❏ scheduled interview appointments?

❏ sent thank-you notes to admissions counselors after interviews?

❏ chosen my audition material?

❏ narrowed my list of colleges?

Have I...

- ❏ considered applying for Early Decision? (Deadlines generally are in early to mid-November.)

- ❏ asked for letters of recommendation from teachers/former employers?

- ❏ drafted my college application essays?

- ❏ finished my essays and applications and photocopied everything before mailing?

- ❏ practiced my audition material regularly?

- ❏ applied for financial aid?

- ❏ requested that ETS, ACT, or TOEFL send official score reports to the colleges which require them?

- ❏ videotaped practice auditions to be critiqued?

- ❏ submitted videotapes for prescreening, if necessary?

- ❏ had necessary photographs taken to submit with applications?

- ❏ prepared a résumé?

- ❏ requested that a copy of my transcript be sent to colleges, as required?

- ❏ communicated regularly with my guidance counselor or college advisor about my progress in school and in college admission?

- ❏ kept up with schoolwork?

- ❏ perfected audition material?

- ❏ prepared a list of extracurricular activities in which I've participated?

- ❏ completed all financial aid documentation?

- ❏ read carefully all audition and schedule information sent to me?

- ❏ arranged for an accompanist for my audition, if necessary?

- ❏ made copies of any original composition I intend to perform?

- ❏ photocopied sheet music for my accompanist, if necessary?

- ❏ responded to colleges about acceptance offers?

- ❏ requested an extension beyond the May 1 Candidates Reply Deadline, if necessary?

- ❏ continued with regular music lessons and ensemble opportunities?

5
Selected Listing of Performing Arts Programs

How These Lists Were Assembled

To assemble these listings, questionnaires were sent to members of the National Association of Schools of Music (NASM), to other well-known music conservatories that are not members of NASM, to Dance and Drama departments at 700 selective colleges and universities, and to organizations listed in *Musical America*, *Stern's Directory* and *Back Stage*, which are recommended by leaders in their respective fields. In the drama section the focus is on acting as a performing art, and not on design, playwriting, or other related drama areas. For schools that did not return the questionnaire but that are considered important to include, limited information is provided.

The information on the questionnaires was supplemented with conversations with performing professionals, faculty members at recognized institutions, and students, who provided candid comments about the strengths and weaknesses of programs. High school guidance counselors and other college personnel also offered helpful suggestions. The author recommendations are based on much personal research and experience as well as knowledge of certain outstanding faculty members who are teaching at a given institution at this time. Faculties do change, however, so if you want to study with a certain teacher, be sure that he or she is still at that school.

These listings are meant to be an aid for counselors, teachers, parents, and students— nothing more. Programs are listed in alphabetical order. If I have overlooked a worthy program, please let me know so that it may be considered for future editions of this book.

This section lists the most highly recommended programs and other noteworthy programs to investigate by major and instrument, for easy reference. Profiles of all programs listed are provided in the next section, in alphabetical order.

Note: The letters following each school indicate the total enrollment at that school, not the enrollment of performing arts majors.

VS = very small (fewer than 1,000 students)
 S = small (1,000–3,000 students)
 M = medium (3,000–8,000 students)
 L = large (8,000–20,000 students)
VL = very large (over 20,000 students)

Dance

Most Highly Recommended Programs (in alphabetical order)

Arizona State, Tempe (AZ)…VL
Barnard (also joint program with Juilliard) (NY)…S
Butler University (IN)…M
California State, Long Beach (CA)…M
Florida State University, Tallahassee (FL)…VL
Harid Conservatory (FL)…VS
Juilliard (NY)…VS
London Contemporary Dance School (London, England)…VS
New World School of the Arts / Miami Dade College (FL)…VL
New York University (NYU) (NY)…L
North Carolina School of the Arts (NCSA) (NC)…VS
Ohio State, Columbus (OH) (modern)…VL
San Francisco State (CA)…L
Southern Methodist University (SMU) (TX)…M
SUNY, Purchase (NY)…M
University of Arizona, Tucson (AZ)…VL
University of California, Irvine (CA)…L
University of California, San Diego (CA)…L
University of Minnesota, Minneapolis (MN)…VL
University of South Florida, Tampa (FL)…VL
University of Utah (UT) (modern)…VL

Other Noteworthy Programs

Adelphi (NY)…L
Amherst College (Part of Five College Dance Department) (MA)…S
Bard (NY)…VS
Bates College (ME)…S
Baylor (TX)…M
Bennington (VT)…VS
Birmingham-Southern (AL)…S
Boston Conservatory (MA)…VS
Brenau College (GA)…VS
Brigham Young University (UT)…VL
Brooklyn College of the City University of New York (NY)…VL
Bucknell College (PA)…S
California Institute of the Arts (CalARTS) (CA)…VS
California State University, Fresno (CA)…L
California State University, Fullerton (CA)…L
Case Western Reserve (OH) (modern)…M
Chapman College (CA)…S
City College of New York (CCNY) (NY)…VL
Colby-Sawyer (NH)…VS
Colorado College (CO) (modern)…S
Columbia College (IL)…M
Connecticut College (CT)…S
Cornell University (NY)…L
Dartmouth (NH)…M
Denison (OH)…S
George Mason University (VA)…L

George Washington University (DC)…M
Goucher (MD)…S
Hamilton (NY)…S
Hampshire (Part of Five College Dance Department) (MA)…S
Hobart / William Smith (NY)…S
Hofstra (NY)…L
Hunter College of the City University of New York (NY)…L
Indiana University, Bloomington (IN) (ballet)…VL
Ithaca (NY)…M
Jacksonville University (FL)…S
Kansas State University, Manhattan (KS)…VL
Kent State (OH)…VL
Michigan State (MI)…VL
Mills College (women) (CA)…VS
Mount Holyoke (women) (Part of Five College Dance Department) (MA)…S
Northern Illinois University, Dekalb (IL)…VL
Ohio University, Athens (OH)…L
Randolph-Macon Women's College (VA)…S
Reed College (OR)…S
Rutgers (NJ)…M
Saint Olaf (MN)…S
Sarah Lawrence (NY)…VS
Scripps (women) (CA)…S
Shenandoah College and Conservatory (VA)…S
Skidmore (NY)…S
Smith (women) (Part of Five College Dance Department) (MA)…S
Stanford University (CA)…M
Stephens College (MO)…S
SUNY, Brockport (NY)…M
SUNY, Potsdam (NY)…M
Temple (PA)…VL
Texas Christian University (TX)…M
Texas Tech University, Lubbock (TX)…M
Towson State (MD)…L
University of Akron (OH)…VL
University of Alabama, Birmingham (AL)…L
University of California, Berkeley (CA)…VL
University of California, Los Angeles (CA)…VL
University of California, Riverside (CA)…L
University of California, Santa Barbara (CA)…L
University of Cincinnati, College-Conservatory (OH)…VL
University of Colorado, Boulder (CO) (modern)…VL
University of Hawaii, Manoa (HI)…VL
University of Iowa, Iowa City (IA)…VL
University of Kansas, Lawrence (KS)…VL
University of Massachusetts, Amherst (Part of Five College Dance Department) (MA)…VL
University of Miami (FL)…L
University of Michigan, Ann Arbor (MI)…VL
University of Nebraska, Lincoln (NE)…VL
University of New Mexico, Albuquerque (NM)…VL
University of North Texas, Denton (TX)…VL
University of Oregon, Eugene (OR)…VL
University of Texas, Austin (TX)…VL

University of the Arts (PA)...VS
University of Washington, Seattle (WA)...VL
University of Wisconsin, Madison (WI)...VL
Washington University, St. Louis (MO)...M
Wayne State (MI)...VL
Wesleyan (CT)...S
Wichita State University (KS) (Mid-America Dance Theater)...L

Summer Programs

Alaska Ballet Fair
2 weeks of intensive dance at
Fairbanks, AK 99775
907-474-7751

American Dance Festival
P.O. Box 6097
College Station
Durham, NC 27708-6097
919-684-6402
6-week summer program plus special
workshops for young dancers.

American University
4400 Massachusetts Avenue, NW
Washington, DC 20016
301-320-2550

Atlanta Ballet
477 Peachtree Street, NE
Atlanta, GA 30308
404-873-5811

Ballet / Aspen Summer Dance School
(may also be referred to as DanceAspen)
Box 8754 D
Aspen, CO 81612
303-925-7718

Bates College Dance Festival
303 Lane Hall
Lewiston, ME 04240
207-786-6077
3-week summer program in ballet and
modern.

Bolshoi Ballet Academy at Vail
Box 309
Vail, CO 81658
303-476-9500

Boston Ballet School Summer Program
42 Vernon Street
Newton, MA 02158
617-964-4070

Briansky Saratoga Ballet Center
Skidmore College
Saratoga Springs, NY 12866
518-584-5000, ext. 2279
Winter address:
220 West 93rd Street
New York, NY 10025
212-799-0341

Burklyn Ballet Theater
P.O. Box 5069
Burlington, VT 05402
802-862-6466
Official School of Vermont Ballet Theater.

Butler University
Jordan College of Fine Arts
Stephan Laurent, Program contact
800-368-6582

Carnegie Mellon University
Pre-College Program in Fine Arts
John Papinchak, contact
412-268-2082

Central Pennsylvania Youth Ballet
107 Meetinghouse Road
Carlisle, PA 17013
717-249-8723

Chautauqua Institute Summer Dance Programs
P.O. Box 1096
Chautauqua, NY 14722
716-357-6200

Danse-Performance Summer Study Program
43, rue de la Republique
30400 Villeneuve les Avignon, France
(90) 25-72-10

Fieldston Summer Performing Arts Institute
Fieldston Road
Riverdale, NY 10471
212-543-5000

Florida State University, Tallahassee
904-644-6200

Harvard Summer Dance Center
Dept. 705
20 Garden Street
Cambridge, MA 02138
617-495-5535 or 2921

Idyllwild School of Music and the Arts
P.O. Box 38
Idyllwild, CA 92349
714-659-2171

Interlochen / National Summer Music Camp
Interlochen Arts Academy
Interlochen, MI 49643
616-276-9221

Jacob's Pillow Dance Festival and School
P.O. Box 287
Lee, MA 01238
413-637-1322

Joffrey Ballet
130 West 56th Street
New York, NY 10019
212-265-7300

Kentucky Governor's School for the Arts Summer Program
David Thurmond, contact
502-562-0148
For sophomores and juniors in Kentucky high schools.

Limon Summer Dance
38 East 19th Street, 9th Floor
New York, NY 10003
212-777-3353
Summer programs at New World School of the Arts, Miami, and SUNY, Purchase.

New Jersey School of the Arts Trenton
NJ Summer Programs
contact—Abraham Beller
609-633-3941

North Carolina School of the Arts
P.O. Box 12189
200 Waughtown Street
Winston-Salem, NC 27117-2189
1-800-282-ARTS
Summer Session Office:
919-770-3293

Princeton Ballet School
262 Alexander Street
Princeton, NJ 08540
609-921-7758

Richmond Ballet
614 North Lombardy Street
Richmond, VA 23220
804-359-0906

Royal Winnepeg Ballet School
Professional Division
380 Graham Avenue
Winnepeg, Manitoba, Canada R3C 4K2
204-956-0183

Rutgers University
New Brunswick
NJ Summer Arts Institute
Jacque Robul, contact
908-463-3640

San Antonio Workshop
2103 Lockhill-Selma
San Antonio, TX 78213
512-656-1334

San Francisco Ballet
455 Franklin Street
San Francisco, CA 94102
415-861-5600

Saratoga Ballet Center at Skidmore College
Saratoga Springs, NY
Winter address:
c/o Carolyn Adams
Juilliard
60 Lincoln Center Plaza
New York, NY 10023

School of American Ballet
70 Lincoln Center Plaza
New York, NY 10023
212-877-0600

South Carolina Governor's School for the Arts
Summer Arts Program—803-271-6488

SUNY, Purchase
Purchase, NY
Norton Owen, contact
Limon Workshop—212-777-3353
For 17 and above: high school seniors and beyond.

Texas Christian University
Summer Dance Workshop
P.O. Box 32889
Fort Worth, TX 76129
817-921-7615
2-week noncredit summer workshop.

Toronto Summer School in Dance
Toronto Regional Ballet
1920 Avenue Road
Toronto, Ontario, Canada M5M 4A1
416-489-7597

University of Utah
1152 Annex Building
Salt Lake City, UT 84112
801-581-7374

Walnut Hill School
Natick, MA
Summer Dance Workshop—508-653-4312

White Mountains Festival, NH
Winter address:
c/o Laura Dean
Juilliard
60 Lincoln Center Plaza
New York, NY 10023

Drama

Most Highly Recommended Undergraduate Programs (in alphabetical order)

Boston University (MA)...L
Catholic University (DC)...L
DePaul University, The Theater School (formerly The Goodman School of Drama) (IL)...L
Duke (NC)...M
Indiana University (IN)...VL
Juilliard (NY)...VS
Northwestern (IL)...L
San Francisco State (CA)...VL
Southern Methodist University (TX)...L
University of California, Los Angeles (CA)...VL
University of Evansville (IN)...M
University of Southern California (CA)...VL
University of Utah (UT)...VL

Other Noteworthy Undergraduate Programs

Alfred University (NY)...S
Amherst College (MA)...S
Arizona State, Tempe (AZ)...VL
Ball State University, Muncie (IN)...L
Barnard College of Columbia University (NY) (women)...S
Bates (ME)...S
Baylor (TX)...L
Bennington (VT)...VS
Boston College (MA)...L
Brandeis (MA)...M
Brigham Young University (UT)...VL
Brown (RI)...M
Bucknell (PA)...S
Butler (IN)...M
California Institute of the Arts (CA)...VS
California State University, Fresno (CA)...L
California State University, Fullerton (CA)...VL
California State University, Long Beach (CA)...VL
California State University, Northridge (CA)...VL
California State University, Santa Barbara (CA)...L
Carnegie-Mellon (PA)...L
Case Western Reserve (OH)...M
Catawba College (NC)...S
Coe College (IA)...VS
College of Charleston (SC)...M

College of Santa Fe (NM)…S
Columbia (NY)…L
Connecticut College (CT)…S
Cornell (NY)…VL
Dartmouth (NH)…M
Dickinson (PA)…S
Drew University (NJ)…M
Emerson (MA)…S
Florida State, Tallahassee (FL)…VL
George Washington University (DC)…L
Goucher (MD)…S
Grambling State University (LA)…M
Hofstra (NY)…L
Howard University (DC)…L
Illinois State University, Normal (IL)…VL
Illinois Wesleyan (IL)…S
Ithaca (NY)…M
James Madison University (VA)…L
Kansas State University, Manhattan (KS)…L
Kenyon (OH)…S
Long Island University / C. W. Post Campus (NY)…VL
Loyola University (LA)…M
Macalester (MN)…S
Marymount Manhattan (NY)…S
Michigan State, East Lansing (MI)…VL
Middlebury (VT)…S
Montclair State College (NJ)…L
Muhlenberg (PA)…S
New York University (NY)…VL
North Carolina School of the Arts (NC)…S
Northern Illinois University, DeKalb (IL)…VL
Occidental (CA)…S
Ohio State, Columbus (OH)…VL
Ohio University, Athens (OH)…L
Princeton (NJ)…M
Reed College (OR)…S
Rollins (FL)…S
Rutgers, New Brunswick (NJ)…VL
San Diego State University (CA)…VL
Sarah Lawrence (NY)…VS
Scripps (CA) (women)…S
Shenandoah College and Conservatory (VA)…S
Skidmore (NY)…S
Smith (MA) (women)…S
SUNY, Buffalo (NY)…VL
SUNY, Fredonia (NY)…M
SUNY, Purchase (NY)…S
SUNY, Stony Brook (NY)…L
Swarthmore (PA)…S
Syracuse (NY)…L
Temple (PA)…VL
Towson State University (MD)…L
Trinity (CT)…S

Tulane (LA)...L
University of Alabama, Tuscaloosa (AL)...VL
University of Arizona, Tucson (AZ)...VL
University of California, Davis (CA)...VL
University of California, Irvine (CA)...L
University of California, Santa Barbara (CA)...L
University of Cincinnati College–Conservatory (OH)...VL
University of Connecticut, Storrs (CT)...VL
University of Georgia, Athens (GA)...VL
University of Hawaii at Manoa, Honolulu (HI)...VL
University of Illinois, Champaign-Urbana (IL)...VL
University of Iowa, Iowa City (IA)...VL
University of Kansas, Lawrence (KS)...VL
University of Maryland, College Park (MD)...VL
University of Massachusetts, Amherst (MA)...VL
University of Miami (FL)...L
University of Michigan, Ann Arbor (MI)...VL
University of Minnesota, Minneapolis (MN)...VL
University of Nebraska, Lincoln (NB)...VL
University of New Mexico, Albuquerque (NM)...VL
University of North Carolina, Chapel Hill (NC)...VL
University of North Carolina, Greensboro (NC)...VL
University of Pittsburgh (PA)...VL
University of Rhode Island, Kingston (RI)...L
University of Southern Florida, Tampa (FL)...VL
University of Tennessee, Knoxville (TN)...VL
University of Texas, Austin (TX)...VL
University of the Arts (PA)...S
University of Virginia, Charlottesville (VA)...L
University of Washington, Seattle (WA)...VL
University of Wisconsin, Madison (WI)...VL
University of Wisconsin, Milwaukee (WI)...VL
Vassar (NY)...S
Virginia Commonwealth University, Richmond (VA)...VL
Wellesley (MA)...S
Wesleyan (CT)...S
West Virginia University, Morgantown (WV)...L
Wheaton College (MA)...S

Most Highly Recommended Graduate Programs (in alphabetical order)

American Conservatory Theater (ACT) (CA)...VS
Brandeis (MA)...S
Catholic University (DC)...M
Indiana University, Bloomington (IN)...VL
Institute for Advanced Theater Training at Harvard (American Repertory Theater) (MA)...VS
Juilliard (NY)...VS
National Theater Conservatory (CO)...VS
New York University, Tisch School of the Arts (NY)...L
Southern Methodist University (TX)...L
University of California, Irvine (CA)...L
University of California, San Diego, La Jolla (CA)...L
University of North Carolina, Chapel Hill (NC)...VL
Yale University School of Drama (CT)...L

Other Noteworthy Graduate Programs

Alabama Shakespeare Festival (AL)...L
California Institute of the Arts (CA)...VS
Case Western Reserve (OH)...M
DePaul University (IL)...L
Florida State University, Asolo Conservatory, Sarasota (FL)...S
Florida State University, Tallahassee (FL)...VL
Illinois State University, Normal (IL)...VL
Kansas State University, Manhattan (KS)...L
Northern Illinois University, DeKalb (IL)...VL
Ohio State University, Columbus (OH)...VL
Ohio University, Athens (OH)...L
Rutgers University, New Brunswick (NJ)...VL
San Francisco State (CA)...VL
SUNY, Binghamton (NY)...VL
SUNY, Buffalo (NY)...VL
University of Alabama, Tuscaloosa (AL)...VL
University of Arizona, Tucson (AZ)...VL
University of California, Davis (CA)...VL
University of Cincinnati, College–Conservatory of Music (OH)...VL
University of Connecticut, Storrs (CT)...VL
University of Delaware, Newark (DE)...L
University of Georgia, Athens (GA)...VL
University of Houston (TX)...VL
University of Illinois, Champaign-Urbana (IL)...VL
University of Iowa, Iowa City (IA)...VL
University of Michigan, Ann Arbor (MI)...VL
University of Minnesota, Minneapolis (MN)...VL
University of Missouri, Kansas City (MO)...L
University of Montana, Missoula...L
University of Nebraska, Lincoln (NB)...VL
University of New Mexico, Albuquerque (NM)...VL
University of North Carolina, Greensboro (NC)...L
University of Pittsburgh (PA)...VL
University of San Diego / Old Globe Theater (CA)...M
University of South Carolina, Columbia (SC)...VL
University of Southern California (CA)...VL
University of Washington, Seattle (WA)...VL
University of Wisconsin, Milwaukee (WI)...L
Wayne State University (MI)...VL
West Virginia University, Morgantown (WV)...L

Noteworthy Nondegree Programs

American Academy of Dramatic Arts (CA and NY)...VS
American Musical and Dramatic Academy (NY)...VS
Circle in the Square Theater School (NY)...VS
CSC Rep—The Actors' Conservatory (NY)...VS
London Academy of Performing Arts (England)...VS
Los Angeles City College: Theater Academy (CA)...VL
National Shakespeare Conservatory (NY)...VS
National Theater Institute, Eugene O'Neill Theater Center (CT)...VS
New Actors Workshop (NY)...VS
Studio of the Actors' Space (NY)...VS

Summary Programs

American Conservatory Theater (ACT)
450 Geary Street
San Francisco, CA 94102
415-771-3880

American University
Washington, DC
Tim Reagan, contact
301-320-2550

Boston University
School of Theater Arts—Summer Program
855 Commonwealth Avenue
Boston, MA 02215
617-353-3390 or 617-353-4363

Carnegie-Mellon Summer Program
Pre-college Program
John Papinchak, contact
412-268-2082

Chapel Hill-Chauncy Hall Summer Theater School
785 Beaver Street
Waltham, MA 02254
617-647-0353

Chautauqua Institute
Summer Programs
P.O. Box 1095
Chautauqua, NY 14722
716-357-6200

Choate Summer Program
185 Christian Street, Box 788
Wallingford, CT 06492
203-269-7722

Circle in the Square Theater School
1633 Broadway
New York, NY 10019
212-307-2732

Fieldston School Summer Program
Fieldston Road
Bronx, NY 10471
212-543-5000

George Washington University
Summer Drama Program
800 21st Street, NW
Washington, DC 20052
202-994-1660

Michael Kahn's Summer Project at the Folger in D.C.
c/o Shakespeare Theater at the Folger
301 East Capital Street, S.E.
Washington, DC 20003
212-547-3230

Northwestern University
Summer Program
1801 Hinman Avenue
Evanston, IL 60201
312-491-7271

Rutgers University
New Brunswick, NJ
Summer Arts Institute
Jacque Robul, contact
908-463-3640

University of the Arts
World of Theater Program for High School Students
Broad and Pine Streets
Philadelphia, PA 19102
215-875-4808

Wayne State University
Department of Theater
Detroit, MI 48202
313-577-3508

Williamstown
Winter:
100 E. 17th Street, 3rd Floor
New York, NY 10003
212-228-2286
Summer:
Box 517
Williamstown, MA 01267
413-458-3200

There is also a very helpful publication, *Summer Theater Directory* (available through Theater Directories, P.O. Box 519, Dorset, VT 05251; 802-867-2223), which is an excellent source of information about summer stock. *Back Stage* also publishes an issue with superb information about summer opportunities.

Drama Classes and Studios

Actor's Studio (Lee Strasberg)
432 West 44th Street
New York, NY 10036
212-757-0870

American Academy of Dramatic Arts
120 Madison Avenue
New York, NY 10016
212-686-9244

**American Academy of Dramatic Arts /
West**
2550 Paloma Street
Pasadena, CA 91107
818-798-0777

Circle in the Square Theater School
1633 Broadway
New York, NY 10019-6795
212-307-2732

Classic Stage Company (CSC)
135 East 13th Street
New York, NY 10003
212-677-4210

HB Studios (Uta Hagen)
120 Bank Street
New York, NY 10014
212-675-2370

National Shakespeare Conservatory
591 Broadway
New York, NY 10012
800-472-6667 or 212-219-9874

Neighborhood Playhouse
340 East 54th Street
New York, NY 10022
212-688-3770

Playwrights Horizons
416 West 42nd Street
New York, NY 10036
212-564-1235

Riverside Shakespeare Company
316 East 91st Street
New York, NY 10128
212-369-2273

Roundabout Theater
1530 Broadway
New York, NY 10036
212-719-9393

Stella Adler Conservatory of Acting
130 West 56th Street, Apt. 1518
New York, NY 10019
212-246-1195

Music

Most Highly Recommended Programs (by instrument in alphabetical order)

Note: An alphabetical listing of all recommended summer music programs, complete with addresses and author comments, appears at the end of the music listings on pages 119–126.

Accompanying Programs

Cleveland Institute (OH)...VS
Eastman School of Music (NY)...M
Florida State, Tallahassee (FL)...VL
Guildhall (England)...VS
Hochschüle, Cologne (Germany)...S
Juilliard (NY)...VS
New England Conservatory (MA)...VS
University of Cincinnati, College–Conservatory of Music (OH)...VL
University of Illinois, Champaign-Urbana (IL)...VL
University of Michigan, Ann Arbor (MI)...VL
University of Minnesota, Minneapolis (MN)...VL
University of Southern California (also undergraduate) (CA)...VL

Accordion

University of Denver (CO)...M
University of Missouri, Kansas City (MO)...VL
Wayne State University (MI)...VL

Bagpipes

Carnegie-Mellon (PA)...M

Bassoon: Undergraduate Programs
Cleveland Institute (OH)...VS
Curtis Institute of Music (PA)...VS
Eastman School of Music (NY)...M
Juilliard (NY)...VS
Manhattan School of Music (NY)...VS
Temple (PA)...VL
University of Cincinnati, College–Conservatory of Music (OH)...VL
University of Southern California (CA)...VL
University of Washington, Seattle (WA)...VL
Yale School of Music (CT)...L

Bassoon: Graduate Programs
Cleveland Institute of Music (OH)...VS
Eastman School of Music (NY)...M
Juilliard (NY)...VS
Manhattan School of Music (NY)...VS
Temple (PA)...VL
University of Cincinnati, College–Conservatory of Music (OH)...VL
University of Southern California (CA)...VL
University of Washington, Seattle (WA)...VL
Yale School of Music (CT)...L

Bassoon: Noteworthy Summer Programs
Aspen (CO)
Banff (Canada)
Blossom (OH)
European International Festival, Geneva (Switzerland)
Montreux Festival (Switzerland)
Mozarteum, Salzburg (Austria)
Tanglewood (MA)

Bass Trombone: *See* Trombone

Choral Conducting
Eastman School of Music (NY)...M
Indiana University, Bloomington (IN)...VL
Luther College (IA)...S
Southern Methodist University (TX)...M
St. Olaf's College (MN)...M
University of Illinois, Urbana-Champaign (IL)...VL
University of Michigan, Ann Arbor (MI)...VL
University of Texas, Austin (TX)...VL
Westminster Choir College (NJ)...VS

Church Music / Sacred Music / Liturgical Music
Baylor (TX)...L
Boston University (MA)...VL
Catholic University (DC)...M
Louisiana State University (LA)...VL
Northwestern University (IL)...M
Southern Methodist University (TX)...M
St. Olaf's College (MN)...M
University of Colorado, Boulder (CO)...VL

University of Michigan, Ann Arbor (MI)…VL
University of Minnesota, Minneapolis (MN)…VL
University of Notre Dame (IN)…L
University of Southern California (CA)…VL
Westminster Choir College (NJ)…VS
Yale Institute of Sacred Music (CT)…L

Clarinet: Undergraduate Programs

Cleveland Institute of Music (OH)…VS
DePaul University (IL)…L
Eastman School of Music (NY)…M
Indiana University, Bloomington (IN)…VL
Juilliard (NY)…VS
Manhattan School of Music (NY)…VS
Michigan State, East Lansing (MI)…VL
North Carolina School of the Arts (NC)…S
Northwestern University (IL)…M
Oberlin (OH)…S
University of Michigan, Ann Arbor (MI)…VL
University of Southern California (CA)…VL
Yale School of Music (CT)…L

Clarinet: Graduate Programs

Cleveland Institute of Music (OH)…VS
DePaul University (IL)…L
Eastman School of Music (NY)…M
Indiana University, Bloomington (IN)…VL
Juilliard (NY)…VS
Manhattan School of Music (NY)…VS
Michigan State, East Lansing (MI)…VL
North Carolina School of the Arts (NC)…S
Northwestern University (IL)…M
SUNY, Stony Brook (NY)…L
University of Michigan, Ann Arbor (MI)…VL
University of Southern California (CA)…VL
Yale School of Music (CT)…L

Clarinet: Noteworthy Summer Programs

Sarasota Music Festival (FL)
Tanglewood (MA)

Composition: Undergraduate Programs

Bennington (VT)…VS
Boston University (MA)…VL
Brandeis (MA)…S
California Institute of the Arts (CA)…VS
Columbia (NY)…M
Duke (NC)…M
Eastman School of Music (NY)…M
Harvard (MA)…M
Juilliard (NY)…VS
Oberlin (OH)…S
Princeton (NJ)…M
Royal College of Music, London (England)…S

University of California, Berkeley (CA)...VL
University of Chicago (IL)...M
University of Miami (FL)...L
University of Michigan, Ann Arbor (MI)...VL
University of Pennsylvania (PA)...L
Yale (CT)...L

Composition: Graduate Programs

California Institute of the Arts (CA)...VS
City University of New York–Graduate Center (NY)...M
Columbia (NY)...M
Eastman School of Music (NY)...M
Harvard (MA)...M
Juilliard (NY)...VS
New York University (NY)...L
Princeton (NJ)...M
University of Illinois, Champaign-Urbana (IL)...VL
University of Michigan, Ann Arbor (MI)...VL
University of Pennsylvania (PA)...L
Yale School of Music (CT)...L

Composition: Noteworthy Summer Programs

Accademia Chigiana, Siena (Italy)
Aspen (CO)
Bard (NY)
Festival at Sandpoint (ID)
IRCOM, Paris (France)
Oberlin (OH)
(2-to-3 week program in electronic and computer music for high school to senior citizens)
Stanford (computer music) (CA)
Tanglewood Institute (composers) (MA)

Double Bass

Curtis Institute of Music (PA)...VS
Indiana University, Bloomington (IN)...VL
Juilliard (NY)...VS
Manhattan School of Music (NY)...VS
Mannes College of Music (NY)...VS
New England Conservatory (NEC) (MA)...S
Queens College of the City College of New York (NY)...VL
University of Southern California (CA)...VL

Double Bass: Noteworthy Summer Programs

Aspen (CO)
Sarasota Music Festival (FL)

Early Music

Boston University (MA)...VL
Brandeis (MA)...S
Brooklyn College of the City of New York (NY)...VL
Brussels Conservatory (Belgium)...S
Case Western Reserve (OH)...L
City University of New York–Graduate Center (NY)...VL
Hochschüle, Freiburg (Germany)...S

Indiana University, Bloomington (IN)...VL
Mannes College of Music (NY)...VS
New England Conservatory (MA)...S
Oberlin (OH)...S
Paris Conservatoire (France)...S
Royal Academy of Music, London (England)...M
Royal College of Music, London (England)...M
Royal Conservatory (Koninklijk), The Hague (Netherlands)...S
Schola Cantorum, Basel (Switzerland)...S
Smith (MA) (women)...S
Stanford (CA)...M
St. Olaf's (MN)...M
University of Southern California (CA)...VL
Wesleyan (CT)...S

Electronic Music: Undergraduate Programs

California Institute of the Arts (CA)...VS
Oberlin College Conservatory (OH)...S

Electronic Music: Graduate Programs

California Institute of the Arts (CA)...VS
IRCOM Center, Paris (France)...VS
Massachusetts Institute of Technology (MA)...M
Northwestern University (IL)...M
Stanford (CA)...M
University of California at San Diego (CA)...L

English Horn: *See Oboe*

Flute

Eastman School of Music (NY)...M
Florida State University, Tallahassee (FL)...L
Indiana University, Bloomington (IN)...VL
Juilliard (NY)...VS
Manhattan School of Music (NY)...VS
New England Conservatory (MA)...S
Northwestern University (IL)...M
Oberlin (OH)...S
Queens College of the City University of New York (NY)...VL
Rice University (TX)...M
Royal Academy of Music, London (England)...S
Royal College of Music, London (England)...S
Royal College of Music, Toronto (Canada)...VL
San Francisco Conservatory (CA)...VS
Southern Methodist University (TX)...M
SUNY, Stony Brook (NY)...L
University of Kansas, Kansas City (MO)...VL
University of New Mexico, Albuquerque (NM)...VL
University of North Texas, Denton (TX)...VL
University of Southern California (CA)...VL

Flute: Noteworthy Summer Programs

Aspen (CO)
Banff (Canada)

Blossom Festival (OH)
Bowdoin (ME)
Colorado Philharmonic (CO)
Eastern Music Festival
Grand Teton Festival
Keith Underwood Seminar in Flute
(write in care of Underwood Enterprises, 760 West End Avenue, New York, NY 10025)
Pacific Music Festival
Sarasota Music Festival (FL)
Tanglewood (MA)
Wildacres (NC)

French Horn

Cleveland Institute of Music (OH)...VS
Conservatory in Oslo (Norway)...S
Curtis Institute of Music (PA)...VS
Eastman School of Music (NY)...M
Hartt School of Music (CT)...VS
Indiana University, Bloomington (IN)...VL
Juilliard (NY)...VS
Manhattan School of Music (NY)...VS
Rice University (TX)...M
San Francisco Conservatory (CA)...VS
University of Houston (TX)...VL
University of Southern California (CA)...VL
University of Wisconsin, Madison (WI)...VL
Yale School of Music (CT)...L

French Horn: Noteworthy Summer Programs

Aspen (CO)
Banff (Canada)
Blossom (OH)
Brevard (NC)
Grand Teton (WY)
Holland Music Sessions (The Netherlands)
Interlochen (MI)
Keystone Brass Institute (Summit Brass) (CO)
Music Academy of the West (CA)
Oklahoma Arts Academy, Quartz Mountain (OK)
Sarasota (FL)
Tanglewood (MA)

Guitar (Classical): Undergraduate Programs

Arizona State University, Tempe (AZ)...VL
Boston Conservatory (MA)...VS
Cleveland Institute of Music (OH)...VS
Florida State University, Tallahassee (FL)...VL
Indiana University, Bloomington (IN)...VL
Macalester College (MN)...S
Manhattan School of Music (NY)...VS
Mannes College of Music (NY)...VS
Mt. Holyoke, University of Massachusetts, Amherst, Hampshire, Smith (MA)...VL
New England Conservatory (MA)...S
North Carolina School of the Arts (NC)...VS

Paris Conservatoire (France)...M
Royal Academy, London (England)...M
Royal Conservatory, London (England)...M
San Francisco Conservatory (CA)...VS
State University of New York, Buffalo (NY)...L
State University of New York, Purchase (NY)...S
University of Arizona, Tucson (AZ)...VL
University of Cincinnati, College–Conservatory of Music (OH)...VL
University of Hartford, Hartt School of Music (CT)...M
University of Miami (FL)...L
University of Minnesota (MN)...VL
University of New Mexico, Albuquerque (NM)...VL
University of Southern California (CA)...VL
University of Texas, Austin (TX)...VL
University of Washington, Seattle (WA)...VL
University of Wisconsin, Milwaukee (WI)...VL
Vanderbilt University, Blair School of Music (TN)...M
Wisconsin Conservatory (WI)...VL

Guitar (Classical): Graduate Programs

While many of the departments listed above also offer graduate degrees, in addition you should
also investigate:
Juilliard (NY)...VS
Yale School of Music (CT)...L

Guitar: Noteworthy Summer Programs:

Mt. Holyoke Guitar Workshop (MA)
National Guitar Summer Institute, New Milford (CT)
Paco Peña International Guitar Festival, Córdoba (Spain)
University of Wisconsin, Milwaukee (WI)

Harp

Brussels Conservatory (Belgium)...S
Curtis Institute of Music (PA)...VS
Eastman School of Music (NY)...VL
Indiana University, Bloomington (IN)...VL
Juilliard (NY)...VS
Manhattan School of Music (NY)...VS
New England Conservatory (MA)...S
Paris Conservatoire (France)...S
Royal Academy, London (England)...S
San Francisco Conservatory (CA)...VS
Temple University (PA)...VL
University of Michigan, Ann Arbor (MI)...VL
University of Southern California (CA)...VL
Yale School of Music (CT)...VL

Harpsichord

Amsterdam with Tom Koopman (Netherlands)...VS
Eastman School of Music (NY)...M
Hochschüle, Freiburg (Germany)...S
Hochschüle für Musik, Vienna (Austria)...M
Indiana University, Bloomington (IN)...VL
Juilliard (NY)...VS

Koninklijk-Royal Conservatory of Music and Dance, The Hague (Netherlands)…VS
Oberlin (OH)…S
Paris Conservatoire (France)…M
Royal Academy of Music, London (England)…S
Royal College of Music, London (England)…S
Schola Cantorum, Basel (Switzerland)…VS
Yale School of Music (CT)…L

Jazz

Berklee College of Music (MA)…S
California Institute of the Arts (CA)…VS
Eastman School of Music (NY)…M
Howard University (DC)…L
Indiana University, Bloomington (IN)…VL
Lawrence University (WI)…M
Loyola University (LA)…M
Manhattan School of Music (NY)…VS
Mannes College of Music (NY)…VS
New England Conservatory (MA)…S
New School of Social Research, Eugene Lang College (NY)…S
Rutgers, Mason Gross School of Music (NJ)…VL
University of Arizona, Tucson (AZ)…VL
University of Hartford, Hartt School of Music (CT)…M
University of Massachusetts, Amherst (MA)…VL
University of Miami (FL)…L
University of North Texas, Denton (TX)…VL
University of Southern California (CA)…VL
Wayne State University (MI)…VL
William Patterson State College (NJ)…M
World School for New Jazz (Holland)…VS

Jazz: Noteworthy Summer Programs

Banff (Canada)
Berklee College of Music (MA)
Clinics all over (usually advertised in *Downbeat* magazine)
Manhattan School of Music (NY)

Musical Theater

American Musical and Dramatic Academy (NY)…S
Arizona State University, Tempe (AZ)…VL
Baldwin-Wallace College (OH)…M
Ball State University (OH)…L
Boston Conservatory (MA)…VS
Brigham Young University (UT)…VL
Brooklyn College of CUNY (NY)…VL
Butler University, Jordan College of Fine Arts (IN)…S
California State University, Fullerton (CA)…VL
Carnegie-Mellon University (PA)…M
Catawba College (NC)…S
Catholic University (DC)…M
Coe College (IA)…S
College of Santa Fe (NM)…S
Cornell College (IA)…S
Drake University (IA)…M

Emerson College (MA)...S
Florida State University, Tallahassee (FL)...VL
Hampshire College (MA)...S
Illinois Wesleyan (IL)...S
Ithaca College (NY)...M
Kansas State University, Manhattan (KS)...VL
Kent State (OH)...VL
Long Island University: C. W. Post Campus (NY)...M
New York University (for undergraduate musical theater) Department of Music and Music
   Professions, School of Education, Health, Nursing, and Arts Professions (NY)...VL
Ohio Wesleyan (OH)...S
Sarah Lawrence (NY)...S
Shenandoah College and Conservatory (VA)...S
SUNY, Fredonia (NY)...M
SUNY, New Paltz (NY)...M
Syracuse University (NY)...L
University of Cincinnati, Cincinnati College–Conservatory of Music (OH)...VL
University of Hartford, Hartt School of Music (CT)...M
University of Miami (FL)...L
University of Michigan, Ann Arbor (MI)...VL
University of Nebraska, Lincoln (NE)...VL
University of Northern Colorado, Greeley (CO)...L
University of the Arts (PA)...VS
West Virginia University (WV)...L

Oboe and English Horn

Cleveland Institute of Music (OH)...VS
Curtis Institute of Music (PA)...VS
Eastman School of Music (NY)...M
Hochschule, Freiburg (Germany)...S
Indiana University, Bloomington (IN)...VL
Juilliard (NY)...VS
Manhattan School of Music (NY)...VS
Oberlin (OH)...S
(Very few schools offer just an English horn major. Most programs require that you major in
   oboe and often play oboe d'amore, also. For other listings, see Oboe. The most highly recom-
   mended program for undergraduate or graduate English horn is Juilliard.)

Oboe: Other Noteworthy Programs

Baylor University (TX)...L
Central Michigan University (MI)...L
Florida State University, Tallahassee (FL)...VL
Louisiana State University, Baton Rouge (LA)...VL
Michigan State, East Lansing (MI)...VL
University of Michigan, Ann Arbor (MI)...VL
University of Minnesota (MN)...VL
University of Wisconsin, Madison (WI)...VL
Wichita State University (KS)...L

Oboe and/or English Horn: Noteworthy Summer Programs

Tom Stacy International English Horn Seminar
(This is advertised in the Double Reed Journal, *or write to Mr. Stacy for more information in*
   care of either the NY Philharmonic or The Juilliard School.)
John Mack Oboe Camp (NC)
(You can write to Mr. Mack in care of the Cleveland Institute for information.)

Aspen (CO)
Banff (Canada)
Chautauqua (NY)
Eastern Music Festival (NC)
National Repertory Symphony (CO)
Orchestra Training Institute, University of Maryland (MD)
Sarasota Music Festival (FL)
Tanglewood (MA)

Orchestral Conducting

Curtis Institute of Music (PA)...VS
Eastman School of Music (NY)...M
Guildhall, London (England)...S
Hochschüle, Berlin (Germany)...S
Hochschüle, Vienna (Austria)...S
Indiana University, Bloomington (IN)...VL
Juilliard (NY)...VS
Mannes College of Music (NY)...VS
New England Conservatory (MA)...S
Northwestern University (IL)...M
San Francisco Conservatory (CA)...VS
Sibelius Academy, Helsinki (Finland)...S
University of Illinois, Champaign-Urbana (IL)...VL
University of Michigan, Ann Arbor (MI)...VL
University of Minnesota (MN)...VL
University of Southern California (CA)...VL
Yale School of Music (CT)...L

Orchestral Conducting: Noteworthy Summer Programs

Accademia Chigiana, Siena (Italy)
American Symphony Orchestra League Seminars (VA)
Aspen (CO)
Bartók Festival (Hungary)
Festival at Sandpoint (ID)
Los Angeles Philharmonic Institute (CA)
Mozarteum, Salzburg (Austria)
(Did not have summer program last summer but may have it again in the future.)
Pierre Monteux, Hancock (ME)
Tanglewood (MA)

Organ

Catholic University (DC)...M
Curtis Institute of Music (PA)...VS
Eastman School of Music (NY)...M
Indiana University, Bloomington (IN)...VL
Juilliard (NY)...VS
Manhattan School of Music (NY)...VS
Oberlin (OH)...S
Royal Northern College of Music, Manchester (England)...S
Southern Methodist University (TX)...M
Syracuse (NY)...L
University of Alabama (AL)...L
University of Iowa, Iowa City (IA)...VL
University of Michigan, Ann Arbor (MI)...VL

University of Southern California (CA)…VL
Westminster Choir College (NJ)…VS

Organ: Noteworthy Summer Programs

Chautauqua (NY)
San Francisco Presbyterian Theological Seminary—Summer Master Classes
University of Kansas, Lawrence (KS)
University of Nebraska, Lincoln (NE)
Westminster Choir College (NJ)

Percussion

California Institute of the Arts (CA)…VS
Cleveland Institute of Music (OH)…VS
Curtis Institute of Music (PA)…VS
Eastman School of Music (NY)…M
Indiana University at Bloomington (IN)…VL
Juilliard (NY)…VS
Manhattan School of Music (NY)…VS
Oberlin (OH)…S
Rice University (TX)…M
San Francisco Conservatory (CA)…VS
Temple University (PA)…VL
University of Hartford, Hartt School of Music (CT)…VL
University of Michigan, Ann Arbor (MI)…VL
Yale School of Music (CT)…L

Piano

Boston University (MA)…VL
City University of New York (NY)…VL
Curtis Institute of Music (PA)…VS
Eastman School of Music (NY)…M
Indiana University, Bloomington (IN)…VL
Juilliard (NY)…VS
Manhattan School of Music (NY)…VS
Mannes College of Music (NY)…VS
New England Conservatory (MA)…S
Northwestern University (IL)…M
Peabody Conservatory (MD)…S
Rice University (TX)…M
Southern Methodist University (TX)…M
SUNY, Stony Brook (NY)…VL
University of Houston (TX)…VL
University of Maryland, College Park (MD)…VL
University of Michigan, Ann Arbor (MI)…VL
University of Texas, Austin (TX)…VL
University of Southern California (CA)…VL
Yale School of Music (CT)…L

Piano: Noteworthy Summer Programs

Aspen (CO)
Banff (Canada)
Bowdoin College Summer Music Festival (ME)
Eastern Music Festival (NC)
Holland Music Sessions (The Netherlands)

Marlboro Festival (VT)
Music Academy of the West (CA)

Saxophone
Baylor University (TX)...L
Boston University (MA)...VL
Brussels Conservatory (Belgium)...S
DePaul (IL)...L
Eastman School of Music (NY)...VL
Florida State, Tallahassee (FL)...VL
Howard University (DC)...L
Indiana University, Bloomington (IN)...VL
University of Arizona, Tucson (AZ)...VL
University of California, Los Angeles (CA)...VL
University of Cincinnati, College–Conservatory of Music (OH)...VL
University of Colorado, Boulder (CO)...VL
University of Hartford, Hartt School of Music (CT)...VL
University of Miami (FL)...L
University of Michigan, Ann Arbor (MI)...VL
University of Wisconsin, Madison (WI)...VL

Trombone: (Tenor and Bass)
Curtis Institute of Music (PA)...VS
Eastman School of Music (NY)...M
Indiana University, Bloomington (IN)...VL
Juilliard (NY)...VS
New England Conservatory (MA)...S
Northwestern University (IL)...M
San Francisco Conservatory (CA)...VS
University of Minnesota (MN)...VL

Trombone: Noteworthy Summer Programs
Aspen (CO)
Grand Teton Festival (WY)
Keystone Brass Institute (Summit Brass), part of the National Repertory Orchestra
Spoleto (South Carolina and Italy)
Tanglewood (MA)

Trumpet
Arizona State University, Tempe (AZ)...VL
Cleveland Institute of Music (OH)...VS
Curtis Institute of Music (PA)...VS
Eastman School of Music (NY)...M
Edward Tarr in Basel (Switzerland)...VS
Indiana University, Bloomington (IN)...VL
Juilliard (NY)...VS
Manhattan School of Music (NY)...VS
New England Conservatory of Music (MA)...S
Northwestern University (IL)...M
Pierre Thibault (France)...VS
University of Michigan, Ann Arbor (MI)...VL
Yale School of Music (CT)...L

Trumpet: Noteworthy Summer Programs
Aspen (CO)
Colorado Philharmonic (CO)
Keystone (CO)
Music Academy of the West (CA)
Roundtop Festival (TX)
Tanglewood (MA)
Waterloo (NJ)

Tuba: Undergraduate Programs
Arizona State University, Tempe (AZ)...VL
Boston Conservatory (MA)...VS
Boston University (MA)...M
Cleveland Institute of Music (OH)...VS
Curtis Institute of Music (PA)...VS
Juilliard (NY)...VS
New England Conservatory (MA)...S
Oberlin (OH)...S
University of North Texas, Denton (TX)...VL
University of Southern California (CA)...VL

Tuba: Graduate Programs
Arizona State University, Tempe (AZ)...VL
Cleveland Institute of Music (OH)...VS
Juilliard (NY)...VS
University of Southern California (CA)...VL

Tuba: Noteworthy Summer Programs
Aspen (CO)
Keystone Summit Brass Symposium (CO)
Roundtop Festival (TX)
Tanglewood (MA)

Viola
Cleveland Institute of Music (OH)...VS
Curtis Institute of Music (PA)...VS
Juilliard (NY)...VS
Mannes College of Music (NY)...VS
New England Conservatory of Music (MA)...S
Oberlin (OH)...S
Royal Academy, London (England)...M
Rutgers, Mason Gross School of the Arts (NJ)...VL
Toho Gakuen School of Music, Tokyo (Japan)...M
University of Cincinnati, College–Conservatory of Music (OH)...VL
University of Minnesota (MN)...VL
University of Southern California (CA)...VL
Yale School of Music (CT)...L
Yehudi Menuhin School of Music, Surrey (England)...VS

Viola: Noteworthy Summer Programs
Banff (Canada)
Sarasota Music Festival (FL)

Violin

Curtis Institute of Music (PA)...VS
Eastman School of Music (NY)...M
Hochschüle, Hannover (Germany)...S
Indiana University, Bloomington (IN)...VL
Juilliard (NY)...VS
Manhattan School of Music (NY)...VS
Mannes College of Music (NY)...VS
Royal College of Music (England)...M
San Francisco Conservatory (CA)...VS
Toho Gakuen School of Music, Tokyo (Japan)...M
University of Cincinnati, College–Conservatory of Music (OH)...VL
University of Minnesota, Minneapolis (MN)...VL
University of Southern California (CA)...VL
Wichita State University (KS)...L
Yehudi Menuhin School, Surrey (England)...VS

Violin: Noteworthy Summer Programs

Alfred University Summer Master Class in Violin (NY)
Aspen (CO)
Holland Music Sessions (The Netherlands)
Interlochen (MI)
Marlboro (VT)
Meadowmount (NY)
Music Academy of the West (CA)
Roundtop Festival (TX)
Sarasota Music Festival (FL)
Tanglewood (MA)
Taos Chamber Music Festival (NM)
Yale at Norfolk (CT)

Violoncello

Boston University (MA)...VL
Curtis Institute of Music (PA)...VS
Hochschüle, Heidelberg (Germany)...M
Illinois State University, Normal (IL)...VL
Indiana University, Bloomington (IN)...VL
Juilliard (NY)...VS
Manhattan School of Music (NY)...VS
Mannes College of Music (NY)...VS
New England Conservatory (MA)...S
Northwestern University (IL)...M
Rice University (TX)...M
San Francisco Conservatory (CA)...VS
University of California, Berkeley (CA)...VL
University of Cincinnati, College–Conservatory of Music (OH)...VL
University of Southern California (CA)...VL
University of Texas, Austin (TX)...VL
Yehudi Menuhin School, Surrey (England)...VS

Violoncello: Noteworthy Summer Programs

Aspen (CO)
Holland Music Sessions (The Netherlands)
Marlboro (VT)

Music Academy of the West (CA)
Rivinia (more advanced players) (IL)
Tanglewood (MA)

Voice: Undergraduate Programs

Barnard (NY) (women)...S
(joint programs with Juilliard and Manhattan School of Music)
Boston University (MA)...VL
College of Wooster (OH)...S
Columbia (NY)...L *(joint program with Juilliard)*
Curtis Institute of Music (PA)...VS
Illinois Wesleyan (IL)...S
Juilliard (NY)...VS
Louisiana State University (LA)...VL
Manhattan School of Music (NY)...VS
Northwestern University (IL)...M
Royal Academy of Music, London (England)...S
Royal Northern College of Music, Manchester (England)...S
Sibelius Academy, Helsinki (Finland)...S
Smith (MA) (women)...S
University of Massachusetts, Amherst (MA)...VL
University of Michigan, Ann Arbor (MI)...VL
University of Southern California (CA)...VL
Westminster Choir College (NJ)...VS

Voice: Graduate Programs

Curtis Institute of Music (PA)...VS
Indiana University, Bloomington (IN)...VL
Juilliard (NY)...VS
(and the Juilliard Opera Center for the most advanced singers)
Manhattan School of Music (NY)...VS
University of Illinois, Champaign-Urbana (IL)...VL
University of Southern California (CA)...VL

Voice: Noteworthy Summer Programs (not apprenticeships)

Abbé de Royamont (France)
Accademia Chigiana (Italy)
AIMS (American Institute of Musical Studies) (Austria)
Aldeborough—Peter Pears School (England)
Aspen (CO)
Banff (Canada)
Brevard (NC)
Chautauqua (NY)
College Light Opera Company, Falmouth, Cape Cod (MA)
Daniel Ferro Summer Program in Voice *(write to him at Juilliard.)*
Holland Music Sessions (The Netherlands)
International Institute of Vocal Arts
(William Woodruff's program in Tampa, FL)
Israel Vocal Arts Institute: Joan Dornemann's program in Tel Aviv *(You can write to her in care of the Metropolitan Opera.)*
Marlena Malas Summer Master Classes *(write to her at Juilliard.)*
Mozarteum, Salzburg (Austria)
Music Academy of the West (CA)
Ohio Light Opera Company (OH)
Tanglewood (MA)

Joint Programs

Tufts University / New England Conservatory

Tufts University	NEC Office of Admissions
Office of Admissions	290 Huntington Avenue
Medford, MA 02155	Boston, MA 02115
617-381-3170	617-262-1120

Barnard–Columbia–Juilliard

Barnard College	Columbia College	Juilliard School
Office of Admissions	Office of Admissions	Office of Admissions
3009 Broadway	212 Hamilton Hall	60 Lincoln Center Plaza
New York, NY 10027	New York, NY 10027	New York, NY 10023-6590
212-854-2014	212-854-2522	212-799-5000, ext 223

University of Rochester / Eastman

University of Rochester	Eastman School of Music
Office of Admissions	Office of Admissions
River Station	26 Gibbs Street
Rochester, NY 14627	Rochester, NY 14604
716-275-3221	716-274-1060

Oberlin / Oberlin Conservatory

Oberlin College	Oberlin Conservatory
Office of Admissions	Office of Admissions
Oberlin, OH 44074	Oberlin, OH 44074
216-775-8411	216-775-8413

Lawrence University / Lawrence Conservatory

Lawrence University	Lawrence University Conservatory
Office of Admissions	Office of Admissions
Appleton, WI 54912	Appleton, WI 54912
414-832-7000	414-832-6611

University of Cincinnati / Cincinnati Conservatory

100 French Hall
Cincinnati, OH 45221
513-475-3425

University of Hartford / Hartt School of Music

200 Bloomfield Avenue
Hartford, CT 06177
203-243-4296

Case Western Reserve / Cleveland Institute of Music

Haydn Hall	11021 East Boulevard
Cleveland, OH 44106	Cleveland, OH 44106
216-368-2400	216-791-5000

Directory of Recommended
Summer Music Programs

Abbé de Royamont
c/o Fondacion de Royamont
Centre de la Voix
95270 Asnieres-sur-Oise, FRANCE
1-30.35.40.18
*AUTHOR'S COMMENT: Recommended for
voice.*

Accademia Chigiana
Via della Città, 89
53100 Siena, ITALY
*AUTHOR'S COMMENT: Recommended for
advanced students, especially in voice,
orchestral conducting, and composition.
The faculty changes fairly frequently, so
be sure to investigate thoroughly.*

Aldeborough—Peter Pears School
High Street
Aldeborough, Suffolk, ENGLAND 1P15 5AX
728-452935   FAX: 728-452715
*AUTHOR'S COMMENT: Recommended for
voice and early music.*

**Alfred University Summer Chamber Music
Institute**
Harder Hall, 444, P.O. Box 826
Alfred, NY 14802
607-871-2219
*AUTHOR'S COMMENT: Highly recom-
mended for violin and chamber music.*

**American Institute of Musical Studies
(AIMS)**
c/o 3500 Maple Avenue, Suite 120
Dallas, TX 75219-3901
214-528-9234   FAX: 214-521-3383
early July to mid-August
*AUTHOR'S COMMENT: This program,
run in Graz, Austria, provides fine
teaching, coaching, and diction classes for
advanced singers. Auditions for European
agents are held each summer and thus
singers have the opportunity to launch a
career in Europe. There is also the AIMS
Chorale and the Festival Orchestra.*

**American Symphony Orchestra League
Conducting Seminars (ASOL)**
c/o ASOL
777 14th Street, NW
Washington, DC 20005
202-628-0099   FAX: 202-783-7228

Appel Farms Arts and Music Center
Box 888
Elmer, NJ 08318
609-358-2472
*AUTHOR'S COMMENT: Recommended
for chamber music. Younger students
especially do quite well here.*

Aspen Music Festival
Winter address:
250 West 54th Street, 10th floor E
New York, NY 10019
212-581-2196   FAX: 212-582-2757
Summer address:
Box AA
Aspen, CO 81612
303-925-3254   FAX: 303-925-3802
late June to late August
*AUTHOR'S COMMENT: Highly
recommended for private instrumental
and vocal instruction, opera workshop,
conducting master classes. Often referred
to as "Juilliard West," as many Juilliard
faculty members teach there during the
summer.*

**Aston Magna Performance Practice
Institute**
P.O. Box 28
Great Barrington, MA 01230
413-528-3595
*AUTHOR'S COMMENT: Highly recom-
mended for early music.*

Bach Aria Festival and Institute
P.O. Box 997
Stony Brook, NY 11790
516-632-7239
mid-June to early July
*AUTHOR'S COMMENT: Recommended for
voice and early music.*

Baldwin-Wallace College
Conservatory of Music
275 Eastland Road
Berea, OH 44017-2088
216-826-2368
*AUTHOR'S COMMENT: Recommended for
the summer Bach Festival.*

Ball State University
Mid-American Summer Music
Muncie, IN 47306
Joe Scagnoli, contact
317-285-5495 or 317-285-5508
*AUTHOR'S COMMENT: Includes the
Musical Theater Institute.*

Banff Center of the Arts
P.O. Box 1020
Banff, Alberta, CANADA
T01 0C0
403-762-6121   FAX: 403-762-6422
June to August
AUTHOR'S COMMENT: A truly magnificent setting for a superbly run program of private instrumental lessons and master classes, opera, and jazz.

Bard Music Festival
Bard College
Annandale-on-Hudson, NY 12504
914-758-2869
AUTHOR'S COMMENT: Recommended for composition and to hear the fine lectures and concerts presented at this beautiful campus on the Hudson River.

Bartók Festival
Interart Festival Center
H-1366, P.O. Box 80
Budapest, HUNGARY
36-1.118.9838   FAX: 36-1.117.9910
AUTHOR'S COMMENT: Recommended for conducting.

Bay View Music Festival
Bay View, MI
616-347-4210
Winter address:
Box 322
Alma, MI 48801
517-463-7221
AUTHOR'S COMMENT: Recommended for younger singers.

Belgium Vocal Arts Institute
c/o Director of Opera
Curtis Institute of Music
1726 Locust Street
Philadelphia, PA 19103
215-893-5252

Berklee College of Music
1140 Boylston Street
Boston, MA 02215
617-266-1400 or 1-800-421-0084
AUTHOR'S COMMENT: Highly recommended for the jazz clinics and courses offered, both on-campus and throughout the world, and for other seminars, workshops, and courses in commercial and popular music.

Blossom Festival School
E101 M and S
Kent State University
Kent, OH 44242
216-672-2613 or 216-566-8184   FAX: 216-920-0968
July to August

Boston Conservatory
8 The Fenway
Boston, MA 02215-4099
617-536-6340
AUTHOR'S COMMENT: Recommended for the musical theater seminar.

Bowdoin Summer Music Festival
Bowdoin College
Gibson Hall
Brunswick, ME 04011
207-725-8731 or 207-725-3322
late June to early August
AUTHOR'S COMMENT: A fine program of private instrumental lessons and master classes with a distinguished faculty.

Brevard Music Festival
Winter address:
P.O. Box 349
Converse Station
Spartanburg, SC 29301
803-585-6482
Summer address:
P.O. Box 592
Brevard, NC 28712
704-884-2011
early July to mid-August

Center for Creative Youth
Wesleyan University
Middletown, CT 06457
203-347-9411 ext. 2684
AUTHOR'S COMMENT: For developing high school students.

Chamber Music Society of Lincoln Center
Performance Awareness Seminar and Composition Studies
Lincoln Center
New York, NY 10023
212-875-5775
AUTHOR'S COMMENT: A new program, run by the composer Bruce Adolphe. Selected New York City high school students will study for free.

Chautauqua Institute
Summer Music Programs
P.O. Box 1095
Chautauqua, NY 14722
716-357-6200   FAX: 716-357-9014
AUTHOR'S COMMENT: Highly recommended for voice, dance, and drama. There is also fine instruction in orchestral instruments.

Cleveland Institute of Music
11021 East Boulevard
Cleveland, OH 44106
216-791-5000
AUTHOR'S COMMENT: The Art Song Festival offered here is truly noteworthy.

College Light Opera Company
Winter address:
162 South Cedar Street
Oberlin, OH 44074
216-774-8485
Summer address:
P.O. Box F
Falmouth, MA 02541
508-548-0668
AUTHOR'S COMMENT: 9 operettas or Broadway shows are presented in 9 weeks, so this is an excellent program for learning to be a "quick study." Highly recommended for musical comedy and light opera experience in a well-run company.

Cullowhee Music Festival
Western Carolina University
Music Department
Cullowhee, NC 28723
704-227-7608
mid-June to early July

Downeast Chamber Music Center
Winter address:
248 East 78th Street
New York, NY 10021
212-734-3904
June to August

Eastern Music Festival
P.O. Box 22026
Greensboro, NC 27420
919-333-7450   FAX: 919-333-7454
late June to early August
AUTHOR'S COMMENT: A superb faculty teaches percussion, violoncello, violin, piano, viola, and flute.

European International Festival
10 Rue des Eaux-Vives
c/o T. Gering, Concerts Atlantique
CH-1207, Geneva, SWITZERLAND
22-786.26.47   FAX: 22-755-1380
North American contact:
54 West 21st Street, Suite 1206
New York, NY 10010
212-633-1128   FAX: 212-633-1129
AUTHOR'S COMMENT: Recommended for bassoon.

Festival at Sandpoint
P.O. Box 695
Sandpoint, ID 83864
208-265-4554
AUTHOR'S COMMENT: Gunther Schuller is the artistic director for this outstanding festival.

Grand Teton Music Festival
P.O. Box 310
Teton Village, WY 83025
307-733-3050 or 1128   FAX: 307-739-9043
AUTHOR'S COMMENT: Recommended for instrumentalists.

Greenwood Music Camp
Haydenville, MA 01039
413-268-7192
AUTHOR'S COMMENT: Recommended for young musicians for chamber music and private instruction.

Holland Music Sessions
Russenplainz, 2, 1861 JR
Bergin, THE NETHERLANDS

Interlochen—The National Music Camp
Interlochen Academy of the Arts
P.O Box 199
Interlochen, MI 49643
616-276-9221   FAX: 616-276-6231
AUTHOR'S COMMENT: An excellent program for high school students in music, dance, and drama.

International Guitar Week at University of Denver
7111 Montview Boulevard
c/o Lamont School of Music
Denver, CO 80220
303-871-6959

International Institute of Vocal Arts
c/o William Woodruff
1805 Hills Avenue
Tampa, FL 33651-0407
813-254-7386
AUTHOR'S COMMENT: Recommended for developing singers for diction and vocal studies.

International Music Festival of Colmar
4, Rue des Unterlinden
6800 Colmar, FRANCE
89-41.02.29   FAX: 89-41.34.13
AUTHOR'S COMMENT: Master classes offered in piano, violin, and violoncello and taught by teachers from the Moscow Conservatory, Curtis, and Manhattan School.

IRCOM
Centre National d'Art et de Culture
Place Pompidou
Paris, FRANCE
011-33-1-278-3942 or 011-33-1-277-1233
AUTHOR'S COMMENT: Recommended for advanced students in composition and electronic music.

Israel Vocal Arts Institute
c/o Joan Dornemann
Metropolitan Opera
Lincoln Center
New York, NY 10023
212-799-3100

Johannesen International School of the Arts
103-3737 Oak Street
Vancouver, British Columbia, CANADA
V6H 2M4
604-736-1611   FAX: 604-736-8018
AUTHOR'S COMMENT: Highly specialized summer program for strings, keyboards, and wind instruments.

John Mack Oboe Camp
c/o Cleveland Institute of Music
11021 East Boulevard
Cleveland, OH 44106
216-791-5000
AUTHOR'S COMMENT: Highly recommended for intensive oboe studies.

Keith Underwood Summer Seminars in Flute
c/o Underwood Enterprises
760 West End Avenue
New York, NY 10025
AUTHOR'S COMMENT: Highly recommended for intensive master classes in flute.

Killington Music Festival
Winter address:
8118 Garland Road
Dallas, TX 75218
214-328-6197
Summer address:
P.O. Box 386
Rutland, VT 05702
late June to early August

Kinhaven Music School
Lawrence Hill Road
Weston, VT 05161
Winter address:
c/o Nancy Midlock
1704 Sycamore Street
Bethlehem, PA 18017
215-868-9200
AUTHOR'S COMMENT: An outstanding program for students ages 13 to 18, in a supportive atmosphere. Recommended for all orchestral instruments, composition, piano, and chamber music.

Kneisel Hall Summer Chamber Music Festival
P.O. Box 648
Kneisel Hall
Blue Hill, ME 04614
207-374-2811
early July to mid-August
AUTHOR'S COMMENT: One of the oldest of festivals, this is a fine program for chamber music. The faculty, especially in violin and viola, seems to be in transition, so be sure to check if you are interested in a particular teacher.

Los Angeles Philharmonic Institute
135 North Grand Avenue
Los Angeles, CA 90012
213-972-7300
late June to mid-August
AUTHOR'S COMMENT: Excellent program for aspiring conductors and instrumentalists.

Luzerne Music Center
Winter address:
5 East Brookhaven Road
Wallingford, PA 19086
215-566-1475
518-696-2771 (Summer telephone)
AUTHOR'S COMMENT: A summer music camp where talented young musicians study with members of the Philadelphia Orchestra. Recommended for orchestral instruments, chamber music, piano, brass, and percussion.

Manhattan School of Music
Summer Sessions Office
120 Claremont Avenue
New York, NY 10027
212-749-2802
AUTHOR'S COMMENT: Has a fine summer jazz program and other studies. Call for exact details.

Marlboro Music Festival
Marlboro School of Music
Marlboro, VT 05344
802-254-2394
Winter address:
135 South 18th Street
Philadelphia, PA 19103
215-569-4690
July to August
AUTHOR'S COMMENT: Perhaps the most renowned chamber music festival, founded by Rudolf Serkin.

Marlena Malas Summer Master Classes in Voice
c/o Manhattan School of Music
Summer Sessions Office
120 Claremont Avenue
New York, NY 10027
212-749-2802
AUTHOR'S COMMENT: Most highly recommended for advanced singers.

Meadowmount School of Music
RFD #2
Westport, NY 12993
518-873-2063
Winter address:
170 West 73rd Street
New York, NY 10023
June to August
AUTHOR'S COMMENT: Highly recommended for intensive study of strings and chamber music.

Mount Holyoke Guitar Workshop
c/o Mount Holyoke College Music Department
Summer Master Classes
South Hadley, MA 01075
413-532-4197

Mozarteum International Summer Academy
Mirabellplatz, 1
A-5020 Salzburg, AUSTRIA
662-88908-400   FAX: 662-872659

Music Academy of the West
1070 Fairway Road
Santa Barbara, CA 93108
805-969-4726   FAX: 805-969-0686
late June to late August
AUTHOR'S COMMENT: A superb faculty and an inspirational setting for advanced instrumentalists, accompanists, singers, and pianists.

National Guitar Summer Workshop
P.O. Box 222
Lakeside, CT 06758
1-800-234-NGSW

National Orchestral Institute
Summer and Special Programs
University of Maryland
College Park, MD 20742-5321
301-405-6540   FAX: 301-314-9572

National Repertory Orchestra
(formerly the Colorado Philharmonic)
P.O. Box 975
Evergreen, CO 80903
303-674-5161
June to August
AUTHOR'S COMMENT: A good program for instrumentalists who want to learn more repertoire and have orchestral experience.

New York State Summer Music Camp
Hartwick College
Oneonta, NY 13920
AUTHOR'S COMMENT: High school music students develop nicely in this program.

Norfolk Chamber Music Festival
Yale School of Music Summer School
96 Wall Street
New Haven, CT 06520
203-436-0336/3690   FAX: 203-432-7542
June to August
AUTHOR'S COMMENT: A wonderful place to play and hear chamber music and be coached by members of the Yale faculty.

North Carolina School of the Arts
P.O. Box 12189
200 Waughtown Street
Winston-Salem, NC 27117-2189
Summer Programs
1-800-282-ARTS

Northwestern University
National High School Music Institute (NHSMI)
School of Music
Evanston, IL 60608-1200
708-491-3141
AUTHOR'S COMMENT: An excellent program that allows high school students to pursue studies in guitar, pop culture, jazz studies, piano, strings, voice, wind, percussion, and chamber music. Living on the campus provides a preview of college life.

Oberlin College Conservatory
Summer Session
Oberlin, OH 44074
216-775-8411
AUTHOR'S COMMENT: Recommended for composition.

Ohio Light Opera Company
College of Wooster
Wooster, OH 44691
216-263-2345   FAX: 216-263-2427
AUTHOR'S COMMENT: A good company for singers to gain valuable experience.

Oklahoma Summer Arts Institute at Quartz Mountain Lodge
c/o P.O. Box 18154
Oklahoma City, OK 73154
405-842-0890   FAX: 405-848-4538

Pacific Music Festival
Japan Center of Western New York
160 Castlebrook Lane
Buffalo, NY 14221
Attn: Dr. Takako Michii
716-633-6755   FAX: 716-626-0504

Paco Peña Summer Workshop in Guitar
Centro Flamenco Paco Peña
Plaza del Potro, 15
14002 Córdoba, SPAIN

Pierre Monteux School for Advanced Conductors and Orchestra Players
P.O. Box 157
Hancock, ME 04640
207-422-3931

Rivinia Festival
Sterns Institute for Young Artists
1575 Oakwood Avenue
Highland Park, IL 60035
312-RAVINIA
AUTHOR'S COMMENT: This is the summer location for the Chicago Symphony. There is an excellent faculty teaching piano, violin, viola, violoncello, and chamber ensembles.

Robert Shaw Choral Institute
Ohio State University
School of Music
1866 College Road
Columbus, OH 43210-1170
614-292-2879
AUTHOR'S COMMENT: The famed conductor Robert Shaw runs a 3-week choral residency in south-central France and also teaches on the Ohio State campus. Highly recommended for choral conductors.

Roundtop—International Festival-Institute
P.O. Drawer 89
Round Top, TX 78954
409-249-3129
AUTHOR'S COMMENT: Located 75 miles east of Austin and 85 miles northwest of Houston, Roundtop offers an extremely well-run music festival and institute on a beautiful campus.

San Francisco Theological Seminary with the Presbyterian Association of Musicians
2 Kensington Road
San Anselmo, CA 94960
Attn: Wilbur F. Russell
415-258-6500

Sarasota Music Festival
709 North Tamiami Trail
Sarasota, FL 34236
813-952-9634   FAX: 813-953-3059
AUTHOR'S COMMENT: An outstanding program for instrumentalists taught by an internationally distinguished faculty.

Sewanee Summer Music Center
University of the South
Sewanee, TN 37375
615-598-5931 or 5881   FAX: 615-598-1145
late June to July

Spoleto Festival USA and Spoleto, Italy
P.O. Box 157
Charleston, SC 29402
803-722-2764
late May to mid-July
AUTHOR'S COMMENT: An outstanding opportunity for advanced undergraduates and graduate orchestral instrumentalists and singers to work with world-class conductors in idyllic settings.

Stanford University
Summer Sessions Office
Stanford, CA 94305
415-732-2091
AUTHOR'S COMMENT: Recommended for summer study in composition and electronic music.

Summit Brass/Keystone Music Festival
Winter address:
c/o Box 26850
Tempe, AZ 85285
602-965-6239
Summer address:
P.O. Box 38
Keystone, CO 80435
303-468-7602
AUTHOR'S COMMENT: An outstanding program for brass players.

SUNY, Cortland
Cortland, NY 13045
518-877-5121

Tanglewood
Boston University Program for High School
Students
855 Commonwealth Avenue, 2nd floor
Boston, MA 02115
617-266-1492 or 617-353-3386
*AUTHOR'S COMMENT: Excellent
programs for advanced high school
students.*

Tanglewood Music Center
c/o Symphony Hall
Boston, MA 02115
617-638-9230   FAX: 617-638-9223
*AUTHOR'S COMMENT: Outstanding
programs for composers, conductors, and
advanced music students.*

Taos School of Music
P.O. Box 1879
Taos, NM 87571
505-776-2388
mid-June to early August
*AUTHOR'S COMMENT: A well-run
chamber music festival in a beautiful
setting.*

**Tom Stacy International English Horn
Seminar**
c/o Mr. Stacy
New York Philharmonic
Lincoln Center
New York, NY 10023
*AUTHOR'S COMMENT: Outstanding
opportunity to study English horn (and
oboe) intensively with a master teacher
and performer.*

**University of Cincinnati, College
Conservatory**
Paul Hillner, contact
513-556-5463
*AUTHOR'S COMMENT: Recommended for
summer program in computers and
synthesizers.*

University of Kansas
Summer Sessions Office
Lawrence, KS 60045
913-864-3911
*AUTHOR'S COMMENT: Recommended for
organ.*

University of Nebraska
Summer Sessions Office
Lincoln, NE 68588
402-472-2503
*AUTHOR'S COMMENT: Recommended for
organ.*

University of Wisconsin, Milwaukee
School of Music—Summer Programs
Milwaukee, WI 53201
*AUTHOR'S COMMENT: Recommended for
summer program in guitar.*

Usdan Center
Winter address:
420 East 79th Street
New York, NY 10021
212-772-6060
Summer address:
185 Colonial Springs Road
Wheatly Heights, NY 11798
516-643-7900
*AUTHOR'S COMMENT: 1,500 students
ages 8 to 19 study music, dance, and
drama on 250 wooded acres in Long
Island, NY.*

Vancouver Early Music
1254 West 7th Avenue
Vancouver, British Columbia
Canada V6H 1B6
604-732-1610

Waterloo Music Festival
c/o Waterloo Foundation for the Arts
Waterloo Village
Stanhope, NJ 07874
201-347-0900
mid-June to late July
*AUTHOR'S COMMENT: Recommended for
advanced players.*

Westminster Choir College
Summer Sessions Office
Hamilton and Walnut Street
Princeton, NJ 08540
609-921-7100
*AUTHOR'S COMMENT: The Summer
Sessions at Westminster include
everything from workshops for teachers to
master classes for choral conductors and
singers. They are well-run and taught by
distinguished teachers.*

Wildacres
c/o Alry Publications
P.O. Box 36542
Charlotte, NC 28236
704-334-3413
*AUTHOR'S COMMENT: Held in the Blue
Ridge Mountains in Little Switzerland,
NC, the music festival is recommended for
flute, but there are often seminars and
master classes in bassoon and other
instruments, so be sure to call for their
summer schedule.*

World School for New Jazz
c/o Rotterdam Conservatory
Pieter de Hoochweg, 222
3024 BJ Rotterdam
Holland
1-800-437-9603
FAX: 31-10-476-8163

6
College and Conservatory Programs in the Performing Arts

Program Profiles

Alabama Shakespeare Festival/University of Alabama

P.O. Box 36120-0350
Montgomery, AL 36120-0350

205-272-1640

Enrollment. University: 16,000. Drama majors: 14.
Drama faculty. 3 full time, 5 part time.
Application deadline. Rolling.
Audition. Required. Call for exact dates and times. Participates in University/Resident Theater Association. Class admitted every other year.
Degrees offered. MFA in Acting, offered through the University of Alabama.
Costs. None. All Professional Actor Training Program/MFA students receive full tuition and fee waiver, plus a monthly stipend.

. . . .

Standardized tests: GRE required.
Interview: Required as part of audition.
Drama facilities: 750-seat theater, 250-seat theater, scene shop, costume shop, prop shops, sound studio, dance studio, rehearsal spaces.

AUTHOR'S COMMENT: This is a highly competitive program for admission, but most worthwhile. Students are able to perform small roles or perform with the Alabama Shakespeare Festival, an Equity company. Recommended for graduate Drama program.

American Academy of Dramatic Arts (CA and NY)

120 Madison Avenue, New York, NY 10016
2550 Paloma Street, Pasadena, CA 91107

212-686-9244 ▪ 818-798-0777

Enrollment. 250 (approximately).
Drama faculty. New York: 13 full time, 8 part time; California: 10 full time, 9 part time.
Application deadline. Rolling.
Audition. Required. Call the school for specific dates and times.
Degrees offered. AA in Acting possible. Certificate in Advanced Studies in Actor Training for students who are invited to complete the third year.
Costs. Tuition: $7,000. Fees: $175. No on-campus housing.

. . . .

Interview: Required as part of the audition process.
Drama facilities: *New York:* 170-seat theater, 169-seat theater, and 150-seat theater, all recently renovated. Library, scene shop, props, sound studio, 3 dance studios, rehearsal spaces, classrooms. *California:* 2 theaters (155-seat proscenium, 74-seat black box), classrooms, dance studios, costume shop, library.
Admissions criteria: Must have high school diploma, recommendations, health certificate, transcripts.
Prominent alumni include: Kirk Douglas, Grace Kelly, Robert Redford, Rosalind Russell.
Financial aid: Merit Scholarships available for second- and third-year students.

AUTHOR'S COMMENT: AADA was founded in New York in 1884 and opened its Los Angeles-area branch in 1974. It is the only conservatory program for actor training with schools in two major centers for the theater. It is possible to transfer between the branches, so a student might study one year in New York and another in California. This is a fine program, primarily nondegree, for serious acting students.

American Conservatory Theater

450 Geary Street
San Francisco, CA 94102

415-749-2350

Enrollment. 64 in the Advanced Theater Training Program.
Drama faculty. 24 full time, 8 part time.
Application deadline. January 15.
Audition. Required.
Degrees offered. MFA in Acting.
Costs. Tuition: $7,000. Fees: $350. No on-campus housing.

• • • • • • • • • • • • • • • •

Interview: Required.
Facilities: 1,300-seat theater, 90-seat theater.
Prominent alumni include: Annette Bening, Julie Brown, Harry Hamlin, Amy Irving, Don Johnson, Elizabeth McGovern, Denzel Washington.

AUTHOR'S COMMENT: This is a highly competitive program for admission. Recommended for graduate studies in Drama.

American Musical and Dramatic Academy

2109 Broadway
New York, NY 10023

212-787-5300; 1-800-367-7908
FAX: 212-799-4623

Enrollment. Ranges from 200–400 students; AMDA has 3 enrollment periods per year.
Application deadline. Rolling.
Audition. Required. Held in New York City, Atlanta, Austin, Chicago, Dallas, Denver, Los Angeles, Orlando, Toronto, and London.
Programs offered. Studio Program—actor training only; Integrated Program—combines the study of acting, musical theater, and dance.
Costs. Tuition: $7,750. Room: $3,200.

• • • • • • • • • • • • • • • •

Tapes and videotapes: Accepted for overseas applicants only.
Admissions criteria: Quality of performance at the audition, recommendations, grades in school, application essay.
Cross-registration: Available through the New School.
Facilities: 70-seat Off-Off Broadway theater, which is used as a performance space and classroom; 70-seat multi-use studio/lab space, which is used as a rehearsal studio and classroom; 6 classrooms; 6 voice studios; dressing rooms; student and faculty lounges.
Housing: 95% receive housing from the school.
Financial aid: FAF required. 10% of scholarships based solely on merit; others based on merit and need. 20% of students receive scholarships from the school.
International students: 12.5% from abroad. Canada and European countries most commonly represented. No special tests required for international students. Financial aid available for international students. Must submit school's own financial aid form.
Prominent Alumni include: Greg Standford Brown, Tyne Daly, Piper Laurie, Victoria Mallory, Dieta Rowe, Paul Sorvino.

AUTHOR'S COMMENT: Recommended for non-degree studies in Drama and Musical Theater.

American University

4400 Massachusetts Avenue, NW
Washington, DC 20016

Admissions: 202-885-6000
Music Dept.: 202-885-3420

Enrollment. University: 11,760; 6,170 undergraduates. Music majors: 23 undergraduates; 10 graduate students.
Music faculty. 6 full time, 30 part time.
Application deadlines. Early Decision: November 15. Regular Decision: February 1.
Audition. Not required for undergraduates in Music unless the applicant wants to be considered for special scholarships, for which there are auditions in early March. Audition required for graduate students.
Degrees offered. BA, BM, MA in Music.
Costs. Tuition: $12,000. Fees: $500. Room: $3,500.

. . . .

Musical instruments taught: All Orchestral, Piano, Organ, Guitar, also Voice.
Facilities include: Recital hall, chapel, theater; new performing arts center to open in 1995.
Financial aid: Submit FAF and University's own form. Merit scholarships available.
International students: 30% from abroad. Korea, South and Central America, Japan, China (PRC), Europe most represented. TOEFL required. Some financial aid for foreign students.
Prominent music alumni include: Earl Miller, William Parker, Georgine Resnick, Rob Rischer.

AUTHOR'S COMMENT: Located near Embassy Row in Washington, American is a fine university with a good music department.

Amherst College

Amherst, MA 01002

Admissions: 413-542-2328
Dept. of Theater and Dance: 413-542-2411
Music Dept.: 413-542-2354

Enrollment. College: 1,600. Drama majors: 15–20. Music majors: 15.
Drama faculty. 5 full time.
Application deadlines. Early Decision: November 15, Regular Decision: January 1.
Audition. Not required.
Degrees offered. BA in Theater. BA in Dance. BA in Music.
Costs. Tuition and fees: $15,785. Room and board: $4,400.

. . . .

Standardized tests: SAT or ACT required. Achievement tests: English plus two others required.
Interview: Recommended with an admissions counselor. Try to arrange ahead to meet a professor in the department while on campus.
Videotapes: Not encouraged.
Admissions criteria: As one of the "small Ivies," Amherst is extremely selective in admissions. Courses and grades, standardized tests, essays, and personal qualities are all considered.
Financial aid: Available. Must submit the FAF by February 1. Scholarships based on need.
Housing: 100% of new students receive on-campus housing.

AUTHOR'S COMMENT: Amherst is a prestigious, highly selective small liberal arts college. As part of the Five College Consortium it is recommended for undergraduate Drama, Dance (part of Five College program), and Guitar. The Music Department in general has strengths for a small liberal arts college.

Arizona State University

Tempe, AZ 85287

Admissions: 602-965-7788 (in-state)
1-800-252-ASU1 (out-of-state)
Dance Dept.: 602-965-5029
Theater Dept.: 602-965-9011
School of Music: 602-965-2816

Dept. of Dance Address:
107 B Physical Education Building East
Zip: 85287-0304

Enrollment. University: 43,000. Dance majors: 69 undergraduates (8 males, 61 females); 14 graduates (4 males, 10 females). Drama majors: 200 students. School of Music: 750 students.

Faculty. Dance: 12 full time, 1 part time. Music: 65 full time, plus Teaching Assistants.

Application deadline. Rolling admissions but recommended before April 15.

Audition. Required for BFA, MFA, and certain scholarships in Drama and Dance. Required for all in Music; held in February–April. Call depts. for exact dates and locations.

Degrees offered. BA in General Theater, BFA in Acting, MA in Theater, MFA in Theater for Youth. BA, BFA, MFA in Dance. BA, BM, MM, DMA in Music.

Costs. Tuition: In-state: $1,278; out-of-state: $4,866.

. . . .

Standardized tests: SAT or ACT required. Achievement tests optional.

Interview: Optional.

Videotapes: Out-of-state applicants applying for scholarship in Dance may send a videotape if unable to attend personal audition. Tapes accepted in Music but personal audition preferred.

Admissions criteria: Grades and courses, rank in class, standardized test scores, audition all considered.

Musical instruments taught: All Orchestral, all Keyboard, Guitar. Also Accompanying, Jazz, Choral and Orchestral Conducting, Voice.

Financial aid: Available. Submit the FAF. Merit- and need-based scholarships available.

Special drama courses taught: Puppetry.

Drama facilities include: 500-seat theater, 160-seat theater, 100-seat theater, scene shop, costume shop, props shop, rehearsal studio, classrooms.

International students: Approximately 5% from abroad. Most commonly represented countries: Taiwan, Canada, Brazil, Greece, Germany, Finland. TOEFL required—550 minimum. Financial aid available for foreign students.

Prominent dance alumni include: members of the Nikolaïs, Limón, Pilobolus, and Repertory Dance Theater.

AUTHOR'S COMMENT: This is a state university in the Sun Belt. The fine arts in general are supported by outstanding facilities and excellent faculty. Recommended highly for Dance. Also recommended for Drama, Guitar, Musical Theater, Trumpet, and Tuba.

Baldwin-Wallace College

275 Eastland Road, Berea, OH 44017

Admissions: 216-826-2222
Conservatory: 216-826-2368

Enrollment. College: 4,713. Conservatory: 165.

Music faculty. 20 full time, 22 part time.

Application deadline. Rolling, but by March 1 or before audition.

Audition. Required. Held in January–March. Call for specific dates and locations.

Costs. Tuition and fees: $9,225. Room and board: $3,675.

. . . .

Interview: Recommended.

Tapes: Accepted from those living far from the campus.

Musical instruments taught: All Orchestral, all Keyboard. Also Voice.

Financial aid: Available. Submit the FAF. Talent scholarships also available.

AUTHOR'S COMMENT: Recommended for Musical Theater.

Ball State University

2000 University Avenue, Muncie, IN 47306

Admissions: 317-285-8300 or 8287
Dept. of Theater and Dance: 317-285-8740
School of Music: 317-285-5502

Enrollment. University: 19,200. Drama majors: 133 undergraduates (63 males, 70 females). Music majors: 442 undergraduates, 70–80 graduate students. Dance majors: 33 undergraduates (4 males, 29 females).

Faculty. Drama: 12 full time, 1 part time. Dance: 4 full time, 1 part time. Music: 52 full time, 8 part time.

Application deadline. March 1. For Music majors, before audition dates preferred; November 1 or January 1 recommended.

Audition. Required for Musical Theater and for the Performance option in the Junior Year for Drama. Required for Music and given in November–March both on campus and in Chicago. Placement tests also given in Music Theory. Auditions, helpful for placement in Dance, held in February.

Degrees offered. BA, BS in Drama. BS, BA, BM, MA, MM, DMA in Music. BA, BS in Dance.

Costs. Tuition and fees: $2,280. Room and board: $3,020 per year.

* * * * * * * * * * * * * * * * * *

Standardized tests: SAT or ACT required.

Videotape: Accepted. Contact the depts. for guidelines. Music tapes or videos must be received by January 31.

Musical instruments taught: All Orchestral, Keyboards. Also has a Jazz program and Voice.

Financial aid: Available. Must complete FAF and department application form by March 1. Merit- and need-based scholarships available.

International students: 2% from abroad. China (PRC), Japan, Argentina, India, Canada represented. TOEFL required—550 minimum. Write to Office of Foreign Student Programs in English at least one year before you hope to enroll.

Prominent alumni include: Drama—Joyce Dewitt. Music—Anthony Knight, Jack Sane, James Trussel. Dance program is only four years old.

AUTHOR'S COMMENT: Recommended for undergraduate Drama and Musical Theater. In general, the School of Music is strong and it is difficult to cite a single department.

Bard College

Annandale-on-Hudson, NY 12504

914-758-7472

Enrollment. College: 1,150.

Faculty. Dance: 6. Music: 7. Drama: 6.

Application deadlines. Early Decision: December 1. Regular Decision: February 15. Also has a unique "Immediate Decision plan" involving daylong interviews and seminars. Call for exact dates and times.

Audition. Not required.

Degree offered. BA.

Costs. Tuition: $16,650. Fees: $460. Room: $2,750. Board: $2,815.

* * * * * * * * * * * * * * *

Standardized tests: SAT or ACT optional. Achievement tests optional.

Interview: Recommended.

Admissions criteria: Courses and grades, essays, personal qualities including intellectual curiosity, creativity, etc.

Financial aid: Submit the FAF and College's own form.

Prominent Drama alumna: Blythe Danner.

AUTHOR'S COMMENT: Bard is about two hours up the Hudson from New York City. The campus is beautiful, the student body interesting and eclectic. Recommended for Dance. Drama and Music in general are worthwhile for a small liberal arts college. Leon Botstein, the president of the college, is a respected musicologist and conductor.

Barnard College of Columbia University

3009 Broadway, New York, NY 10027

Admissions: 212-854-2014
Dance Dept.: 212-854-2995
Drama Dept.: 212-854-2079
Music Dept.: 212-854-5096

Enrollment. College: 2,200 undergraduate women. Drama majors: 20. Dance majors: 16. Music majors: 15.
Faculty. Dance: 4 full time, 8 part time. Drama: 5 full time. Music: faculty primarily at Columbia.
Application deadlines. Early Decision: November 15 or January 15. Regular Admissions: February 15.
Audition. Required for exchange programs with Juilliard and Manhattan School of Music.
Degrees offered. BA, Theater major. BA, Dance major. BA in Music.
Costs. Tuition: $15,874. Room: $4,332. Board: $2,560.

• • • • • • • • • • • • •

Standardized tests: SAT required and 3 achievement tests, one of which must be English.
Interview: Recommended. Required of Dance applicants to exchange program with Juilliard.
Videotapes: Accepted; send to the Office of Admissions, which will refer to the department for an evaluation.
Admissions criteria: Courses and grades in school, application essay, recommendations, standardized test scores, extracurricular activities, special talents, character.
Facilities: Minor Latham Theater, a proscenium theater. Also black box and workshop space.
Financial aid: Must submit the FAF and Barnard Supplement by February 1 deadline. All financial aid is need-based and Barnard is need-blind.
International students: 8% of student body is from abroad. Most commonly represented countries include: Canada, Japan, Taiwan, Great Britain, Switzerland, Hong Kong. TOEFL required. No financial aid available for students from abroad.
Housing: 100% of new students receive on-campus housing.

Prominent alumnae include: Dance—Sally Hess, Sara Rudner, Twyla Tharp. Drama—Cynthia Hamilton, Ellen Novak, Linda Yellin. Music—Rita Shane, Suzanne Vega.

AUTHOR'S COMMENT: Barnard is one of the Seven Sisters and is affiliated with Columbia University. Recommended for undergraduate Drama, Dance, and all musical studies due to joint programs with Juilliard and Manhattan School of Music.

Bates College

Lewiston, ME 04240

Admissions: 207-786-6000
Dance Dept.: 207-786-6157
Theater Dept.: 207-786-6187

Theater Dept. Address: 300 Schaeffer Theater

Enrollment. College: 1,450. Drama majors: 20. Dance majors: 15.
Drama faculty. 3 full time, 1 part time.
Application deadlines. Early Decision: December 1 and January 1. Regular Decision: February 1.
Audition. Not required.
Degrees offered. BA.
Costs. Tuition, room, and board: $21,400.

• • • • • • • • • • • • •

Standardized tests: SAT or ACT optional. Achievement tests: optional.
Interviews: Recommended.
Videotapes: Not encouraged.
Drama facilities include: New Olin Arts Center. 324-seat theater, 106-seat theater, 50-seat theater, scene shop, costume shop, sound studio, video studio, dance studio, rehearsal space, classrooms.
Financial aid: Available. Submit FAF by February 1.

AUTHOR'S COMMENT: A small liberal arts college in Maine, Bates is a warm, intellectual, and vigorous campus. Recommended for undergraduate Drama and Dance.

Baylor University

Waco, TX 76798

Admissions: 817-755-1811
School of Music: 817-755-1161
Theater Dept.: 817-755-1861

Theater Dept. Address: BU, Box 7262

Enrollment. University: 12,000. Drama majors: 60. School of Music: 350.

Faculty. Drama: 6 full time, 1 part time. Music: 52 full time.

Admissions deadlines. Rolling admissions but by March 1 recommended.

Audition. Required. Held in January–March. Call department for exact date and location.

Degrees offered. BA, BFA.

Costs. Tuition: $185 per credit hour or approximately $5,550 to $5,920 per year. Fees: $60 per semester hour in Music; also $255 general fees. Room: $1,795. Board: $955.

• • • • • • • • • • • • • • • • • • • •

Standardized tests: SAT or ACT required.

Interview: Recommended.

Admissions criteria: High school grades, standardized tests scores, essays, evidence of a student's desire for a "Christian education with academic excellence."

Musical instruments taught: All Orchestral, all Keyboard. Also Voice.

Drama facilities include: 352-seat proscenium theater, 250-seat thrust stage, 75 to 100 flexible seating, scene shop, costume shop, dance studio.

AUTHOR'S COMMENT: Owned and supported by Southern Baptists, Baylor can be recommended for undergraduate Drama, Church Music, Oboe, and Saxophone. There is also a Dance Dept.

Bennington College

Bennington, VT 05201

Admissions: 802-442-6349

Enrollment. College: 600 students.

Application deadlines. Early Decision: December 1. Regular Decision: March 1.

Audition. Not required.

Costs. Tuition: $19,400. Room and board: $3,900.

• • • • • • • • • • • • • • • • • • • •

Interviews: Required.

Videotapes: Encouraged.

Admissions criteria: High school grades and courses, evidence of intellectual curiosity and ability to assume responsibility for education.

Financial aid: Available, based on need. FAF due by March 1.

AUTHOR'S COMMENT: Bennington, located in a lovely area in southwest Vermont, is generally considered preeminent among the progressive colleges. It enrolls creative, self-motivated students. Recommended for undergraduate Drama, Dance (modern), Composition.

Berklee College of Music

1140 Boylston Street
Boston, MA 02215

617-266-1400 or 1-800-421-0084

Enrollment. College: 2,734 undergraduates.
Music faculty. 197 full time, 107 part time.
Application deadline. Rolling until March 1 for fall, but recommended to file in January for scholarship consideration. Rolling deadline for spring.
Audition. Required for scholarship; held in Boston and regionally throughout the United States in February.
Degrees offered. BM, Professional diploma.
Costs. Tuition and fees: $8,990. Room and board: $6,190.

. . . .

Standardized tests: SAT or ACT required.
Interview: Required.
Tapes: Cassette tapes accepted with 15 to 20 minute musical limit, or 3 songs.
Instruments taught: All except Harp and Harpsichord. Also has programs in Composition, Film Scoring, Electronic Music, Jazz.
Financial aid: Submit FAF and College's own form. Merit scholarships also available.
Housing: 65% of new students offered on-campus housing.
International students: 26% from abroad. Japan, Canada, Germany, Italy, Brazil most represented. TOEFL required—450 to 500 minimum. Financial aid available for foreign students.
Prominent alumni include: Gary Burton, Keith Jarrett, Quincy Jones, Arif Mardin, Branford Marsalis, John Scofield, Steve Vai.

AUTHOR'S COMMENT: Recommended for Jazz, Popular, and Commercial music.

Boston College

140 Commonwealth Avenue
Chestnut Hill, MA 02167-3100

Admissions: 617-552-3100
Theater Dept.: 617-552-4609

Enrollment. College: 14,000. Theater majors: 40.
Theater faculty. 4 full time, 6 part time.
Application deadlines. Early Decision: November 1 and 15. Regular Decision: January 10 and 25.
Audition. Not required.
Degrees offered. BA.
Costs. Tuition: $13,790. Room: $3,360. Board: $2,600.

. . . .

Standardized tests: SAT or ACT required. Achievement tests: English, Math, and one other Achievement test required.
Interview: Recommended.
Videotapes: Send to Office of Admissions for referral to the Department for evaluation.
Theater facilities: 620-seat proscenium theater, black box theater.
Financial aid: FAF due by February 2.
International students: 3% of undergraduates. China (PRC), Canada, Japan, India, Spain most represented. No Financial Aid for foreign students.

AUTHOR'S COMMENT: BC is a Catholic college run by the Jesuits, but many non-Catholics now seek enrollment. There is a fairly new Theater Complex and there are plans for expanding the program and facilities; thus BC is recommended for undergraduate Drama.

Boston Conservatory

8 The Fenway
Boston, MA 02215-4099

Admissions: 617-536-6340, ext. 15 or 16
Dance Dept.: 617-536-6340, ext. 37

Enrollment. Conservatory: 320 students. Music majors: 100 undergraduates, 30 graduate students. Dance majors: 68 (8 males, 60 females).
Application deadline. Rolling.
Audition. Required. Held in Boston November–March. Call for exact dates.
Degrees offered. BM, MM, CDP, GPC, ADP in Music. BFA in Dance.
Costs. Tuition: $9,900. Fees: $345. Room and board: $5,300.

. . . .

Tapes: Cassette accepted in Music. Videotape accepted in Dance.
Musical instruments taught: All Orchestral, Guitar, Piano. Also Composition and Voice.
Financial aid: Submit school's application and FAF. Some merit scholarships available.
Housing: 33% receive on-campus housing.
International students: 15% to 17% from abroad. China (PRC), Mexico, Japan, and Turkey most represented. TOEFL required—500 minimum. Apply by June 1 for fall enrollment. No financial aid available for foreign students.

AUTHOR'S COMMENT: Recommended for Dance, Guitar, Musical Theater, and Tuba.

Boston University

121 Bay State Road
Boston, MA 02215-9949

Admissions: 617-353-2300 or 4241
School of Music: 617-353-3341
School of Theater Arts: 617-353-3390

School of Theater Arts and School of Music Address: 855 Commonwealth Avenue

Enrollment. University: 27,630. Drama majors: 190. Music majors: 215 undergraduates, 215 graduate students.

Faculty. Drama: 21 full time, 11 part time. Music: 40 full time, 60 part time.
Application deadlines. Early Decision: November 15. Regular Decision: January 15 or February 15 (School of Music).
Audition. Required.
Degrees offered. BFA in Acting. BM, MM, DMA, Artist Diploma Certificate, Opera Institute Certificate all available in Music.
Costs. Tuition and fees: undergraduate—$14,950, graduate—$8,000. Room and board: $6,500.

. . . .

Standardized tests: SAT or ACT required. Achievement tests: Required, but vary according to School. GRE required for some graduate students in Music.
Interview: Required as part of audition.
Tapes: Videotapes accepted for Conducting. Cassettes for other music majors.
Drama facilities: 850-seat proscenium theater, 100-seat theater, 100-seat flexible space.
Financial aid: Submit FAF. Merit awards available.
International students: 30% from abroad. China (PRC), Canada, France, Korea, Japan most represented. TOEFL required—550 minimum. Limited financial aid available for foreign students.
Prominent music alumni include: Parature Brothers, Laurel Ohlson.

AUTHOR'S COMMENT: BU is located across the Charles River from Harvard and MIT, in a busy section of Boston. Students in the Theater program have the advantage of working with the Huntington Theater Company, an Equity professional theater company in residence at BU, which provides advanced students with many opportunities. The actor training in general is quite good. The School of Music faculty includes many members of the Boston Symphony. BU is also recommended for Church Music, Composition, Early Music, Piano, Saxophone, Tuba, Violoncello, and undergraduate Voice.

Bowdoin College

Brunswick, ME 04011

Admissions: 207-725-3100
Music Dept.: 207-725-3321

Enrollment. College: 1,250. Music majors: 20.
Music faculty. 4 full time, 12 part time.
Application deadlines. Early Decision: November 15.
Regular Decision: January 15.
Audition. Not required.
Degrees offered. BA.
Costs. Tuition: $16,070. Fees: $300. Room and board: $5,590.

. . . .

Standardized tests: Optional.
Interviews: Recommended. Call ahead to make arrangements to speak to the Department.
Videotapes: Send to Admissions to be referred to the department for evaluation.
Musical instruments taught: All Orchestral, Piano, Harpsichord, Organ, Guitar, Saxophone. Also Early Music, Jazz, Electronic Music, Voice.
Financial aid: Available. Based on need. File FAF and Bowdoin form by March 1.
Housing: 100% of new students receive on-campus housing.
International students: 5% from abroad. Limited financial aid for foreign students.
Prominent music alumnus: Kurt Ollmann.

AUTHOR'S COMMENT: *An excellent small liberal arts college with a strong Music department. Also has a very good summer Music program.*

Bradley University

Peoria, IL 61625

Admissions: 1-800-447-6460
Music Dept.: 309-677-2595

Enrollment. University: 4,700 undergraduates, 800 graduate students. Music majors: 55 undergraduates, 2 graduate students.
Music faculty. 10 full time, 9 part time.
Application deadline. Rolling, but apply before auditions.
Audition. Required. Held in February and March on campus.
Degrees offered. BA, BS, BM, MM in Music.
Costs. Tuition: $8,550. Fees: $34. Room and board: $3,750.

. . . .

Interview: Required.
Videotapes: Accepted.
Musical instruments taught: All Orchestral and Band Instruments, Organ, Piano. Also Composition, Voice, Accompanying, Jazz Ensemble.
Music facilities include: Constance Hall, classrooms, practice rooms. Dingeldine Music Center: Concert Hall, rehearsal hall, practice rooms.
Financial aid: Submit FAF. Merit awards also available.
Prominent music alumnus: Jerry Hadley.

AUTHOR'S COMMENT: *Has a solid Music program.*

Brandeis University

415 South Street
Waltham, MA 02154-2700

Admissions: 617-736-3500
Dept. of Music: 617-736-3311
Dept. of Theater Arts: 617-736-3340

Enrollment. University: 3,700; Drama majors: 20. Music majors: 15.
Faculty. Drama: 14 full time, 11 part time. Music: 8.
Application deadlines. Early Decision: January 1. Regular Decision: February 1.
Auditions. Required for MFA.
Degrees offered. BA in Theater Arts, MFA in Acting. BA in Music.
Costs. Tuition and fees: $15,320. Room and board: $5,960.

. . . .

Standardized tests: SAT or ACT required. Achievement tests required: English plus two others.
Interviews: Recommended. Required as part of audition for MFA.
Drama facilities include: 748-seat theater, 160-seat theater, 125-seat theater. Scene shops, costume shops, dance studios, rehearsal spaces.
Financial aid: Available. Submit the FAF.

AUTHOR'S COMMENT: Founded in the 1950s by a group of Jewish intellectuals, including Supreme Court Justice Louis Brandeis, Brandeis is a nonsectarian, intense, socially conscious school. The architecture on campus is unusual, with the music building, for instance, built in the shape of a grand piano. The Drama program has a relationship with the Brandeis Repertory Company, a professional Equity company in residence, and is recommended at both the undergraduate and graduate levels. The Music program was founded by the late Leonard Bernstein and is recommended for the study of undergraduate Composition and Early Music. The Lydian String Quartet is also in residence.

Brigham Young University

Provo, UT 84602

Admissions: 801-378-2507
Theater and Film Dept.: 801-378-6645
Music Dept.: 801-378-3294
Dance Dept.: 801-378-5086

Music Dept. Address:
C550 Harris Fine Arts Center

Enrollment. University: 28,000 undergraduates; 2,600 graduate students. Drama program: 232 undergraduates; 29 graduate students. Music program: 600 undergraduates; 30 graduate students. Dance program: 200 students.
Faculty. Drama: 17 full time, 2 part time. Music: 43 full time, 37 part time. Dance: 37 full and part time.
Application deadline. February 15. Transfer: April 15.
Auditions. BFA program requires audition and interviews after student is accepted to the University. Auditions are held on campus in September, December, and April. Music requires an audition.
Degrees offered. BA in Theater, MA in Theater and Film. BFA in Musical Dance Theater. BA, BM, MM in Music.
Costs. Tuition: Church of Jesus Christ of Latter-Day Saints members—$2,000 per year. Non-members—$3,000 per year. Fees: Private music lessons—$175 per semester. Room and board: $3,900 per year.

. . . .

Standardized tests: ACT required. Achievement tests: Recommended.
Videotapes: Not accepted in Drama. Music will accept audiotapes but prefers videotapes.
Admissions criteria: Acceptance into the University, quality of the audition, previous training, experience in productions, recommendations, male/female ratio, standardized test scores, grades in school, body type, age of performer.
Musical instruments taught: All Orchestral, Band, and Keyboard Instruments, Guitar. Also Jazz Studies, Media Composition, Voice.

(continued on next page)

Facilities: Drama: 612-seat proscenium theater, 250-seat proscenium theater, 150-seat black box, 1,400-seat concert hall, theater. Music: Harris Fine Arts Center, 5 theaters, two large rehearsal halls, practice space, two piano labs, recording studio, electronic music studio, music performance library, instrument shop, music library. Knight Mangum Building for Musical-Dance-Theater students.

Financial aid: Must submit FAF by March 1. Many merit-based scholarships and some based on need.

Housing: 24% of new students receive on-campus housing.

International students: 20% from abroad. Most commonly represented countries include Great Britain, Canada, China, South Africa, Australia. TOEFL required—550 minimum. Special deadline: All applications from outside the U.S. must arrive 2½ months before the deadline. Some financial aid available for foreign students, but never full support. An application for aid will influence admissions decision.

Prominent alumni include: Drama—Orson Scott Card, Carol Lynn Pierson. Music—Kurt Bestor, Ariel Bybee, Sam Cardon, Merrill Jenson, Lawrence Vincent.

AUTHOR'S COMMENT: BYU is supported by the Mormon Church and the majority of students are Mormon. Students sign an honor code promising to "Observe the Word of Wisdom" and abstain from drugs, alcohol, tobacco, tea, and coffee. If you can uphold this Code of Ethics, BYU is recommended for undergraduate Drama, Dance, and Musical Theater. The Music program in general has strengths.

Brooklyn College of the City University of New York

Bedford Avenue and Avenue H
Brooklyn, NY 11210-2893

Admissions: 718-780-5001 or 5044
Conservatory of Music: 718-780-5286
Drama Dept.: 718-780-5666

Enrollment. College: 16,040. Music majors: 90 undergraduates, 100 graduates. Drama: 24 undergraduates, 20 graduates.

Faculty. Music: 18 full time, 35 part time. Drama: 12 full time, 12 part time.

Application deadlines. Early Action: January 15. Rolling admissions to April 1.

Audition. Required in Music; held in January, March, May, and August on the campus. Required for BFA in Acting (held in August) and MFA in Acting (held in early March).

Degrees offered. BA, BM, MA, MM in Music. BA in Theater, BFA, MFA in Acting.

Costs. Tuition: undergraduates—$1,850; graduates—$2,604.

· · · · · · · · · · · · · · · · · · · ·

Standardized tests: SAT recommended. Achievement tests: optional.

Interview: Required of MFA in Acting applicants.

Tapes: Accepted in Music. Contact the Conservatory Office for information. Accepted in Drama only if a personal appearance is impossible; should include two contrasting monologues and a short summary of your background and goals.

Musical instruments taught: All standard Orchestral Instruments. Also has programs in Contemporary Music, Computer Music, American Music, Voice.

Facilities: Gershwin Theater, 500-seat proscenium; New Workshop Theater, 100-seat black box; costume and scene shops.

Financial aid: Available. Some merit-based awards also. Submit FAF and CUNY financial aid forms.

Housing: Not available.

International students: 33% from abroad. Taiwan, China (PRC), Latin America, Korea, France most represented. TOEFL required—500 minimum. Limited financial aid available for foreign students. Apply for admission and financial aid by April 1 for fall enrollment.

Prominent alumni include: Music—Eddie Daniels, Ray Marchica, Eddie Salkin, Stephan Tran-Ngoc. Drama—Herb Edelman, Michael Lerner, Jimmy Smits.

AUTHOR'S COMMENT: The New England-style campus is located in Midwood, a residential section of Brooklyn. Because it is part of the City University system, most of the students come from the five boroughs of New York City. Brooklyn College is very affordable, has an excellent faculty, and can be recommended for Early Music, Musical Theater, and the Music program in general.

Brown University

45 Prospect Street
Providence, RI 02912

Admissions: 401-863-2378
Drama Dept.: 401-863-3283

Theater Department Address: Dept. of
Theater, Speech, and Dance, P.O. Box 1897

Enrollment. University: 5,250 undergraduates; 1,500 graduate students. Drama students: 15 to 20 undergraduates, 8 graduate students.
Drama faculty. 12 full time; 2 part time.
Application deadline. January 1.
Audition. Not required.
Degrees offered. BA, MA, and Ph.D with concentration in Theater.
Costs. Tuition: $15,871; Fees: $1,499. Room and board: $4,980. Total expenses: approximately $22,350.

. . . .

Standardized tests: SAT and Achievements. GRE for graduate students.
Interviews: Not required, but useful for the student and can result in a departmental assessment for the Office of Admissions.
Videotapes: Not encouraged.
Criteria for admissions: Brown is a highly selective liberal arts university. Students are admitted into the college, not to the department, and competition is keen. Grades and courses in school, standardized test scores, application essay, recommendations, and personal profile are all considered.
Facilities: 4 theaters including 350-seat proscenium, 200-seat arena and two flexible spaces, plus a large dance studio, costume shop, scenery construction space.
Financial aid: Determined by the University. Financial Aid Form (FAF) required.
International students: Must submit SAT, TOEFL, and for graduate students, GRE scores. Limited financial aid available for foreign students.
Prominent drama alumni include: Bess Armstrong, John Lee Beatty, Kate Burton, Richard Foreman, James Naughton, Alfred Uhry, JoBeth Williams.

AUTHOR'S COMMENT: Recommended as a good Drama Department within a demanding Ivy League liberal arts school. Graduates of Brown have done well in all areas of theater, including acting, directing, theater scholarship, playwriting, and design.

Brussels Conservatory (Belgium)

Conservatoire Royal de Musique de
Bruxelles—French section
30 rue de la Regence
1000 Bruxelles, BELGIUM

02-512-2369

Koninklijk Muziekconservatorium van Brussels

Regentschapstraat, 30
1000 Brussel, BELGIUM

02-513-4587

Enrollment. 720 French-speaking, 550 Flemish-speaking, 70 international students.
Application deadline. September 1.
Degrees offered. Higher Diploma/Certificate.
Costs. Belgium tuition: 1,800 Belgian francs. International students: 40,000 Belgian francs per year.

. . . .

Admissions procedures: File application. Students from non-European Economic Community countries must possess an authorization for provisional stay in Belgium.
Music facilities include: 2 organ practice rooms, 1 percussion practice room, 50 practice pianos, 3 concert halls, music library.
Financial aid: Available. Must file special scholarship application.
Prominent alumni and faculty include: Adolphe Sax, Henri Vieuxtemps, Henry Wieniawsky, Eugene Ysaye.

AUTHOR'S COMMENT: The Conservatory, located near the Royal Palace and Park, is internationally recognized. It has two autonomous sections, the French and Flemish, and it is important to know on which faculty a particular faculty member teaches. The French side is recommended for Harp, and the Flemish side is recommended for Viola da Gamba, Baroque Flute, Early Music.

Butler University

Jordan College of Fine Arts
4600 Sunset Avenue
Indianapolis, IN 46208

Admissions: 317-283-9255 or 1-800-368-6852
Dance Dept.: 317-283-9341
Drama Dept.: 317-283-9655
Music Dept.: 317-283-9656

Enrollment. University: 2,600 full-time undergraduate students; 1,600 graduate and part-time students. Dance majors: 90 undergraduates (13 males, 77 females). Drama majors: 40 undergraduate (11 males, 29 females). Music majors: 350 undergraduates, 75 graduate students.

Faculty. Dance: 6 full time, 5 part time. Drama: 6 full time. Music: 35 full time, 50 part time.

Application deadlines. June 1 or August 1 for fall semester; November 1 or January 1 for spring semester.

Audition. Required. Held in Indianapolis from October–April. Regional auditions may be announced.

Degrees offered. BA in Theater. BA in Musical Theater, Performing Arts, Music Performance, Theory and Composition. BFA in Dance Performance, BA in Dance.

Costs. Tuition: $10,500. Fees: $100. Room: $1,700. Board (20 meal): $2,140.

. . . .

Standardized tests: SAT or ACT required. GRE for graduate students.

Interview: Required as part of audition process.

Videotapes: Accepted in Drama and Music only if live audition is impossible; send to Admissions, Jordan College of Fine Arts. Dance will accept videotape for international students and Summer Session only.

Musical instruments taught: All, except no Early Music program.

Facilities: 1 small proscenium theater, 1 medium-sized black box, 1 large proscenium theater, 3 dance studios.

Financial aid: Must file FAF. Scholarships: 38% receive academic and/or audition awards. 53% receive academic, audition, scholarship, grant and/or departmental awards.

International students: 4% from abroad. Must submit TOEFL—550 minimum score. Most commonly represented countries: England, Scotland, Germany, Denmark, Korea, Malaysia. Apply at least 2 months before the beginning of the term of entrance. For financial aid consideration, FAF must be submitted at least 4 to 6 months before the beginning of the term. Butler actively recruits students from abroad with travel to Japan, Taiwan, Korea, Singapore, Malaysia, Indonesia, Thailand, Hong Kong, and Central and South America.

AUTHOR'S COMMENT: Recommended for undergraduate Drama. Highly recommended for Dance. Also recommended for Musical Theater.

California Institute of the Arts (CalARTS)

24700 McBeam Parkway
Valencia, CA 91355

General Switchboard: 805-255-1050
Admissions: 805-253-7865
Theater: 805-253-7862
Music: 805-253-7816
Dance: 805-253-7898

Enrollment. Institute: 955; Drama majors: 180. Music majors: 136. Dance majors: 66.

Faculty. Drama: 19 full time, 6 part time. Dance: 16. Music: 65.

Audition. Required.

Degrees offered. Cerficate, BFA, MFA in Acting. BFA, BM in Music.

Costs. Tuition: $12,875. Room: $1,875 to $3,050. Board: $2,500 to $3,200.

. . . .

Interview: Required.

Drama facilities include: 300-seat theater, 90-seat theater, 80-seat theater.

Musical instruments taught: All Orchestral, Voice, Composition, Electronic Music, Jazz. No Organ.

Financial aid: Available. Submit FAF.

Prominent alumnus: Adam Klein.

AUTHOR'S COMMENT: CalARTS is one of the more progressive conservatories. Located outside Los Angeles, it is recommended for Drama, Dance, Composition, Electronic Music, Jazz, Percussion.

California State University, Fresno

Fresno, CA 93740

Admissions: 209-278-2261

Enrollment. University: 19,100. Drama majors: 90.
Drama faculty. 12 full time, 4 part time.
Audition. Not required.
Degrees offered. BA in Theater.
Costs. Tuition: In-state—$916; out-of-state—$5,670. Room and board: $3,450.

· · · · · · · · · · · · · · · ·

Standardized tests: SAT or ACT required.
Interview: Not required.
Drama facilities include: 420-seat theater, 200-seat theater, 100-seat theater, scene shop, costume shop, welding area, video studio, dance studio, classrooms.
Financial aid: Available. Submit FAF and California State form. Merit scholarships also available.

AUTHOR'S COMMENT: Not far from Yosemite and Sequoia national parks, CSU, Fresno also has its own school winery. The undergraduate programs in Drama and Dance are recommended.

California State University, Fullerton

800 North State College
Fullerton, CA 92634-3599

Admissions: 714-773-2086
Dept. of Theater and Dance: 714-773-3628

Enrollment. 23,034 undergraduates. Drama majors: 290.
Drama faculty. 15 full time, 4 part time.
Audition. Required.
Degrees offered. BA in Acting, MFA in Drama. BA in Dance. BA in Musical Theater, MFA in Music.
Costs. Tuition: In-state—$916; out-of-state—$5,670. Room and board: Not available.

· · · · · · · · · · · · · · · · ·

Standardized tests: SAT required.
Interview: Required as part of audition.
Drama facilities include: 500-seat theater, 200-seat theater, 135-seat theater, 55-seat workshop theater, scene shop, costume shop, props shop, 4 dance studios, 2 rehearsal studios, 10 classrooms.
Financial aid: Available. File FAF and California form (SAAC). Some merit scholarships available, based on GPA, recommendations, audition.

AUTHOR'S COMMENT: Theater students at CSU, Fullerton, also have the opportunity to work with the Grove Shakespeare Company, a professional Equity company. In general, this branch of the California State system can be recommended for undergraduate Drama, Dance, and Musical Theater.

California State University, Long Beach

1250 Bellflower Boulevard
Long Beach, CA 90840-7101

Admissions: 213-985-5471
Music Dept.: 213-985-4781

Enrollment. University: 26,600 undergraduates, 6,500 graduate students. Music majors: 250 undergraduates, 75 graduate students.
Music faculty. 20 full time, 40 part time.
Application deadlines. December Varies.
Audition. Required in Music; given in December, April, and May. Also Music Theory placement exam given.
Degrees offered. BA in Performance. BA, MA in General Theater, MFA in Acting. BA, BM, MA, MM in Music.
Costs. Tuition: In-state—$862; out-of-state—$5,670. Room and board: $4,400.

· · · · · · · · · · · · · · · ·

Tapes and Videotapes: Accepted for Music. Mail to the Department of Music.
Musical instruments taught: Orchestral Instruments and Voice. Also Choral Conducting, Composition, Orchestral Conducting, and Commercial Music.
Facilities include: Recital Hall, 400 seats, two small theaters, 100 and 120 seats, respectively; new theater, seating 1,200 to open in March 1993.
Financial aid: Available. Based on merit and need. Some merit scholarships available.
Housing: 50% of new students receive on-campus housing.
International students: 12% from abroad. China (PRC), Japan, and Mexico most represented. TOEFL required—500 minimum. File application by December 1.

AUTHOR'S COMMENT: Recommended for undergraduate Drama. Highly recommended for Dance. Music department well regarded.

California State University, Northridge

18111 Nordhoff Street
Northridge, CA 91330

Admissions: 818-885-3700
Theater Dept.: 818-885-3086
Music Dept.: 818-885-3181

Enrollment. University: 3,153. Drama majors: 235. Music majors: 550 undergraduate, 50 graduate students.
Faculty. Drama: 14 full time, 19 part time. Music: 30 full time, 20 part time.
Application deadlines. November for fall semester; August for spring semester.
Audition. Required in Music; given in November and August. Also Music Theory and Piano placement exams.
Degrees offered. BA, MA in Drama. BA, BM, MA, MM in Music.
Costs. Tuition: In-state—$1,400; out-of-state—$5,670. Room and board: $4,900.

· · · · · · · · · · · · · · · ·

Standardized tests: SAT or ACT required. GRE for graduate programs recommended.
Tapes or videotapes: Accepted in Music. Prefer videotape.
Musical instruments taught: All Orchestral Instruments, Guitar, Piano, Saxophone, Organ. Also has programs in Electronic Music and Jazz.
Drama facilities include: 400-seat theater, 209-seat theater, 100-seat theater.
Financial aid: Available, both need- and merit-based. Merit-based: consider faculty nomination, artistic promise, achievement, and GPA.
International students: 2% from abroad. Japan, Taiwan, Iran, China (PRC), Korea most represented. TOEFL required—500 minimum for undergraduate, 550 minimum for graduate students. Applications should be submitted by November 30 or August 31.
Prominent music alumni include: Robert Babko, Beverly Grigsby, James O'Neal, Toshiyuki Shimada, Carol Vaness, Michael Wolf.

AUTHOR'S COMMENT: Located not far from Los Angeles, CSU, Northridge, has ongoing relationships with a number of professional companies in the area in which students may be cast in small roles or be in internship or apprentice programs. Recommended for undergraduate Drama. Music department also noteworthy.

Carnegie Mellon University

5000 Forbes Avenue
Pittsburgh, PA 15213-3890

Admissions: 412-268-2082
Dept. of Drama, College of Fine Arts:
412-268-2392
Music Dept.: 412-268-2372 or 2385

Enrollment. University: 4,327 undergraduates, 2,708 graduate students. Drama majors: 150 undergraduates, 35 graduate students. Music majors: 135 undergraduates, 65 graduate students.

Application deadlines. Early Decision: December 1; Regular Admissions: January 1. April 1 for graduate students in Music.

Audition. Required. For Drama: held in New York City, Chicago, San Francisco, Los Angeles, Houston, and Miami in February. For Music: held on campus and in Boston, New York City, Detroit, Chicago, Interlochen, Cleveland, Washington, D.C., Philadelphia, Miami, Atlanta, and Charlotte, November–February. Also holds Music audition in Taipai, Taiwan. Music applicants must also take Music Theory and ear-training examinations.

Degrees offered. BFA, MFA in Acting. BFA in Music Performance and Composition, MM in Music Performance, Composition, and Conducting.

Costs. Tuition: $14,000 for undergraduates, $8,016 for graduate students; Fees: $100. Room and board: $4,720. (No on-campus housing for graduate students.)

Standardized tests: SAT or ACT required. Achievement tests: required but specific requirements vary according to department

Interview: Recommended.

Videotapes: Not accepted for Drama. Music will accept tapes or videotapes.

Musical instruments taught: All Orchestral Instruments, Piano, Organ, Saxophone, Guitar, Bagpipes. Also has a program in Jazz, Computer and Electronic Music, Voice.

Facilities: Drama: 320-seat, 110-seat theater. Music: 250-seat Recital Hall, 325-seat Chamber Music Hall, 1,900-seat Concert Hall.

Financial aid: Available. Must submit FAF and 1040. Applications due February 15. 10% of financial aid decisions based on merit; 90% based on need.

International students: In Drama, 5% of student body from abroad. Great Britain, Canada, Egypt, Costa Rica, New Zealand, most commonly represented. TOEFL required. No financial aid available for foreign students. In Music, 10% from abroad. Asia, Europe, Central and South America most represented. TOEFL required—550 minimum. Financial aid is granted to graduate foreign students only in the Department of Music.

Housing: 100% of freshmen receive on-campus housing.

Prominent alumni: Music—Phil Myers, Conrad Sousa, Earle Wilde. Drama—William Atherton, Rene Auberjonois, Ted Danson, Jennifer Darling, Barbara Feldon, Shari Belafonte Harper, Mariette Hartley, Jack Klugman.

AUTHOR'S COMMENT: Recommended for undergraduate Drama, Bagpipes (a new major), Musical Theater.

Case Western Reserve University

10900 Euclid Avenue
Cleveland, OH 44106-1712

Undergraduate Admissions: 216-368-4450
Graduate Admissions: 216-368-4390
Dept. of Theater: 216-368-5923
Dance Program: 216-368-2854
Music Dept.: 216-368-2400

Enrollment. University: 8,000. Drama majors: 56. Dance majors: 15 to 17 graduates (2 to 4 males, 11 to 13 females). Music majors: 25.
Faculty. Drama: 10 full time, 8 part time. Dance: 3 full time, 2 part time. Music: 8 full time, 5 part time.
Application deadlines. Early Decision: January 15. Regular Decision: March 15.
Audition. Required. Call for dates and locations.
Degrees offered. BA in General Theater. BA, MFA in Acting. MFA in Modern Dance. BA, MA in Music and joint program with Cleveland Institute of Music.
Costs. Tuition and fees: $12,800. Room and board: $4,620.

. . . .

Standardized tests: SAT or ACT required. Achievement tests: recommended.
Interview: Recommended.
Videotapes: Not accepted.
Admissions criteria: GPA, rank in class, courses and grades, standardized test scores, recommendations.
Drama facilities include: 152-seat theater, 1 flexible space, scene shop, costume shop, props shop, 3 dance studios, 2 rehearsal studios, classrooms.
Financial aid: Submit FAF. Merit awards available.
International students: 1% from abroad. Japan, China (PRC), Colombia most represented. TOEFL required—550 minimum. Apply by January 31. Limited financial aid available for foreign students.
Prominent alumni include: Gary Gailbraith, Gina Gibney, Billy Gornell, Gail Heilbron, Jan Hyatt, Karen Nazor, Frank Roth.

AUTHOR'S COMMENT: Case Western Reserve has apprenticeships/internships with Cleveland's professional theaters. Modern Dance students have gone on to companies including Paul Taylor and Erick Hawkins. The joint program with the Cleveland Institute of Music make the music program strong. Recommended for Dance (modern), Drama, Early Music, Oboe (joint program with Cleveland Institute of Music).

Catholic University

620 Michigan Avenue, NE
Washington, DC 20064

Undergraduate Admissions: 202-319-5305
Graduate Admissions: 202-319-5057
Drama Dept.: 202-319-5358
Benjamin T. Rome School of Music:
202-319-5414

Enrollment. University: 6,580. Drama majors: 90 undergraduates (40 males, 50 females); 40 graduate students (20 males, 20 females). Music majors: 122 undergraduates, 187 graduate students.
Faculty. Drama: 9 full time, 12 part time. Music: 18 full time, 75 part time.
Application deadlines. Early Action: November 15. Regular Decision: February 15. Transfers: April 1.
Audition. Required for MFA in Acting and for Music applicants. Master's and doctoral candidates in Music also have an entrance recital requirement and further required music examinations. Music auditions are held on campus October–April.
Degrees offered. BA, MA in Drama, MFA in Acting. BM, MM, DMA, Ph.D in Music. Also MLM (Master of Liturgical Music).
Costs. Tuition: $11,630. Fees: $170 to $400. Room: $3,200. Board: $2,400.

. . . .

Standardized tests: SAT required. Achievement tests: required. GRE required for graduate students.
Interview: Optional.
Videotapes: Accepted for applicants in Drama who live far from campus and whose applications show a range of performing experience and potential for graduate study. Videotapes in Music accepted for conductors. Cassettes accepted for Voice and other instrumental candidates, but live audition preferred.
Musical instruments taught: All Orchestral Instruments, Guitar, Harpsichord, Organ, Piano, Saxophone, Also Composition, Accompanying, Choral and Instrumental Conducting, Musical Theater, Voice.
Drama facilities include: 550-seat proscenium theater, 80-seat theater, 40-seat theater, black box.
Financial aid: Available. Submit FAF or GAPSFAS and University form by February 15. Merit scholarships also available.
Housing: 100% of new students receive on-campus housing.

(continued on next page)

International students: Approximately 10% from abroad. Korea, Argentina, Brazil, China, Poland most represented. TOEFL required—500 minimum. Some financial aid available for foreign students.

Prominent alumni include: Drama—Philip Bosco, Pat Carroll, John Heard, Laurence Luckinbill, Ed McMahon, Susan Sarandon, Jon Voight. Music—John Aler, Carmen Balthrop, Harolyn Blackwell, Richard Buckley, Kevin McCarthy.

AUTHOR'S COMMENT: Located next to the largest Catholic church in the United States, the Shrine of the Immaculate Conception, Catholic University is a surprisingly sprawling campus in a residential section of the nation's capital. The performing arts programs do not seem to be concerned about an applicant's religious affiliation and admit many talented students who are not Catholic. The Drama program has had some changes in faculty in recent years but remains extremely strong. The National Players, a touring group with many actors from the school, tours nationally for 9 months each year. There is also an affiliation with the Olney Theater in Olney, Maryland, a summer Equity theater. Highly recommended for undergraduate and graduate Drama. Also recommended for Church Music, Organ, and Musical Theater. The School of Music in general is strong.

Central Michigan University

105 Warriner Hall
Mount Pleasant, MI 48859-0001

Admissions: 517-774-3076
Music Dept.: 517-774-3281

Enrollment. University: 16,788. Music majors: 327.
Audition. Required. Held in January–March. Call for exact dates.
Degrees offered. BA, BM.
Costs. Tuition: $70.50 per credit hour.

* * * * * * * * * * * * * * * *

AUTHOR'S COMMENT: Recommended for Oboe.

Chapman College

333 North Glassell Street
Orange, CA 92666-1099

Admissions: 714-997-6711
School of Music: 714-997-6871

Enrollment. College: 1,500; Music majors: 120. Dance majors: 40.
Faculty. Music: 7 full time, 25 part time. Dance: 18.
Application deadline. March 1.
Audition. Required. Held by arrangement on campus.
Degrees offered. BA, BM.
Costs. Tuition: $12,974. Fees: $250. Room and board: $5,000.

* * * * * * * * * * * * * * * * * * *

Standardized tests: SAT or ACT required.
Interview: Recommended.
Tapes or videotapes: Accepted in Music by arrangement with the School of Music.
Musical instruments taught: All Orchestral Instruments, Harp, Guitar, Piano, Organ, Saxophone. Also has an Early Music and Contemporary Music program, Voice.
Facilities include: Auditorium, 100-seat recital hall.
Financial aid: Available. Both need- and merit-based. File FAF and SAAC (California residents).
Housing: 60% of new students receive on-campus housing.
International students: 12% from abroad. Japan, Korea, France, Taiwan, Indonesia most represented. TOEFL required—500 minimum. Financial aid available after first year.

AUTHOR'S COMMENT: Recommended for undergraduate Dance, taught in the Department of Movement and Exercise Science. The Department of Music has been in transition and has just restructured as a School of Music within a liberal arts setting.

Circle in the Square Theater School

1633 Broadway
New York, NY 10019

212-307-2732

Enrollment. 70.
Drama faculty. 22 part time.
Application deadline. Rolling but before June 1.
Audition. Required. Held in March–June.
Degrees offered. Certificate.
Costs. Tuition: $5,000.

• • • • • • • • • • • • • • • • • •

Interview: Required.
Admissions criteria: Audition most important; recommendations also considered.
Drama facilities include: 700-seat theater.

AUTHOR'S COMMENT: Circle in the Square Theater School students are connected with the Equity Broadway theater of the same name. All faculty are practicing professionals. Recommended for non-degree Drama studies.

City College of The City University of New York (CCNY of CUNY)

Convent Avenue at West 138th Street
New York, NY 10031

Admissions: 212-650-6977 or 6448
Dance Dept.: 212-650-6635
Music Dept.: 212-650-5411

Enrollment. College: 14,000 undergraduates; 2,000 graduates. Dance majors: 15 undergraduates (3 males, 12 females); 18 graduates (4 males; 14 females). Music majors: 100 undergraduates, 30 graduate students.
Faculty. Dance: 4 full time; 8 part time. Music: 16 full time, 12 part time.
Application deadlines. February 15 recommended deadline for fall, but will accept applications until May 1; November 1 for spring semester.
Auditions. Required for Dance and for BFA and MA in Music. Music auditions held in November; call for details. Dance auditions held in March and November at the City University campus. Special arrangements may be made if these dates are impossible to meet. Dance audition consists of ballet barre and center and short modern class.
Degrees offered. BA, BFA, MA.
Costs. Undergraduate tuition: In-state—$972; out-of-state—$2,225. Fees: $47.35. Graduate tuition: In-state—$1,302; out-of-state—$2,550. Fees: $15.35.

• • • • • • • • • • • • • • • • • •

Interview: Required for graduate program.
Tapes: Videotapes accepted in Dance for international students only; should show performance ability clearly. Performance of the student's own choreography is encouraged. Tapes in Music are accepted only for those applicants living at a great distance from the campus.
Musical instruments taught: Piano, Clarinet, Violin, Viola, Violoncello, Double Bass. Others arranged through associated private instructors. Also has a full Jazz program, Electronic Music, and Composition.
Cross-registration: Available through the Dance Notation Bureau, NYU, CUNY Graduate Center, University of Surrey, School of the Hartford Ballet.

(continued on next page)

Facilities: 4 dance studios—2 are 30 x 40, one is 40 x 50, one is 15 x 25. All have sprung wood floors. One fully equipped performance studio, one 200-seat dance theater, and one 850-seat proscenium theater. New music recital hall to be completed in fall 1992.
Financial aid: 20% receive tuition assistance; 10% based on merit; 90% based on need.
Housing: None available.
International students: Approximately 20% in Dance from abroad, about 40% of music majors from abroad. China (PRC), Japan, European countries most represented. TOEFL of 550 required. Videotape accepted.
Prominent alumni: Dance—Sandra Burton, Danny McKayle, Daniel Nagrin. Music—Verna Gillis, Joel Lester, Muzz Skillings.

AUTHOR'S COMMENT: Recommended for Dance, Jazz, Electronic Music, and Piano.

City University of New York (CUNY) – Graduate Center

33 West 42nd Street
New York, NY 10036

Admissions: 212-642-2812
Music Dept.: 212-642-2301

Enrollment. 3,300 graduate students. Music department: over 100.
Application deadline. Before January 1.
Audition. Required. Also various Music tests required; given in December and January or by special arrangement.
Degrees offered. Ph.D, DMA.
Costs. Tuition: In-state—$2,604; out-of-state—$5,600.

AUTHOR'S COMMENT: Recommended for Composition and Early Music.

Cleveland Institute of Music

11021 East Boulevard
Cleveland, OH 44106

216-791-5000

Enrollment. 271 undergraduates, 158 graduate students.
Music faculty. 38 full time, 72 part time.
Application deadlines. February 1 for fall, November 1 for spring semester.
Audition. Required. Held in Cleveland February–early March. Music Theory placement and Music History assessment exams also required.
Degrees offered. BM, MM, DMA, Artist Diploma, Undergraduate Diploma, Professional Studies.
Costs. Tuition: $11,500. Fees: $300. Room: $2,575. Board: $2,000.

Tapes: Not accepted in all departments.
Musical instruments taught: All Orchestral Instruments, Guitar, Piano. Also Composition, Choral and Orchestral Conducting, Early Music, and Voice.
Financial aid: Submit FAF and Institute's own form. Financial aid based on merit and need.
International students: 25% from abroad. Taiwan, China (PRC), Germany, Hong Kong, Canada most represented. TOEFL required—500 minimum for undergraduates, 550 for graduate students. Financial aid available; file Foreign Student Financial Aid application and supporting documents.
Prominent alumni include: Ward Davenny, Donald Erb, Maria Ewing, Sydney Harth, Anton Kuerti, Kermit Moore, Howard Swanson, Lyndon Woodside.

AUTHOR'S COMMENT: Recommended for Accompanying, Bassoon, Clarinet, French Horn, Guitar, Oboe, Percussion, Trumpet, Tuba, and Viola.

Coe College

1220 First Avenue, N.E.
Cedar Rapids, IA 52402

Admissions: 319-399-8500
Music Dept.: 319-399-8521
Theater Arts Dept.: 319-399-8624

Enrollment. College: 1,217. Drama majors: 29.
Drama faculty. 3 full time, 1 part time.
Audition. Required for some merit scholarships.
Degrees offered. BA in Acting. BA in Musical Theater.
Costs. Tuition: $10,280. Room: $1,750. Board: $2,090.

. . . .

Standardized tests: SAT or ACT required.
Interview: Recommended; required for some merit scholarships.
Admissions criteria: Courses and grades, SAT or ACT scores, recommendations.
Drama facilities include: 302-seat proscenium theater, 90-seat theater, 1,110-seat theater, scene shop, costume shop, props shop, welding shop, 2 dance studios, 3 rehearsal studios, classrooms.
Financial aid: Available. Submit FAF. Merit scholarships also available.

AUTHOR'S COMMENT: Recommended for undergraduate Drama and Musical Theater, as an interdisciplinary major between the Drama and Music departments.

College of Charleston

66 George Street
Charleston, SC 29424

Admissions: 803-792-5670
Dept. of Fine Arts: 803-792-8218

Enrollment. College: 7,000. Drama majors: 40.
Drama faculty. 5 full time, 3 part time.
Degrees offered. BA in Theater or Acting/Directing.
Costs. Tuition: In-state—$2,300; out-of-state—$4,550. Room and board: $2,850.

. . . .

Drama facilities include: Simmons Arts Center, 290-seat theater, 100-seat theater, flexible space, scene shop, costume shop, design studio.

AUTHOR'S COMMENT: In May the world-renowned Spoleto Festival uses many of the facilities of the College of Charleston, and students may be used as interns. Recommended for undergraduate Drama.

College of Santa Fe

1600 St. Michael's Drive
Santa Fe, NM 87501

Admissions: 1-800-456-2673
Performing Arts Dept.: 505-473-6439

Enrollment. College: 1,500. Drama Department: 120 (50 males, 70 females).
Faculty. Drama: 7 full time. Music: 2 full time, 15–20 part time.
Application deadlines. February 28 for fall semester.
Audition. Required. Make appointment through the Department.
Degrees offered. BFA, BA.
Costs. Tuition: $8,200. Fees: $1,000. Room: $1,446. Board: $1,478.

· · · · · · · · · · · · · ·

Videotapes: Accepted.
Admissions criteria: Audition, letters of recommendation, SAT or ACT scores, previous training, grades in school, essays.
Cross-registration: Available with British American Drama Academy.
Facilities include: 500-seat Greer Garson Theater, 100-seat Weckesser Studio Theater, dance studio, costume shop, scene shops.
Financial aid: Available. Must submit the FAF. Both merit- and need-based scholarships available.
Housing: 100% of new students receive on-campus housing.
International students: 1% of student body. Israel, Japan, Canada represented. SAT of 1020 minimum or ACT of 21 required. Application must be filed in early February. Financial aid available for foreign students only after student has been enrolled a year.
Prominent drama alumni include: Ray Buktanica, Lauren Klein.

AUTHOR'S COMMENT: Recommended for undergraduate Drama, Musical Theater.

College of Wooster

Wooster, OH 44691

Admissions: 216-263-2323 or 1-800-877-9905
Music Dept.: 216-263-2418

Enrollment. College: 1,800. Music majors: 50.
Application deadlines. Early Decision: December 15. Regular Decision: February 15.
Audition. Required for Music scholarships; scheduled in February.
Music degrees offered. BA, BM.
Costs. Tuition and fees: $12,470. Room and board: $3,950.

· · · · · · · · · · · · · ·

Standardized tests: SAT or ACT required. Achievement tests: Recommended.
Interviews: Recommended.
Instruments taught: All Orchestral Instruments, Piano, Organ, Saxophone, Guitar. Also Voice.
Music facilities include: 300-seat Gault Recital Hall, 1,400-seat McGaw Chapel, and a new Music Center.
Financial aid: File FAF by February 1.
International students: 8% from abroad. Pakistan, India, Malaysia most represented. TOEFL required. Must submit Certificate of Finances by February 15.
Prominent music alumni include: Lee Merrill, Erie Mills.

AUTHOR'S COMMENT: College of Wooster is a beautiful campus and a demanding school. The Music program is strong for a small liberal arts college.

Colorado College

14 East Cache la Poudre
Colorado Springs, CO 80903-3298

Admissions: 719-389-6344
Dance Dept.: 719-389-6637

Enrollment. College: 1,850. Dance majors: 5 to 10.
Application deadlines. Early Action: December 1.
Regular Decision: February 1.
Audition. Not required.
Costs. Tuition and fees: $12,710. Room and board: $3,410.

. . . .

Standardized tests: SAT or ACT required. Achievement tests: optional.
Interview: Optional.
Videotapes: Accepted and referred to Dance department.
Financial aid: Available; submit FAF by February 15.
Housing: 100% of new students receive on-campus housing.
International students: 2% from abroad. TOEFL required. Limited financial aid available and will affect candidacy.

AUTHOR'S COMMENT: Colorado College is particularly distinctive for its curriculum: the Colorado College Plan, wherein students study one area in depth for a block. It is a beautiful campus in the Rocky Mountains. Recommended for undergraduate Dance (modern).

Columbia College of Columbia University

212 Hamilton Hall
New York, NY 10027

Admissions: 212-854-2522
School of the Arts: 212-854-3408

Enrollment. University: 15,000. Columbia College: 3,200.
Application deadlines. Early Decision: November 1.
Regular Decision: January 1.
Audition. Required for joint or exchange program with Juilliard.
Degrees offered. BA. (MFA program is not actor training).
Costs. Tuition and fees: $15,520. Room and board: $6,122.

. . . .

Standardized tests: SAT required. Achievement tests: English Composition and two others required.
Interviews: Recommended.
Tapes: Not encouraged but may be sent to the Office of Admissions to be referred to the proper department for evaluation.
Financial aid: Available; submit FAF by February 1.
Facilities include: MacMillan theater, another 110-seat theater, 20-seat flexible space.

AUTHOR'S COMMENT: Located on the Upper West Side of Manhattan, Columbia is an intense, politically active campus. Recommended for undergraduate Drama, Composition, and all musical studies due to double degree and exchange program with Juilliard.

Connecticut College

270 Mohegan Avenue
New London, CT 06320-4196

Admissions: 203-439-2200

Enrollment. College: 1,650. Dance majors: 25.
Application deadlines. Early Decision: November 15.
Regular Decision: January 15.
Audition. Not required for Drama. Required for Dance; held in fall and spring.

• • • • • • • • • • • • • • • • • •

Standardized tests: SAT or ACT required. Achievement tests: required (English Composition and two others).
Interview: Recommended.
Tapes: Not encouraged for Drama but may be sent to the Office of Admissions, which will refer them to the proper department for evaluation. Dance will accept a videotape under special circumstances when a personal audition is impossible; call for specifics.
Housing: 100% of new students receive on-campus housing.

AUTHOR'S COMMENT: Formerly an all-women's college, Connecticut College is a fine small liberal arts college, midway between Boston and New York. Recommended for undergraduate Dance. Drama is also strong and students have the opportunity to work with the Eugene O'Neill Theater Institute.

Conservatory in Oslo (Norway)

Norges Musikkhogskole
(The Norway State Academy of Music)
Nordahl Brunsgt, 8
Postboks, 6877, St. Olavs Pl
N-0130 Oslo, 1, NORWAY

02-20.70.19

Enrollment. Conservatory: 350 (approximately), including 40 foreign students.
Music faculty. 58 full time, 121 part time.
Application deadline. December 15.
Audition. Required.
Costs. Student fee: $70.

• • • • • • • • • • • • • • • • • •

Interview: Not required.
Admissions criteria: Must be a high school graduate. Quality of the audition most important, tests in music theory, ear training.
Facilities include: 61 practice rooms, 2 organs, 4 percussion practice rooms, music library, listening library, special collection of historical instruments.
Financial aid: Not available.
International students: Admitted. Must take audition and tests. Write well in advance of deadline for special information and acceptability of tapes.

AUTHOR'S COMMENT: Recommended for French Horn.

Cornell University

410 Thurston Avenue
Ithaca, NY 14850

Admissions: 607-255-5241
Dept. of Theater Arts: 607-254-2700

Dept. of Theater Arts Address:
104 Lincoln Hall

Enrollment. University: 18,000. Drama majors: 50. Dance majors: 3.
Application deadlines. Early Decision: November 1. Regular Decision: January 1.
Audition.   Not required but recommended for Dance.
Degrees offered. BA.
Costs. Tuition: $16,170. Room and board: $5,300.

. . . .

Standardized tests: SAT or ACT required. Achievements: vary with program.
Interview: Recommended.
Financial aid: Submit FAF.

AUTHOR'S COMMENT: Cornell is an Ivy League school with a beautiful campus. The performing arts have been receiving some attention in recent years, and the University can be recommended for undergraduate Drama and Dance.

CSC Rep—The Actors' Conservatory

Classic Stage Company
135 East 13th Street
New York, NY 10003

212-677-4210

Enrollment. 30 acting students.
Drama faculty. 3 full time, 7 part time.
Application deadline. Rolling.
Audition. Required and determines admission. Held once a month January–March.
Costs. Tuition: $3,000.

. . . .

Facilities: 180-seat theater.

AUTHOR'S COMMENT: Students in the two-year actor training program have the opportunity to earn Equity points while working with the Classic Stage Company. Although the program is only 4 years old, it is recommended for nondegree Drama.

Curtis Institute of Music

1726 Locust Street
Philadelphia, PA 19103

Admissions: 215-893-5262

Enrollment. 145 undergraduates, 20 graduate students.
Music faculty. 75.
Application deadline. January 15.
Audition. Required. Held in March in Philadelphia.
Degrees offered. BM, Diploma. MM in certain areas.
Costs. Tuition: $0. Fees: $400. Room and board: $6,000– $7,000 for 9 months. (No dormitory.)

- - - - - - - - - - - - - - - - -

Tapes: Not accepted.
Musical instruments taught: All Orchestral Instruments, Piano, Organ, Harpsichord. Also Orchestral Conducting, Composition, Opera training, Voice.
Financial aid: FAF and Curtis form required.
International students: 40% from abroad. Korea, Canada, China (PRC), Taiwan, Hong Kong, Japan, Europe and Latin America most represented. TOEFL required for BM students only.
Prominent music alumni include: Leonard Bernstein, Jorge Bolet, Gary Graffman, Ned Rorem, Benita Valente.

AUTHOR'S COMMENT: A small, prestigious conservatory. Highly recommended for Bassoon, Composition, Double Bass, French Horn, Harp, Oboe, Organ, Percussion, Piano, Trombone, Trumpet, Tuba, Viola, Violin, Violoncello, Voice, and Opera training.

Dartmouth College

Hanover, NH 03755-1477

Admissions: 603-646-2875
Drama Dept.: 603-646-3104
Dance Dept.: 603-646-3438

Enrollment. College: 5,300. Dance majors: 15. Drama majors: 40.
Faculty. Dance: 3 full time, 2 part time. Drama: 7 full time, 2 part time.
Application deadlines. Early Decision: November 10. Regular Decision: January 1.
Audition. Not required.
Degrees offered. BA.
Costs. Tuition: $15,372 . Room and board: $5,124.

- - - - - - - - - - - - - - - - -

Standardized tests: SAT or ACT required. 3 achievement tests required.
Interview: Recommended.
Tapes: Not encouraged but may be sent to the Office of Admissions to be referred to the proper department for evaluation.
Facilities: Hopkins Center for the Arts; 460-seat theater, 181-seat theater, flexible space.
Financial aid: Available. Based on need. Submit FAF by February 1.

AUTHOR'S COMMENT: Although Dartmouth has undergone some difficult times in recent years, especially because of the ultra–right-wing Dartmouth Review, it is seeking peace among its diverse student body. Ensconsed in the wilds of northern New England, it is one of the Ivy League colleges and can be recommended for undergraduate Drama and Dance. The dance company Pilobolus was born at Dartmouth.

Denison University

P.O. Box H
Granville, OH 43023

Admissions: 614-587-6276
Dance Dept.: 614-587-6712

Enrollment. University: 2,000. Dance majors: 18.
Application deadlines. Early Decision: January 1.
Regular Decision: February 1.
Audition. Not required.
Costs. Tuition and fees: $13,510. Room and board:
$3,740.

. . . .

Standardized tests: SAT or ACT required. Achievement tests recommended.
Interview: Recommended.
Tapes: May be sent to the Office of Admissions to be referred to the proper department for evaluation.
Financial aid: Available. File FAF by April 1. Some merit scholarships available.
Housing: 100% of new students receive on-campus housing.

AUTHOR'S COMMENT: Denison is a fine liberal arts college in a beautiful midwestern small town. Recommended for undergraduate Dance.

DePaul University

Chicago, IL 60604

Admissions, in-state: 312-362-8374
Admissions, outside Illinois: 1-800-4-DEPAUL
School of Music: 312-362-8373
FAX, School of Music: 312-362-8215

*Theater School (formerly The Goodman
School of Drama) Address:*
2135 North Kenmore Avenue
Chicago, IL 60614
Located at DePaul's Lincoln Park campus.

School of Music Address:
804 West Belden Avenue
Chicago, IL 60614-3296

Enrollment. University: 15,720. Drama majors: 174 undergraduates (82 males, 92 females); 40 graduate students (23 males, 17 females). Music majors: 300 undergraduates, 45 graduate students.
Faculty. Drama: 38 full time, 20 part time. Music: 17 full time, 53 part time.
Application deadlines. Early Decision: November 15. Regular Decision: Rolling, but no later than a month before the last audition date.
Audition. Required for music and drama; held October–April in Chicago and regionally in New York City, New Orleans, Los Angeles, San Francisco. Contact the school for exact dates.
Degrees offered. BFA, Certificate (undergraduate 3-year program), MFA (3 years) in Drama. BA in Music, BM in Music Performance, Composition, Jazz Studies, MM in Performance, Composition, Jazz Studies, Performers Certificate.
Costs. Tuition and fees: Undergraduates—$10,989; Graduates—$11,289. Room and board: $4,500.

. . . .

(continued on next page)

Standardized tests: SAT or ACT required. Achievement tests: recommended.

Interview: Recommended.

Videotapes: Not accepted for Drama. Accepted for Music only with the permission of the Coordinator of Admissions.

Admissions criteria: Quality of audition, grades in school, standardized test scores, recommendations, application essay.

Musical instruments taught: All Orchestral Instruments, Saxophone, Classical and Jazz Guitar, Piano, Electric Bass. Also Voice.

Facilities: Drama: Blackstone Theater, 1,300-seat proscenium, classroom black box spaces. Music: 500-seat concert hall, 750-seat opera theater, 150-seat recital hall, 15-seat performance parlor.

Financial aid: Must submit the FAF. Due by May 1. Some merit scholarships available, most based on need.

Housing: 100% of undergraduates receive on-campus housing.

International students: 10% from abroad. Canada, German, China (PRC), Taiwan, Great Britain, Japan most represented. Must take TOEFL—550 minimum. No financial aid available for foreign students. Applications must be received at least 2 months prior to matriculation.

Prominent alumni include: Drama—Theoni V. Aldredge, Kevin Anderson, Bruce Boxleitner, Melinda Dillon, Harvey Korman, Eugene Lee, Joe Mantegna, Kevin J. O'Connor, Geraldine Page, Elizabeth Perkins, Michael Rooker. Music—Members of Chicago Symphony.

AUTHOR'S COMMENT: *DePaul is affiliated with the Catholic Church, but many of the students are non-Catholic. It has a strong regional representation among the student body. Highly recommended for undergraduate and graduate Drama; also recommended for Clarinet and Saxophone.*

DePauw University

Greencastle, IN 46135

School of Music, Admissions: 317-658-4118
Music Dept.: 317-658-4380

Enrollment. University: 2,350. Music majors: 110 undergraduates.

Music faculty. 15 full time, 14 part time.

Application deadlines. Early Action: December 1. Regular Decision: February 15.

Audition. Required. Call for exact dates and locations.

Degrees offered. BA, BM.

Costs. Tuition: $13,000. Room and board: $4,420.

• • • • • • • • • • • • • • • • • • •

Standardized tests: SAT or ACT required.

Interview: Required.

Tapes: Videotapes or cassettes accepted.

Musical instruments taught: Piano, Organ, Harpsichord, Guitar, All Orchestral Instruments. Also has a Jazz program.

Financial aid: Submit FAF. Some merit awards given.

International students: Very few from abroad. TOEFL required. Limited financial aid available for foreign students.

Prominent music alumni include: Joseph Flummerfeld, Wesley Tower.

AUTHOR'S COMMENT: *Has a solid Music program.*

Dickinson College

Carlisle, PA 17013

Admissions: 717-245-1231

Enrollment. College: 2,000 students. Drama majors: 7.
Drama faculty. 1 full time, 3 part time.
Application deadlines. Early Decision: December 15 and February 1. Regular Decision: March 1.
Audition. Not required.
Degrees offered. BA in Acting/Directing. BA in Dance.
Costs. Tuition and fees: $14,600. Room and board: $4,230.

• • • • • • • • • • • • • • • • • •

Standardized tests: SAT or ACT required. Achievement tests optional.
Interviews: Recommended.
Facilities: Relatively new Fine Arts building. 244-seat theater, 1 flexible space.
Financial aid: Available; file FAF by February 15.

AUTHOR'S COMMENT: Recommended for undergraduate Drama. Dickinson also sponsors many noteworthy programs abroad.

Drake University

25th Street and University Avenue
Des Moines, IA 50311-4505

Admissions: 515-271-3181
Music Dept.: 515-271-3975

Enrollment. 4,000.
Music faculty. 20
Application deadline. Rolling, but before March 1 highly recommended.
Audition. Required.
Degrees offered. BA, BFA, BM.
Costs. Tuition, room, board, and fees: $15,995.

• • • • • • • • • • • • • • • • • •

Standardized tests: SAT or ACT required.
Interview: Encouraged.
Financial aid: Available. Submit the FAF or FFS.
International students: 2% from abroad.
Musical instruments taught: Many Orchestral, Piano, Church Music, Piano Pedagogy, Conducting.

AUTHOR'S COMMENT: Recommended for Church Music and Musical Theater.

Drew University

36 Madison Avenue
Madison, NJ 07940-1493

Admissions: 201-408-3739
Theater Arts Dept.: 201-377-3000, ext. 326

Enrollment. University: 2,200. Drama majors: 40.
Drama faculty. 3 full time, 9 part time.
Application deadlines. Early Decision: January 15.
Regular Decision: February 15.
Audition. Not required.
Degrees offered. BA in Theater Arts.
Costs. Tuition and fees: $14,926. Room and board: $4,475.

• • • • • • • • • • • • • • • • • •

Standardized tests: SAT or ACT required. Achievement tests: English Composition and two others recommended.
Interview: Required for department.
Facilities: 225-seat Brown Theater, 125-seat Commons Theater, 60-seat studio.
Financial aid: Submit FAF by March 1.

AUTHOR'S COMMENT: Drew is located in a suburban town about 30 miles outside of New York City. Internships are available with New Jersey Shakespeare Festival, an Equity theater. Recommended for undergraduate Drama.

Duke University

Durham, NC 27706

Admissions: 919-684-3214
Drama Dept.: 919-684-2306
Music Dept.: 919-684-2534

Drama Dept. Address:
206 Bivings Building.

Enrollment. University: 7,000 undergraduates; 2,500 graduates. Drama majors: 30 undergraduates (10 males, 20 females). Music majors: 20 undergraduates; 35 graduate students.
Faculty. Drama: 13 full time, 1 part time. Music: 21 full time, 18 part time.

Application deadlines. Early Decision: November 1.
Regular Decision: January 1.
Audition. Not required.
Degrees offered. BA, Drama major. BA, Music major.
MA in Composition, Performance Practice.
Costs. Tuition: $14,700. Room: $3,000. Board: $2,780.

• • • • • • • • • • • • • • • • • •

Standardized tests: SAT or ACT required and 3 achievement tests, one of which must be English Composition.
Interview: Recommended.
Videotapes: Accepted only to enhance the chances of being admitted to the University. The Drama faculty will review the video and give an assessment to the Office of Admissions. Music Department welcomes tapes.
Admissions criteria: Students must be admitted into the University and admission is highly competitive. Grades in school, standardized test scores, application essays, recommendations all of importance.
Musical instruments taught: All Orchestral Instruments, Piano, Organ. Courses available also in Jazz, Performance Practice, Composition including Electronic Music, Collegium Musicum (Early Music), Voice.
Drama facilities include: Black box theater, proscenium theater, classrooms.
Financial aid: Available. Must submit FAF by February 15. Music Department has some merit scholarships.
Housing: 100% of new students offered on-campus housing.
Prominent drama alumni include: Simon Billig, Jack Coleman, Kevin Gray.

AUTHOR'S COMMENT: Duke is a prestigious university with a beautiful campus that attracts extremely bright students from around the world. Recommended for undergraduate Drama, Composition.

Eastman School of Music

26 Gibbs Street
Rochester, NY 14604

Admissions: 716-274-1060
Music General number: 716-274-1000

Enrollment. University of Rochester: 5,327 undergraduates; 4,299 graduate students. Eastman: 465 undergraduates; 280 graduate students.
Music faculty. 88 full time, 43 part time.
Application deadlines. February 1.
Audition. Required. Held in November–March in Rochester and regionally in Atlanta, Boston, Chicago, Cincinnati, Cleveland, Dallas, Denver, Greensboro, Houston, Los Angeles, Minneapolis, New Orleans, New York City, Philadelphia, San Francisco, Sarasota, Seattle, St. Louis, Washington, D.C. Auditions also held in Hong Kong, Japan, Korea, and Taiwan. Applicants must also take a Music Theory test and be interviewed. Doctoral applicants must submit research papers.
Music degrees offered. BA, Music Concentration, BM, MA, MM, DMA, Ph.D.
Costs. Tuition: $13,960. Fees: $325. Room and board: $5,750.

. . . .

Musical instruments taught: All Orchestral Instruments, Organ, Piano, Harpsichord, Euphonium, Saxophone, Guitar, Composition, Conducting, Jazz, Accompanying, Opera. Also has programs in Computer and Electronic Music, Early Music, Jazz Studies, Sacred Music, Voice.
Facilities include: 3,100-seat Eastman Theater, 460-seat Kilbourn Hall, 100-seat Schmitt Organ Hall, 80-seat Howard Hanson Hall.
Financial aid: Available; file the FAF and 1040. Some merit scholarships available.
Housing: 100% of new students receive on-campus housing.
International students: 14% from abroad. Canada, Korea, Japan, Taiwan, Singapore most represented. TOEFL required—500 minimum for undergraduates; 550 for graduate students. Must file special financial aid form to be considered for financial aid.

AUTHOR'S COMMENT: Recommended for Accompanying, Bassoon, Choral Conducting, Clarinet, Composition, Flute, French Horn, Harp, Harpsichord, Jazz, Oboe, Orchestral Conducting, Organ, Percussion, Piano, Saxophone, Trombone, Trumpet, and Violin.

Emerson College

100 Beacon Street
Boston, MA 02116-1596

Admissions: 617-578-8600
Division of Performing Arts: 617-578-8780

Enrollment. College: 1,750 undergraduates; 350 graduate students. Drama majors: 285 undergraduates (100 males, 185 females); 20 graduate students (8 males, 12 females).
Drama faculty. 17 full time, 16 part time.
Application deadline. March 1 for fall semester.
Audition. Required. Held in Boston and regionally throughout the United States from December–March. Contact the Office of Admissions for exact dates and locations.
Drama degrees offered. BA, BS, BFA, MA.
Costs. Tuition: $12,695. Fees: $250. Room: $4,358. Board: $2,762.

. . . .

Standardized tests: SAT required.
Videotapes: Accepted in special circumstances. Contact Admissions.
Financial aid: FAF required. Some merit scholarships available.
Housing: 100% who request housing receive it.
International students: 5% from abroad. Canada most represented. TOEFL required—550 minimum. Must submit application by November 15 for fall enrollment. No financial aid for foreign students.
Prominent drama alumni include: Richard Dysart, Spalding Gray, Henry Winkler, Stephen Wright.

AUTHOR'S COMMENT: Located in a series of brownstones in historic Back Bay Boston, Emerson is recommended for undergraduate Drama, Musical Theater.

Emory University

Department of Music
535 North Kilgo Circle
Atlanta, GA 30322

Undergraduate Admissions: 404-727-6036
Graduate Admissions: 404-727-0184
Dept. of Music: 404-727-6445

Enrollment. University: 9,390. Music majors: 66 undergraduates, 7 graduate students.
Music faculty. 12 full time, 42 part time.
Application deadlines. Early Decision: November 15. Regular Decision: February 1. Transfers: July 1.
Audition. Required. Held in March and September on the campus.
Degrees offered. BA in Music, MM in Conducting, Organ, and MSM (Master of Sacred Music).
Costs. Tuition: $14,580. Fees: $400. Room and board: $3,500.

. . . .

Standardized tests: SAT or ACT required. Achievement tests: recommended.
Tapes: Cassettes or videotapes accepted; should include 2 or 3 contrasting pieces.
Musical instruments taught: All Orchestral Instruments, Viola da Gamba, Organ, and Guitar. Also Choral and Orchestral Conducting.
Financial aid: Sumbit FAF. Music is the only deparment that provides merit scholarships.
International students: 10% from abroad. Korea, China (PRC), Japan, Caribbean, and former USSR most represented. TOEFL required.

AUTHOR'S COMMENT: Recommended for Church Music and Music in general.

Florida State University

Asolo Conservatory
Postal Drawer E
Sarasota, FL 33578

General Number: 813-355-7115
Drama Dept.: 813-355-0994

Enrollment. Professional Actor Training Program (PATP): 20 to 25.
Drama faculty. 6 full time.
Audition. Required.
Degrees offered. MFA.
Costs. All students accepted into the Conservatory are on full scholarship which includes tuition waivers, assistantships, stipends from Florida State University, and work stipends from Asolo Performing Arts Center.

. . . .

Standardized tests: GRE required.
Drama facilities include: 500-seat theater, 110-seat theater.

AUTHOR'S COMMENT: Students accepted into this highly selective actor training program are eligible for earning Equity points while working as part of the Asolo State Theater, an Equity company that works in conjunction with the Conservatory. Recommended for graduate Drama.

Florida State University

Tallahassee, FL 32306

Admissions: 904-644-6200
School of Theater: 904-644-6795
Undergraduate Music: 904-644-3424
Graduate Music: 904-644-5848
Dance Dept.: 904-644-1023

School of Music Address:
School of Music, Tallahassee, FL 32306-2098

School of Theater Address:
216 B, William Johnston Building

Enrollment. University: 23,000 undergraduates; 5,500 graduates. Dance majors: 45 undergraduates; 15 graduates. Drama majors: 210. Music majors: 520 undergraduates; 310 graduates.
Faculty. Dance: 10 full time, 3 part time. Drama: 23 full time. Music: 71 full time, 5 part time, 125 graduate assistants.
Application deadlines. Rolling admissions, but be sure to apply before auditions and no later than March 1 recommended. Transfers: May 20.
Audition. Required for BFA and MFA and for all Music applicants. Music auditions held in Tallahassee in October–June.
Degrees offered. BA in General Theater, BFA, MFA in Acting. BFA, MFA in Dance. BA, BM, MM, DM, Ph.D, and numerous Certificate programs in Music.
Costs. Tuition: In-state—$1,350; out-of-state— $3,000. Room and board: $3,280.

. . . .

Standardized tests: SAT or ACT required. Achievement test optional.
Interview: Required for BFA and MFA as part of the audition.
Tapes: Cassettes acceptable for Music applicants.
Admissions criteria: Audition and evaluation of academic record and recommendations.
Musical instruments taught: All Orchestral Instruments, all Keyboard, Non-Western instruments, Guitar, Historic instruments. Also has programs in Church Music, Piano Pedagogy, Computers in Music, Early Music, Music of the Americas, Jazz, Contemporary Media, Voice.

Drama facilities: 500-seat theater, 245-seat theater, 200-seat theater.
Financial aid: Available; file FFS and School of Music application. University has need-based scholarships and School of Music has some merit scholarships.
International students: 5% from abroad. China, Korea, Canada, Japan, Australia most represented. TOEFL required—550 minimum. Application must be filed 6 months prior to matriculation. A special University form must also be filed for financial aid.
Prominent alumni include: Charles Rex, Ellen Taaffe Zwilich.

AUTHOR'S COMMENT: *Recommended for Drama. Highly recommended in Dance. Also recommended for Accompanying, Flute, Guitar, Musical Theater, Oboe, Saxophone, and Choral Conducting.*

George Mason University

4400 University Drive
Fairfax, VA 22030-4444

Admissions: 703-993-2400

Enrollment. University: 19,000. Dance majors: 36.
Dance faculty. 10.
Application deadlines. Early Decision and Early Action: December 1. Regular Decision: February 1.
Degrees offered. BA, BFA.
Costs. Tuition: In-state—$2,496; out-of-state— $4,665. Room and board: $4,470.

. . . .

Standardized tests: SAT required. Achievement tests required for certain majors.
Facilities: New Center for the Arts.
Financial aid: Available; file FAF by March 1.
Housing: Limited and most students commute.

AUTHOR'S COMMENT: *Recommended for undergraduate Dance. Music Department allows for cross-registration with Shenandoah College and Conservatory.*

George Washington University

2121 I Street, NW
Washington, DC 20052

Admissions: 202-994-6040
Dept. of Theater and Dance: 202-994-1660
Dept. of Music: 202-994-6245

Dept. of Theater and Dance Address:
800 21st Street, NW

Enrollment. University: 18,960. Dance majors: 8 undergraduates, 5 graduates. Drama majors: 40. Music majors: 32 undergraduates, 4 graduate students.
Faculty. Drama: 6 full time, 1 part time. Music: 5 full time, 43 part time.
Application deadlines. Early Decision and Early Action: December 1. Regular Decision: February 1.
Audition. Required for Music applicants; held on campus in November and January. Theory exam also required for BM.
Degrees offered. BA in Theater. BA in Dance. MFA in Theater/Dance. BA, BM in Music.
Costs. Tuition and fees: $13,950. Room and board: $6,040.

• • • • • • • • • • • • • • • •

Standardized tests: SAT required. Achievement tests in English and math required for BA applicants.
Interview: Required for graduate admission in Drama.
Tapes: Videotapes and cassettes accepted in Music.
Drama and dance facilities: 484-seat theater, 50-seat theater, 3 dance studios.
Financial aid: Submit FAF and Music Department Application for merit scholarships in music.
International students: 21% from abroad. Korea, Japan most represented. TOEFL required—600 minimum. Application should be submitted one month prior to regular deadline.
Prominent alumni include: Music—William Rust, William Toutant. Dance—Liz Lerman.

AUTHOR'S COMMENT: GWU, just down the road from the White House, is truly an urban campus. The Drama program has relationships with Washington Stage Guild and Horizon's Theater, two Equity companies, and students may find internships with them. Recommended for undergraduate Drama and Dance. The Music department in general has strengths.

Goucher College

Dulaney Valley Road
Towson, MD 21204

Admissions: 301-337-6100
Dance Dept.: 301-337-6390
Theater Dept.: 301-337-6273

Enrollment. College: 900 students. Drama majors: 20. Dance majors: 18.
Faculty. Drama: 3 full time, 3 part time. Dance: 6 full time, 2 part time.
Application deadlines. Early Decision: November 15. Early Action: December 15. Regular Decision: December 15.
Audition. Not required. Placement audition given.
Degrees offered. BA.
Costs. Tuition and fees: $11,950. Room and board: $5,380.

• • • • • • • • • • • • • • • •

Standardized tests: SAT or ACT required. Achievement tests required (English composition and two others).
Interview: Recommended.
Tapes: Submit videotapes to the Office of Admissions to be referred to the appropriate department for evaluation.
Facilities: Meyerhoff Arts Center.
Financial aid: Submit the FAF. Some merit scholarships also available.

AUTHOR'S COMMENT: Goucher, formerly an all-women's college, is located on a beautiful campus, just outside Baltimore and not far from Washington, D.C. Recommended for undergraduate Drama and Dance.

Grambling State University

Brown Hall, Room 109
Grambling, LA 71245

318-869-5075

Dept. of Speech and Theater Address:
P.O. Box 417

Enrollment. University: 6,000. Drama majors: 12.
Drama faculty. 4 full time.
Degrees offered. BA in Theater.
Costs. Tuition and fees: $1,766. Room and board: $4,170.

. . . .

Standardized tests: SAT or ACT required.
Interview: Required for theater program.
Facilities: 210-seat theater, 2,200-seat theater, scene shop, costume shop, rehearsal spaces, classrooms.
Financial aid: Submit the FAF. Merit scholarships also awarded.

AUTHOR'S COMMENT: Grambling State is a historically black university. Recommended for undergraduate Drama; has a highly regarded Band program.

Guildhall School of Music and Drama

Barbican
London EC2Y 8DT, ENGLAND

01-628-2571

Enrollment. School: 1,300 (approximately).
Application deadline. Rolling admissions.
Audition. Required. Contact the Principal or Admissions Office about cassettes and exact dates and times of auditions.
Costs. UK residents: $5,500 per year; foreign students approximately $9,000 per year. Room: approximately $5,500.

. . . .

Admissions criteria: High school diploma; Music Perception and ear-training tests required.
Facilities: Music hall, 2,000-seat Barbican Hall, St. Giles, Cripplegate, and other City Halls. School is part of the Barbican Centre, an arts complex located in the heart of London. 70 practice rooms, percussion and organ practice rooms, recording studio, music library, listening facilities.
Financial aid: Limited scholarships available. Submit application by June 25.
Housing: Available.

AUTHOR'S COMMENT: Recommended for Drama, Accompanying, and Orchestral Conducting.

Hampshire College

Amherst, MA 01002

Admissions: 413-549-4600
Music: 413-549-4600

Enrollment. College: 1,250. Dance concentrations: 15. Music concentrations: 22.
Application deadlines. Early Decision: December 1. Early Action: January 1. Regular Decision: February 1.
Audition. Not required.
Costs. Tuition and fees: $16,430. Room and board: $4,240.

. . . .

Standardized tests: SAT, ACT, and achievement tests all optional.
Interviews: Recommended.
Tapes: Encouraged.
Admissions criteria: Essays, recommendations, grades and courses, and evidence of intellectual curiosity and ability to take responsibility for educational plans.

AUTHOR'S COMMENT: Started by some visionary educational leaders from the other four colleges in the Connecticut Valley (Amherst, Mt. Holyoke, Smith, and University of Massachusetts), Hampshire is one of the "progressive" or alternative colleges. It offers a superb education to motivated students. Recommended for undergraduate Dance (part of Five College department), Guitar, and Musical Theater.

Harid Conservatory

P.O. Box 1754
Boca Raton, FL 33429

407-997-2677

Enrollment. Music: 19; Dance: 38 (high school). No Drama.
Application deadline. Rolling, but before March preferred.
Audition. Required. Held in January, February, and March. Call for exact dates and locations.
Degrees offered. BM, 3-year Performance Certificate in Music.
Costs. Harid has a full-tuition scholarship program.

. . . .

Standardized tests: SAT or ACT required.
Tapes: Accepted but personal audition preferred.

AUTHOR'S COMMENT: Harid was started only a few years ago and its benefactor chooses to remain anonymous. There has been turnover already in the Dance Department, and it currently has just a high school program, but the direction seems strong, so that the Conservatory can be highly recommended for Dance for high school students. It is too early to evaluate how the Music Department is progressing.

Hartford Ballet—School of

224 Farmington Avenue
Hartford, CT 06105

203-525-9396

Enrollment. 2 males, 15 females.
Dance faculty. 6 full time, 12 part time.
Application deadlines. July 1 for fall; November 1 for spring; April 30 for summer.
Audition. Required.
Degrees offered. Certificate in Performance. BFA program in conjunction with the University of Hartford in process.
Costs. Tuition: $5,100. Fees: $50.

. . . .

Interview: Required.
Videotapes: Accepted.
Cross-registration: University of Hartford, Trinity College (CT).

AUTHOR'S COMMENT: Hartford is a fine ballet school.

Hartford Conservatory of Music and Dance

834-846 Asylum Avenue
Hartford, CT 06105

203-246-2588

Enrollment. School: 50. Dance majors: 18 females.
Dance faculty. 3 full time, 5 part time.
Application deadline. Rolling.
Audition. Required. Made by appointment in Hartford.
Degrees offered. Diploma in Performance.
Costs Tuition: $5,900. Fees: $100.

. . . .

Interview: Required.
Videotapes: Accepted for those for whom travel is impossible.
Prominent dance alumni: Members of Graham, Hartford, Limón, Nikolaïs, and Stuttgart Companies.

AUTHOR'S COMMENT: Hartford Conservatory celebrated its 100th anniversary in 1990. It has the longest continuously serving dance department in Connecticut and has offered modern dance since 1936. Many alumni transfer into BFA dance programs.

Hartt School of Music

(Sometimes listed as University of Hartford-Hartt School of Music)

200 Bloomfield Avenue
West Hartford, CT 06117

Admissions: 203-243-4465
FAX: 203-243-4441
Music Dept.: 203-243-4454

Enrollment. University: 6,000 undergraduates; 2,000 graduate students. Music majors: 360 undergraduates; 150 graduate students.
Music faculty. 47 full time, 52 part time.
Application deadlines. February 1 for graduate students. April 15 for fall semester for undergraduates.
Audition. Required. Music applicants also take music theory, ear training, and music history exams. Auditions are held on campus and regionally December–February. Call the school for exact dates and locations.
Degrees offered. BM, BA, BS, MM, DMA, Undergraduate Diploma, Graduate Artist Diploma, Certificate of Advanced Graduate Study.
Costs. Tuition: $12,990. Fees: $550. Room and board: $6,000.

. . . .

Standardized tests: SAT or ACT required.
Interview: Required as part of audition.
Tapes: Accepted from applicants living more than 300 miles from the campus.
Admissions criteria: High school graduation with rank in upper 40%.
Musical instruments taught: All Orchestral Instruments, Organ, Harpsichord, Piano, Guitar. Also Composition, Jazz studies, Electronic Music, Opera, Musical Theater, Voice.
Facilities: Hartt is located in the Alfred C. Fuller Music Center, a 3-building complex. Paranov Hall: classrooms, teaching studios, rehearsal rooms, recording studio, library. O'Connell Hall: organ studio, Berkman Recital Hall, practice rooms, teaching studios, 428-seat Millard Auditorium, 700-seat Lincoln Theater, music library, listening library.
Financial aid: Available. Talent-based scholarships also available. File FAF.

International students: 3% of undergraduates and 37% of graduate students from abroad. Korea, Taiwan, Brazil, Canada, China (PRC), France, Germany, Japan most represented. TOEFL required—500 minimum. Some financial aid for foreign students available.
Prominent alumni include: Stan Freeman, Neal Gittleman, Cornell MacNeil, Dionne Warwick.

AUTHOR'S COMMENT: Recommended for French Horn, Guitar, Jazz, Percussion, and Saxophone. The Emerson String Quartet is in residence.

Harvard–Radcliffe College

Byerly Hall
8 Garden Street
Cambridge, MA 02138-6534

Admissions: 617-495-1551

Enrollment. University: 17,500; 6,500 undergraduates. Music majors: 38.
Music faculty. 22.
Application deadlines. Early Action: November 1. Regular Decision: January 1.
Audition. Not required.
Degrees offered. BA.
Costs. Tuition and fees: $15,530. Room and board: $5,125.

. . . .

Standardized tests: SAT required. 3 achievement tests required. GRE required for graduate students.
Interviews: Optional campus interviews; required alumni interview.
Tapes: May be submitted to the Office of Admissions to be referred to the appropriate department for evaluation.
Financial aid: Available. File FAF by January 1. Scholarships based on need.
Prominent alumni include: Yo Yo Ma, Leonard Bernstein, and many others.
Housing: 100% of new students receive on-campus housing.

AUTHOR'S COMMENT: Recommended for Composition.

Hobart and William Smith Colleges

Geneva, NY 14456

Hobart Admissions: 315-781-3622 or
1-800-852-2256
William Smith Admissions: 315-781-3472 or
1-800-245-0100
Dance Dept.: 315-781-3495

Enrollment. Colleges (coordinate system): 1,900. Dance majors: 5 to 10.
Dance faculty. 3.
Application deadlines. Early Decision: January 1. Regular Decision: February 15.
Audition. Not required.
Degrees offered. BA.
Costs. Tuition and fees: $15,296. Room and board: $4,899.

. . . .

Standardized tests: SAT or ACT required. Achievement tests: English composition and two others required.
Interview: Recommended.
Tapes: Videotape may be sent to the Office of Admissions who will refer it to the department for evaluation.
Facilities: Bartlett Theater.
Financial aid: Submit the FAF by February 15.

AUTHOR'S COMMENT: Recommended for undergraduate Dance.

Hochschule, Cologne

(Also known as Staatliche Hochschule für Musik, Köln)
Dagobertstrasse, 38
D-5000 Köln, 1, GERMANY

221-12.40.33

Enrollment. 1,300 students.
Music faculty. 98 full time, 141 part time.
Audition. Required.
Degrees offered. Diplomas.

. . . .

Admissions criteria: High school diploma, comprehensive examinations.
Facilities: 3 major concert halls, large music library, listening facilities, practice rooms, electronic music studio, organ and percussion practice rooms.

AUTHOR'S COMMENT: Recommended for Accompanying.

Hochschule, Freiburg

(Sometimes listed as Musik Hochschule, Freiburg or Staatliche Hochschule für Musik, Freiburg)
Schwarzwaldstrasse, 141
D-7800 Freiburg, GERMANY

0761-31.91.50

Enrollment. 600.
Application deadlines. July 15 or January 31.
Audition. Required. Music theory and piano proficiency exam also required.
Music degrees offered. Diploma, Postgraduate degree.

. . . .

Facilities include: New school building (1983), practice rooms, organ practice rooms, percussion practice rooms, studios for new music, opera, electronic studio, music library, concert halls.
International students: Foreign students come from the United States, Korea, Japan, Switzerland, Great Britain. The School does not offer financial aid for foreign students.

AUTHOR'S COMMENT: Freiburg has an international reputation and an extremely strong and renowned faculty. Especially recommended for Early Music, Harpsichord, and Oboe. (Composition seems to be in transition right now.)

Hochschule für Musik, Berlin (Germany)

(Sometimes the name is listed as: Musik Hochschule/BERLIN or as Hochschule der Künste, Berlin)
Ernst-Reuter-Platz, 10
1000 Berlin 10, GERMANY

030-3185-0

Audition. Required.
Degrees offered. Diploma.

. . . .

International students: Accepted.

AUTHOR'S COMMENT: Recommended for Orchestral Conducting.

Hochschule für Musik und Darstellende Kunst, Wien

(College for Music and Performing Arts, Vienna)
Lothringerstrasse, 18
1030 Vienna (Wien), AUSTRIA

222-56.16.85/87

Music degrees offered. Diploma.
Audition. Required.

. . . .

Facilties: Music library, concert halls.
International students: Welcome. Contact the Rector for exact dates and times of auditions. Music theory and ear training exams are usually part of the admissions process.
Prominent alumni: Fritz Kreisler, Gustav Mahler.

AUTHOR'S COMMENT: The school has an international reputation. Recommended for Harpsichord and Orchestral Conducting.

Hochschule für Musik und Theater, Hannover

Emmichplatz, 1
3000 Hannover, 1, GERMANY

511-31001

Enrollment. 200 students.
Application deadline. May 30.
Audition. Required. Ear training, music theory, and piano proficiency exams also required.

. . . .

Facilities: 2 concert halls, music library, listening library, practice rooms, 6 organs, percussion practice rooms.
Financial aid: Scholarships and loans are available.

AUTHOR'S COMMENT: Recommended for Violin.

Hochschule, Heidelberg

(Sometimes listed as: Staatliche Hochschule für Musik, Heidelberg)
Friedrich-Ebert-Anlage, 62, GERMANY

06221-200.40

Degrees offered. Diplomas.

∙ ∙ ∙ ∙ ∙ ∙ ∙ ∙ ∙ ∙ ∙ ∙ ∙ ∙ ∙ ∙ ∙

AUTHOR'S COMMENT: Recommended for Violoncello.

Hofstra University

Hempstead, NY 11550

Admissions: 516-463-6700
Drama and Dance Dept.: 516-463-5444

Enrollment. University: 12,230. Drama majors: 88 undergraduates (40 males, 48 females). Dance majors: 42 undergraduates (4 males, 38 females).
Faculty. Drama: 7 full time, 2 part time. Dance: 3 full time, 4 part time.
Application deadlines. Early Decision: December 1. Regular Decision: Rolling, but by February 15 highly recommended.
Audition. Required for talent scholarships; held in February at the campus.
Degrees offered. BA, BFA.
Costs. Tuition: $8,570. Fees: $245. Room: $2,780. Board: $2,150.

∙ ∙ ∙ ∙ ∙ ∙ ∙ ∙ ∙ ∙ ∙ ∙ ∙ ∙ ∙ ∙ ∙

Standardized tests: SAT or ACT required.
Videotape: Accepted. Should be standard 4-minute audition format for Drama. In Dance should show 20 minutes from a ballet or modern class and a 3-minute solo. Audition in person highly recommended.
Admissions criteria: Students must be accepted into the University first. Then "trainability is assessed."
Drama facilities include: West End Theater, flexible stage, seats 150; John Cranford Adams Playhouse, proscenium theater, seats 1,134; Speigel Theater, thrust stage, 110 seats.
Financial aid: Available. Must submit the FAF by February 15. Approximately 75% of students receive financial aid. Merit-based scholarships available.
Housing: 40% of new students receive on-campus housing.
International students: 1 or 2% of student body. TOEFL required—450 minimum. High school grades very important. Must file all documents early. Recruiters sent to Europe, Asia, and Latin America. No financial aid available for foreign students.
Prominent drama alumni include: Margaret Colin, Francis Ford Coppola, Peter Friedman, Madeline Kahn, Lainie Kazan, Irene Lewis, Joe Morton, Susan Schulman, Susan Sullivan. Dance program is only 5 years old.

AUTHOR'S COMMENT: Recommended for undergraduate Drama, Dance.

Howard University

2400 Sixth Street, NW
Washington, DC 20059

Admissions: 202-806-2755
Dept. of Drama: 202-636-7050
Dept. of Music: 202-806-7080 or 7082

Enrollment. University: 12,510. Drama majors: 81.
Faculty. Drama: 12 full time. Music: 21 full time, 20 part time.
Application deadline. Rolling admissions.
Audition. Required.
Degrees offered. BA, BFA.
Costs. Tuition and Fees: $5,905. Room and board: $3,200.

. . . .

Standardized tests: SAT or ACT required. Achievement tests required, but vary according to major.
Interview: Required for Drama.
Tapes: May be sent to the Office of Admissions to be forwarded to the department for evaluation.
Drama facilities include: 300-seat theater, 75-seat theater, flexible space, scene shop, costume shop, dance studio, classrooms.
Musical instruments taught: Piano, Guitar, Jazz, Voice.
Financial aid: FAF and Merit scholarships available.
International students: 20% from abroad.
Prominent alumni: Jesse Norman, Roberta Flack, Harold Wheeler, Angela Winbush, Shelton Becton, Thomas Flagg, Dr. Doris McGinty.

AUTHOR'S COMMENT: Howard is a leading historically black university. Recommended for undergraduate Drama, Jazz, Saxophone. The Music Department in general is strong.

Hunter College of the City University of New York

695 Park Avenue
New York, NY 10021-5085

Admissions: 212-772-4490
Dance Dept.: 212-772-5012

Enrollment. College: 19,600. Dance majors: 30.
Application deadlines. Regular Decision: January 15.
Costs. Tuition: In-state—$1,320.

. . . .

Standardized tests: SAT and achievement tests optional.
Admissions criteria: Academic record most important, personal qualities.
Financial aid: Submit College's own form and FAF.

AUTHOR'S COMMENT: Located on the Upper East side of Manhattan, Hunter is a strong liberal arts college. Recommended for undergraduate Dance.

Illinois State University

201 Hovey Hall
Normal, IL 61761-2993

Admissions: 309-438-2181
Dept. of Theater: 309-438-8786
Dept. of Music: 309-438-7631

Enrollment. University: 22,300. Drama majors: 225. Music majors: 300.
Faculty. Drama: 22 full time, 1 part time. Music: 45.
Audition. Required for MFA; held in conjunction with the U/RTA auditions or as scheduled on campus.
Degrees offered. BA, BS, MFA in Acting. BA, BS, BM, MM in Music.
Costs. Tuition and fees: In-state—$2,272; out-of-state—$3,015. Room and board: $2,560.

. . . .

Standardized tests: SAT or ACT required.
Interview: Required as part of audition.
Admissions criteria: GPA, class rank, recommendations, standardized test scores, talent.
Musical instruments taught: All Orchestral Instruments, Piano, Voice, Organ, Harpsichord
Drama facilities include: 450-seat theater, 135-seat theater, flexible space.
Financial aid: File FAF or FFS.
Prominent alumni: Drama—Gary Cole, Judith Ivey, Terry Kinney, John Malkovich, Laurie Metcalf. 70% of the original Steppenwolf company were alumni of the Illinois State Theater Department.

AUTHOR'S COMMENT: Recommended for Drama and Violoncello.

Illinois Wesleyan University

210 East University
Bloomington, IL 61701

309-556-3031

Enrollment. University: 1,740. Drama majors: 78. Music majors: 126.
Faculty. Drama: 12. Music 33.
Application deadline. Rolling admissions, but by March 1 recommended.
Audition. Not required.
Degrees offered. BA, BFA, BM, B. Sacred Music.
Costs. Tuition and fees: $10,085. Room and board: $3,475.

. . . .

Standardized tests: SAT or ACT required.
Interview: Recommended.
Musical instruments taught: Violin, Viola, Double Bass, Violoncello, Piano, Harpsichord, Organ, Trumpet, Clarinet, Saxophone, Flute, Trombone, Tuba, Oboe, Bassoon, Voice, Percussion, French Horn, Harp. No Guitar.
Financial aid: Submit FAF by March 1.
Prominent alumni: Drama—Frankie Faison, Stephanie Faracy, Katherine James, Sam Smiley. Music—Dawn Upshaw.

AUTHOR'S COMMENT: Recommended for undergraduate Drama, Musical Theater, and Voice.

Indiana University

300 North Jordan Avenue
Bloomington, IN 47405

Admissions: 812-855-0661
School of Music: 812-855-1582
Dept. of Theater and Drama: 812-855-4535
Dept. of Ballet: 812-855-6787

Enrollment. University: 34,860. Drama majors: 200.
School of Music: 1,500.
Faculty. Drama: 25 full time. Music: 145.
Application deadlines. Rolling admissions but recommended by February 15 or before auditions.
Audition. Required for graduate Drama and for all Music applicants.
Degrees offered. BA in Theater and Drama, MFA in Acting. BA, BM, MM, DMA in Music.
Costs. Tuition and fees: In-state—$2,310; out-of-state—$6,845. Room and board: $3,159.

. . . .

Standardized tests: SAT or ACT required. Achievement tests optional.
Interview: Required for graduate Drama as part of audition.
Tapes: Accepted, but personal audition preferred. Call for tape or videotape requirements.
Musical instruments taught: All Orchestral, Jazz, Choral Conducting, Composition, Early Music, Organ, Saxophone, Voice.
Admissions criteria: Academic record, rank in class, standardized tests scores.
Facilities include: 383-seat theater, 66-seat theater, 423-seat theater.
Financial aid: Submit the FAF by March 1.
International students: Submit international application. Canada, Korea, Taiwan, Japan, Germany most represented. TOEFL required.
Prominent alumni: Drama—Kevin Kline, Stephen Macht, Patricia Kalember. Music—Joshua Bell, Sylvia McNair, Timothy Noble.

AUTHOR'S COMMENT: Recommended for undergraduate and graduate Drama; Dance (ballet); Choral Conducting, Clarinet, Double Bass, Early Music, Flute, French Horn, Guitar, Harp, Harpsichord, Jazz, Oboe, Orchestral Conducting, Organ, Piano, Saxophone, Trombone, Trumpet, Violin, Violoncello, graduate Voice.

Institute for Advanced Theater Training at Harvard

(American Repertory Theater)

64 Brattle Street
Cambridge, MA 02138

617-495-2668

Enrollment. Institute: 40 students.
Drama faculty. 8 full time, 3 part time.
Application deadline. January 1.
Audition. Required.
Degrees offered. Certificate. (Actors get Equity card at the end of the 2 years.)
Costs. Tuition: $7,200. No housing.

. . . .

Admissions criteria: Quality of audition most important; statement of purpose, recommendations, transcripts also considered.
Drama facilities include: 550-seat theater, 80-seat theater, 200-seat theater; scene, costume, props shops.
Financial aid: Available. File GAPSFAS.

AUTHOR'S COMMENT: This is Robert Brustein's program, transported from Yale in the early to mid-1980s. Students receive superb training and are often cast in the productions of the American Repertory Theater (ART). Highly recommended for graduate Drama.

IRCOM Center

Centre Nationale d'Art et de Culture,
Georges Pompidou
Place Pompidou
Paris, FRANCE

011-33-1-278-3942 or
011-33-1-277-1233

. . . .

AUTHOR'S COMMENT: Recommended for graduate studies in Electronic Music.

Ithaca College

Ithaca, NY 14850

Admissions: 607-274-3124
Dept. of Theater Arts: 607-274-3345 or 3919

Enrollment. College: 6,000. Drama majors: 169. Music majors: 430 undergraduates; 28 graduate students.
Faculty. Drama: 16 full time, 2 part time. Music: 54.
Application deadlines. Early Decision: November 1. Regular Decision: March 1.
Audition. Required for Music and Theater program; held on campus and regionally. Sightsinging also required of Music applicants.
Degrees offered. BA in Drama, BFA in Acting. BFA in Musical Theater, BA in Music, BM in Music, Performance, Composition, Jazz Studies.
Costs. Tuition and fees: $11,070. Room: $2,500. Board: $2,604.

• • • • • • • • • • • • • • •

Standardized tests: SAT or ACT required. Achievement tests recommended.
Interview: Required for Theater program.
Tapes: Accepted from applicants far from audition site, but personal audition preferred. Call for tape or videotape requirements.
Musical instruments taught: All Orchestral Instruments, Organ, Piano. Also Voice.
Facilities: Drama: 535-seat theater, 300-seat theater, scene shop, costume shops, 2 dance studios, rehearsal spaces. Music: 740-seat concert hall, 150-seat recital hall.
Financial aid: Based on need; submit FAF.
International students: Korea, Germany, Japan, and South Africa most represented. TOEFL required—550 minimum. Faculty recruit abroad and may hear a Music audition.

AUTHOR'S COMMENT: Ithaca was originally founded as a Conservatory of Music and the Music program remains strong. Especially recommended for undergraduate Drama and Musical Theater.

Jacksonville University

2800 University Boulevard, North
Jacksonville, FL 32211-3396

General Information: 904-744-3950
Dance Division: 904-744-3950 or 3374

Enrollment. University: 2,500. Dance majors: 45.
Application deadline. Rolling, but by March for scholarship consideration.
Audition. Required. Call for exact dates.
Degrees offered. BA, BFA.
Costs. Tuition and fees: $7,960. Room and board: $3,580.

• • • • • • • • • • • • • • •

Standardized tests: SAT or ACT required.
Interview: Recommended.
Videotapes: Accepted for those at great distance, but personal audition preferred. Call for guidelines for the videotape.
Financial aid: Submit the FAF by March 1.

AUTHOR'S COMMENT: Jacksonville University is a private university with a generally strong performing arts program. Recommended for undergraduate Dance.

James Madison University

Harrisonburg, VA 22807

Admissions: 703-568-6147
Dept. of Theater and Dance: 703-568-6342

Enrollment. University: 11,000. Drama majors: 80 undergraduates (30 males, 50 females).
Drama faculty. 6 full time, 2 part time.
Application deadlines. Early Action: December 1; Regular Decision: February 1.
Audition. Not required but recommended for "entry preference." Scheduled through the Theater Office.
Degrees offered. BA, Theater major.
Costs. Tuition and fees: In-state—$3,016; out-of-state—$6,004. Room and board: $3,908.

. . . .

Standardized tests: SAT required. Achievement tests optional.
Videotapes: Not accepted.
Admissions criteria: Grades in school, standardized tests scores, previous training, audition, recommendations.
Drama facilities include: 1 experimental theater, 1 proscenium theater, 1 dinner theater.
Financial aid: Available. Must submit the FAF by March 15.
International students: Very few enrolled.

AUTHOR'S COMMENT: Recommended for undergraduate Drama.

Joffrey II Dancers (Company)

130 West 56th Street
New York, NY 10019

212-265-7300

Enrollment. 8 Dancers ages 17 to 22; half male, half female.
Application deadline. Résumés and pictures are accepted year-round for consideration.
Audition. Required. Arranged on an individual basis and evaluated by the artistic staff.

. . . .

Videotapes: Recommended for dancers who live outside the metropolitan New York area for pre-screening.
Admissions criteria: Must be high school graduate. Performance at audition most important.
Recent choreographers: Has a choreographer workshop. This year the choreographers were Daniel Peizig, Diane Coburn Bruning, and Mark Haim.

AUTHOR'S COMMENT: Upon completion of 1 or 2 years in Joffrey II the dancers (if not "graduated" into the main Joffrey Ballet Company) almost always go on into other top-level professional dance companies in the U.S. or abroad. A fine company for studying primarily classical ballet.

Juilliard (The Juilliard School)

60 Lincoln Center Plaza
New York, NY 10023-6590

Admissions: 212-799-5000, ext. 223

Enrollment. School: 800. Dance division: 100. Drama division: 100. Music division: 600 students.

Application deadlines. January 8 for February auditions in Drama and March auditions in Dance and Music; March 15 for May auditions in Dance and Music.

Audition. Required. Drama: Scheduled for February in New York City, Chicago, and San Francisco. Dance and Music: March and May in New York. Dance also holds auditions in other cities around the United States in February and March. Call for specific dates and locations.

Degrees offered. BFA in Drama. BFA in Dance. BM, MM, and DMA in Music. Non-degree programs: Certificate (undergraduate in Dance, Drama, and Music), Advanced Certificate in Music, Professional Studies in Music.

Costs. Tuition: $9,800. Fees: $550. Room and board: $5,500.

. . . .

Standardized tests: Not required.

Interview: Required as part of the audition for certain departments and for all DMA applicants.

Videotapes: Required for first-time college Voice and all Opera applicants. (Audio tapes also accepted, but videos in American format VHS preferred.) Not accepted for Drama. Accepted as prescreening in Dance.

Admissions criteria: Audition most important. Academic profile and personal qualities also considered.

Musical instruments taught: All Orchestral, All Keyboard, Classical Guitar (graduate level only). Also Orchestral Conducting, Voice, Composition, Accompanying. No Jazz and No Saxophone.

Facilities include: 5 major theaters and concert and recital halls located at Lincoln Center for the Performing Arts, black box theaters, flexible space, electronic music studio, music library, video library, listening library, archives, instrument rental library, rehearsal spaces, practice rooms, organ and percussion practice rooms, dance studios with sprung floors; costume, props, wig, and scene shops.

Financial aid: Available. File FAF, Juilliard Financial Aid application, and supporting documents. Based on merit and need. Merit scholarships awarded on occasion.

Housing: New Meredith Willson Residence Hall houses 375 students in luxury suites overlooking Lincoln Center. All freshmen who do not reside with their parents in Manhattan are required to live in the Residence Hall.

International students: 33% of the student body is from abroad. Korea, Japan, Canada, Germany, China (PRC) most represented. For Dance, a videotape of the applicant performing both modern dance and ballet will be accepted with the application for prescreening to inform the applicant if it is worthwhile to make the trip for the personal audition. Music also accepts audio tapes or videotapes of the audition repertoire for prescreening. Financial aid is available for foreign students. The FAF and supporting documents must be filed. TOEFL or Juilliard's English Proficiency Exam required.

Prominent alumni include: Drama—Kevin Kline, Patty LuPone, Kelly McGillis, Christopher Reeve, Robin Williams. Dance—Pina Bausch, Martha Clark, Bruce Marks, Dennis Nahat, Paul Taylor, Michael Uthoff. Music—Yo Yo Ma, Wynton Marsalis, Itzhak Perlman, Leontyne Price, Leonard Slatkin.

AUTHOR'S COMMENT: Highly recommended for Drama and Dance. Highly recommended for graduate programs in Accompanying, Guitar, Orchestral Conducting, and Voice. Highly recommended for undergraduate and graduate programs in Bassoon, Clarinet, Composition, Double Bass, English Horn, Flute, French Horn, Harp, Harpsichord, Oboe, Organ, Percussion, Piano, Trombone, Trumpet, Tuba, Viola, Violin, Violoncello, and Voice.

Kansas State University

Manhattan, KS 66506

Admissions: 913-532-6250
Dept. of Music: 913-532-5740
Dept. of Theater and Speech: 913-532-6875
Dept. of Dance: 913-532-6875

Enrollment. University: 36,449 undergraduates, 6,905 graduates. Drama majors: 60 undergraduates (25 males, 35 females); 15 graduate students (6 males, 9 females). Music majors: 120 undergraduates, 25 graduate students.
Music faculty. 21 full time, 3 part time.
Application deadline. Rolling to April 1.
Audition. Not required in general, but held for certain scholarships.
Degrees offered. BA, BS in Theater. BA in Musical Theater. MA, BA, BM, MM in Music.
Costs. Tuition: In-state—$1,600 per year; out-of-state—$4,800. Room and board: $2,640.

• • • • • • • • • • • • • • • • • •

Standardized tests: SAT or ACT required.
Tapes: Not accepted in Drama. Tapes or videos accepted in Music.
Musical instruments taught: All Band and Orchestral, All Keyboard, Early Music Instruments, Guitar. Also has programs in Early Music, Electronic Music, Jazz, and Marching Band.
Facilities include: Drama—250-seat thrust theater, 1,800-seat proscenium theater, 100-seat thrust theater. Music—2,000-seat auditorium, 400-seat recital hall, 300-seat theater.
Financial aid: Must submit the FFS. Merit scholarships also available.
Housing: 100% of new students offered on-campus housing.
International students: 6% of entire student body is from abroad. 4% of Drama students are from abroad. TOEFL required—550 minimum. June 1 application deadline for fall semester. International students must have a guarantee of sufficient finances to complete the year. Limited financial aid available for foreign students.
Prominent alumni include: Matt Betton, Gordon Jump, Samuel Ramey, Jerry Wexler.

AUTHOR'S COMMENT: *Recommended for Drama, Dance, and Musical Theater.*

Kent State University

Kent, OH 44242

Admissions: 216-672-2444
School of Music: 216-672-2172
School of Theater: 216-672-2082
School of Dance: 216-672-2069

Enrollment. University: 23,000. Drama majors: 142. Music majors: 220 undergraduates; 80 graduate students.
Faculty. Dance: 5 full time, 3 part time. Drama: 11 full time, 1 part time. Music: 36 full time, 10 part time.
Application deadlines. Undergraduates in Music: June 1 for fall, December 1 for spring. Graduate students in Music: August 1 for fall, December 1 for spring. March 1 for Dance majors.
Audition. Required. Music applicants must also take music theory, music history, and piano placement exams. Auditions are held November-May on campus.
Degrees offered. BS in Dance. BA in General Theater, BFA in Acting. BFA in Musical Theater, BA, BM, MM, MA, Ph.D in Music.
Costs. Tuition and fees: $3,006. Room and board: $2,678.

• • • • • • • • • • • • • • • • • •

Standardized tests: SAT or ACT required.
Tapes: Accepted in Music when personal audition is impossible.
Musical instruments taught: All Orchestral, Harpsichord, Guitar, Various Ethnic Instruments. Also Composition, Electronic Music, Jazz Studies, Voice.
Facilities: Drama: 525-seat theater, 199-seat theater, 60-seat theater, scene, costume, props shops, dance studio. Music: Ludwig Recital Hall, Stump Theater, Student Center, ballroom, Kiva.
Financial aid: Available; submit the FAF. Merit scholarships also available.
Housing: Freshmen and sophomores must live in campus housing.
International students: 5% from abroad. China (PRC), Japan, Greece, Malaysia most represented. TOEFL required—525 minimum. Some financial aid available for foreign students.
Prominent music alumni include: Susan Banks, Bill Dobbins, Donald Erb, Eugene Hartzell, Andrew Parr, Susan Wallin, Sally Wolff.

AUTHOR'S COMMENT: *Recommended for Dance, Drama, and Musical Theater.*

Kenyon College

P.O. Box 708
Gambier, OH 43022-9624

Admissions: 614-427-5776
Dance and Drama Depts.: 614-427-5531

Enrollment. 1,500. Drama majors: 25.
Drama faculty. 6 full time, 1 part time.
Application deadlines. Early Decision I: December 1, Early Decision II: February 1. Regular Decision: February 15.
Audition. Not required.
Degrees offered. BA.
Costs. Tuition, room, board, and fees: $21,180.

. . . .

Standardized tests: SAT or ACT required. Achievement tests optional.
Interview: Recommended.
Videotape: Accepted. Send to the Office of Admissions to be referred to the department for evaluation.
Financial aid: Available. Submit the FAF.
Housing: 100% of new students receive on-campus housing.
Prominent drama alumnus: Paul Newman, Jonathan Winters.

AUTHOR'S COMMENT: Kenyon is a very strong small liberal arts college. Recommended for undergraduate Drama.

Koninklijk Conservatorium voor Musiek en Dans (Royal Conservatory of Music and Dance, The Hague)

1 Juliana van Stolberglaan
2595 CA The Hague, NETHERLANDS

070-63-99-25 or 070- 81-42-51

Enrollment. Conservatory: 850.
Music faculty. 200.
Audition. Required.

. . . .

Facilities: Music library, concert halls, studios.
Financial aid: Some scholarships from the Dutch government are awarded to foreign students.

AUTHOR'S COMMENT: Recommended for Harpsichord and Early Music.

Lawrence University Conservatory of Music

P.O. Box 599
Appleton, WI 54912-0599

Admissions: 1-800-227-0982
Music Dept.: 414-832-6612

Enrollment. University: 1,250. Music majors: 200 undergraduates.
Music faculty. 26 full time.
Application deadlines. Early Decision I: December 1. Early Decision II: January 15. Regular Decision: February 15. Transfer deadlines: December 5 and May 15.
Audition. Required. Held in November–February on campus and regionally in Boston, New York City, Interlochen, St. Louis, San Francisco, Seattle. Call University for exact dates and locations. Music theory exam also required.

(continued on next page)

Degrees offered. BA in Music. BM in Performance, 5 year BA/BM.
Costs. Tuition: $14,685. Fees: $650. Room: $1,461. Board: $1,902.

. . . .

Standardized tests: SAT or ACT required.
Interview: Required as part of audition.
Music facilities include: 250-seat recital hall, 1,250-seat concert hall, 350-seat flexible space.
Musical instruments taught: All Orchestral Instruments, Classical Guitar, Piano, Organ, Harpsichord. Also Voice.
Financial aid: FAF and Lawrence University form must be filed. All admissions are need-blind. Academic scholarships and performance awards are merit-based.
Housing: 100% of new students receive on-campus housing.
International students: 8% from abroad. India, Pakistan, China, Netherlands, Japan, and Korea most represented. TOEFL required—575 minimum. Applications due by January 15. Full and partial scholarships are available.
Prominent alumni include: Dale Duesing, Robert McDonald, Richard Westenburg.

AUTHOR'S COMMENT: The Conservatory in general is strong and it is difficult to cite a single department.

London Academy of Performing Arts

861/863 Fulham Road
London SW6 5HT, ENGLAND

44-71-736-0121

Enrollment. 40 acting students.
Drama faculty. 7 full time, 2 part time.
Audition. Required for full-time students and for scholarship consideration.
Degrees offered. Diploma, Postgraduate Diploma.
Costs. £6,000.

. . . .

Admissions criteria: Audition, interview, recommendations, résumé, experience.
Facilities: 100-seat theater, 50-seat theater.

AUTHOR'S COMMENT: Recommended for non-degree Drama.

London Contemporary Dance School

The Place, 17 Duke's Road
London, WC1H 9AB, ENGLAND

01-071-387-0152

Enrollment. 55 Dance majors (15 males, 40 females).
Dance faculty. 6 full time, 4 part time.
Application deadlines. July 15 for September entry.
Audition. Required. Dates and locations to be announced.
Degrees offered. BA, M.Ph., MA, 4th year Diploma, 1- and 3-year Certificates.
Costs. Tuition: £6,500.

. . . .

Interview: Required.
Videotapes: Accepted in exceptional circumstances.
Exchange programs with: CalARTS, Juilliard, SUNY Purchase, and University of Utah.
Prominent alumni include: Kim Brandstrup, Síobhán Davies, Robert North.

AUTHOR'S COMMENT: Highly recommended for undergraduate Dance (modern).

Long Island University/C.W. Post Campus

Route 25A
Brookville, NY 11548

Admissions: 516-299-2413
Dept. of Theater and Film: 516-299-2353

Enrollment. University: 22,000. Drama majors: 90.
Drama faculty. 6 full time, 7 part time.
Audition. Required.
Degrees offered. BA in Theater, BFA in Acting, MA in Acting.
Costs. Tuition and fees: $9,170. Room and board: $4,360.

. . . .

Interview: Required.
Drama facilities include: 120-seat theater, 60- seat theater, scene and costume shops, dance studios.
Financial aid: Submit the FAF.

AUTHOR'S COMMENT: Recommended for undergraduate Drama and Musical Theater.

Los Angeles City College Los Angeles Theater Academy

855 North Vermont Avenue
Los Angeles, CA 90029

Production Office: 213-953-4382 or
213-953-4336

Enrollment. Academy: 80 students (30 males, 50 females).

Deadline for applications. June 1 for fall semester, December 1 for spring semester.

Audition. Required. Held in May, June, August, and September.

Degrees offered. AA and Academy Certificate of completion.

Costs. California residents: Tuition—$100 per year. Out-of-state tuition—approximately $2,000 per year.

. . . .

Interview: Required; held at time of the audition.

Videotapes: Not accepted.

Admissions criteria: Quality of the audition, previous training in Drama, application essay, grades in school.

Drama facilities include: 325-seat theater, 49-seat theater, 75-seat theater.

Financial aid: Available; handled through the Financial Aid Office: 213-953-4441.

Housing: Not available through the school.

International students: 10% to 15% of student body is from abroad. Mexico, China, Denmark, Iceland, Holland, France most represented. No financial aid available for foreign students.

Prominent drama alumni include: Diana Canova, James Coburn, Charles Gordone, Mark Hamill, Hugh O'Brian, José Quintero, Donna Reed, Paul Winfield.

AUTHOR'S COMMENT: A limited number of talented actors participate in an intensive professional actor training program. Located near television and film studios.

Louisiana State University

110 Thomas Boyd Hall
Baton Rouge, LA 70803

Admissions: 504-388-1175
School of Music: 504-388-3261

School of Music Address:
ZIP Code: 70803-2504

Enrollment. University: 21,000 undergraduates, 4,000 graduates. Music majors: 220 undergraduates, 130 graduates.

Music faculty. 48 full time, 1 part time.

Application deadline. Rolling admissions but before July 1.

Audition. Required. Undergraduate transfer students must also take placement test in music theory. Graduate students must take advisory exams in music history and music theory.

Degrees offered. BM, BA, MM, Ph.D.

Costs. Tuition and fees: $1,802. Room and board: $4,748.

. . . .

Standardized tests: ACT required. Achievement tests optional.

Videotapes: Contact Dr. John Raush at the School of Music about submitting audition tapes.

Interviews: Optional.

Musical instruments taught: Piano, Organ, All Orchestral Instruments, Saxophone, Composition. Also Voice.

Music facilities include: 300-seat Music School Recital Hall, Union Theater and University Theater for large groups and opera.

Financial aid: Available; submit the FAF.

International students: TOEFL required—550 minimum.

Prominent alumni include: Alvin Batiste, Bill Conti, Anne Epperson, Carl Fontana, James King, Marguerite Piazza, Travis Paul Groves.

AUTHOR'S COMMENT: Some fine musicians teach here and the school has produced some excellent students. Recommended for Church Music, Oboe, and Voice.

Loyola University of New Orleans

3363 St. Charles Avenue
New Orleans, LA 70118-6195

Admissions: 504-865-3240
Dept. of Drama and Speech: 504-865-3840

Enrollment. University: 5,400. Drama majors: 36. Music majors: 175 undergraduates, 23 graduates.
Faculty. Drama: 6 full time, 2 part time. Music: 20 full time, 22 part time.
Application deadline. Rolling admissions, but by August 1.
Degrees offered. BA in Drama. BM, MM in Music.
Costs. Tuition and fees: $8,698. Room and board: $4,748.

. . . .

Standardized tests: SAT or ACT required. Achievement tests optional.
Interviews: Recommended.
Drama facilities include: 154-seat theater, 80-seat theater, scene shop, mime studio, classrooms.
Financial aid: Submit the FAF.

AUTHOR'S COMMENT: A Jesuit university, Loyola can be recommended for undergraduate Drama and Jazz. Its College of Music also has some other strong departments.

Luther College

Decorah, IA 52101-1045

Admissions: 319-387-1287

Enrollment. College: 2,300.
Application deadline. Rolling, but by March 1 recommended.
Audition. Not required.
Costs. Tuition and fees: $10,600. Room and board: $3,300.

. . . .

Standardized tests: SAT or ACT required.
Interview: Recommended.
Tapes: Cassettes or videotapes may be sent to the Office of Admission to be referred to the Music Department.
Financial aid: Submit the FAF by March 1.

AUTHOR'S COMMENT: Affiliated with the Lutheran Church, this small liberal arts college is recommended for undergraduate Choral Conducting.

Macalester College

1600 Grand Avenue
St. Paul, MN 55105-1899

Admissions: 612-696-6357 or 1-800-231-7974

Enrollment. College: 1,700.
Application deadlines. Early Decision: December 1 and January 15. Regular Decision: February 1.
Audition. Not required.
Costs. Tuition and fees: $12,471. Room and board: $3,714.

• • • • • • • • • • • • • • • •

Standardized tests: SAT or ACT required. Achievement test optional.
Interview: Recommended.
Tapes: Cassettes or videotapes may be sent to the Office of Admissions to be referred to the department for evaluation.
Financial aid: Available. Submit FAF by March 1.
International students: 10% from abroad; 65 different countries represented.

AUTHOR'S COMMENT: A wonderful Midwestern small liberal arts college, Macalester is recommended for undergraduate Drama and Guitar.

Manhattan School of Music

120 Claremont Avenue
New York, NY 10027

Admissions: 212-749-3025
General number: 212-749-2802

Enrollment. 400 undergraduates, 418 graduate students.
Music faculty. 25 full time, 220 part time.
Application deadlines. July 1 for fall semester; December 1 for spring semester.
Audition. Required. Held in New York in January, March, May, and August. Also held regionally; call for exact dates and locations.
Degrees offered. BM, MM, DMA. Nondegree programs: Diploma, Postgraduate Diploma, Professional Studies, Certificate.
Costs. Tuition and fees: $9,650.

• • • • • • • • • • • • • • • •

Tapes: Cassettes and videotapes accepted for those residing outside of North America.
Musical instruments taught: All Orchestral Instruments, Piano, Classical Guitar, Organ, Harpsichord. Also Accompanying, Composition, Jazz Program Including All Major Instruments, Voice.
Cross-registration: With Barnard College.
Exchange program: Royal Conservatory, Toronto.
Facilities include: 1,000-seat Borden Auditorium; 250-seat Hubbard Hall, a recital hall with organ; 60-seat Pforzheimer Hall; Myers Hall and recording studio.
Financial aid: FAF required. Some merit-based scholarships available.
Housing: 5% of new students receive on-campus housing.
International students: 34% from abroad. Korea, Taiwan, Canada, Japan, Israel most represented. TOEFL required—600 minimum for DMA, 550 minimum for Professional Studies Certificate, 450 minimum for all other programs. No financial aid for foreign students. Some merit awards available.
Prominent alumni include: Ron Carter, Harry Connick Jr., John Corigliano, Timothy Eddy, Catherine Malfitano, Johanna Meier, Abby Simon, Dawn Upshaw.

AUTHOR'S COMMENT: Recommended for Bassoon, Clarinet, Double Bass, Flute, French Horn, Guitar, Harp, Jazz/Commercial music, Oboe, Organ, Percussion, Piano, Saxophone, Trombone, Trumpet, Violin, and Violoncello. Highly recommended for Voice.

Manhattanville College

Purchase, NY 10577

914-694-2200

Enrollment. College: 2,050. Music majors: 40.
Music faculty. 14 full time, 17 part time.
Application deadlines. Early Decision: December 1. Regular Decision: March 1.
Audition. Required in Music.
Degrees offered. BA, BM.
Costs. Tuition and fees: $11,660. Room and board: $5,250.

. . . .

Standardized tests: SAT or ACT required. English and math achievement tests required.
Interview: Recommended.
Tapes: Cassettes or videotapes accepted. Call department for guidelines. Personal audition preferred.
Financial aid: Submit the FAF by March 1.

AUTHOR'S COMMENT: Located about 45 minutes outside New York City and down the street from SUNY, Purchase, Manhattanville, once a Catholic, all-female college, is now co-ed and has a fine Music Department.

Mannes College of Music

150 West 85th Street
New York, NY 10024

Admissions: 212-580-0210 or 1-800-292-3040

Enrollment. 103 undergraduates, 122 graduate students.
Music faculty. 25 full time, 125 part time.
Application deadlines. Rolling for fall semester; December 1 for spring semester.
Audition. Required. Held in New York in March, May, and August and regionally in February. Call Admissions for exact dates and locations. Applicants also required to take placement examinations in music theory, ear training, piano proficiency, and English (for international applicants).
Degrees offered. BM, BS, MM. Non-degree programs: Undergraduate Diploma, Postgraduate Diploma, Professional Studies diploma.
Costs. Tuition: $10,100. Fees: $150. Room: $4,500.

. . . .

Tapes: Accepted for prescreening only. Personal audition required before acceptance is granted.
Instruments taught: All Orchestral Instruments, Piano, Saxophone, Guitar, Jazz, Composition, Orchestral and Choral Conducting. Also Early Music and Voice.
Cross-registration: Available with New School for Social Research, Hunter College, and Marymount Manhattan College.
Financial aid: Submit FAF and College's own form. Merit awards available.
International students: 47% from abroad. Korea, Taiwan, Japan, Israel, Canada most represented.
Prominent alumni include: Richard Goode, Eugene Istomin, Murray Perahia, Eve Queler, Julius Rudel, Frederica von Stade.

AUTHOR'S COMMENT: Recommended for Double Bass, Early Music, Guitar, Jazz, Orchestral Conducting, Percussion, Piano, Viola, Violin, and Violoncello.

Marymount Manhattan College

221 East 71st Street
New York, NY 10021

Admissions: 212-517-0555
Drama Dept.: 212-517-0475

Enrollment. College: 1,400. Drama majors: 175 undergraduates (70 males, 105 females).
Application deadlines. Rolling; for best chance for scholarships and financial aid apply by March 1, for fall semester, November 1 for spring semester.
Audition. Required for BFA and for scholarships; Held at the campus November through March.
Degrees offered. BA in Theater. BFA in Acting.
Costs. Tuition and fees: $8,800.

. . . .

Videotapes: Accepted. Must include 2 short, contrasting monologues.
Admissions criteria: Quality of the audition, grades in school, standardized test scores, previous training, and consideration of the "total person."
Drama facilities include: Modern proscenium, Off-Broadway theater, black box, studio spaces.
Financial aid: Available. About 80% of students receive some form of financial aid. Must file FAF. Based on merit and need.
Housing: 85% of those who request housing are accommodated.
International students: 5% from abroad. Greece, England, Germany, Spain most represented. TOEFL required. No financial aid available for foreign students.
Prominent alumni include: Kelly Coffield, Moira Kelly.

AUTHOR'S COMMENT: Recommended for undergraduate Drama.

Massachusetts Institute of Technology (MIT)

77 Massachusetts Avenue
Cambridge, MA 02139-4307

Admissions: 617-258-5515
Music Dept.: 617-253-3210

Enrollment. Institute: 10,210. Music majors: 10.
Music faculty. 11 full time.
Application deadlines. Early Action: December 15. Regular Decision: January 1.
Auditions. Required for scholarships for private lessons; held before registration for admitted students only.
Degrees offered. BS, MM, Ph.D in Music.
Costs. Tuition, room, and board: $24,250.

. . . .

Standardized tests: SAT or ACT required. GRE required for graduate students. Achievement tests required: one in math, others in science, English, or history.
Interview: Alumni interview required.
Musical instruments taught: All. Also has an Electronic Music program.
Cross-registration: With Wellesley College and Harvard.

AUTHOR'S COMMENT: Recommended for Electronic Music.

Miami University
Oxford, OH 45056

Admissions: 513-529-2531
Dept. of Music: 513-529-3014

Enrollment. University: 13,000 undergraduates, 3,000 graduate students. Music majors: 200 undergraduates, 30 graduate students.
Music faculty. 30 full time, 7 part time.
Application deadlines. Early Decision: November 1. Regular Decision: January 31.
Audition. Required. Music theory exam also required.
Degrees offered. BA, BM, MM in Music.
Costs. Tuition and fees: In-state—$3,388; out-of-state—$7,368. Room and board: $3,100.

• • • • • • • • • • • • • • • •

Standardized tests: SAT or ACT required. GRE required for graduate students.
Tapes: Accepted. Contact Music department for guidelines.
Musical instruments taught: All Orchestral Instruments, Keyboards. Also Composition and Voice.
Financial aid: Submit FAF. Some Music merit awards available.
International students: 4% from abroad. Luxembourg, Taiwan, and Canada most represented. TOEFL required. Some financial aid available for foreign students.

AUTHOR'S COMMENT: Music department is strong.

Michigan State University
East Lansing, MI 48824

Admissions: 517-355-8332
Dept. of Theater: 517-355-6690

Music Dept. Address:
105 Music Building

Dept. of Theater Address:
149 Auditorium Building

Enrollment. University: 42,780.
Application deadline. Rolling admissions. Must apply 1 month prior to the start of the term, however.
Audition. Not required for admission to the University but may be required by the department. Call the department for guidelines.
Costs. Tuition, room and board: In-state—$6,900; out-of-state—$12,127.

• • • • • • • • • • • • • • • •

Standardized tests: SAT or ACT required. Achievement tests optional.
Interview: Not required.
Financial aid: Submit the FAF.

AUTHOR'S COMMENT: Recommended for undergraduate Drama, Dance, Clarinet, Double Bass, and Oboe.

Middlebury College

Middlebury, VT 05753-6001

Admissions: 802-388-3711, ext. 5153
Dept. of Theater, Dance, and Film/Video:
802-388-3711, ext. 5601
Dept. of Music: 802-388-3711, ext. 5221

Enrollment. College: 1,950 undergraduates. Drama majors: 25 (10 males, 15 females).
Faculty. Drama: 5 full time, 1 part time. Music: 5 full time, 15 part time.
Application deadline. Early Decision: November 15. Regular Decision: January 15.
Audition. Not required.
Degrees offered. BA.
Costs. Tuition, room, and board: $21,200.

• • • • • • • • • • • • • • • • • • •

Standardized tests: SAT, ACT, or five achievement tests (English composition and four others) required.
Videotapes: Accepted by Theater Department to give Office of Admissions an assessment. Department prefers medium close-up of a naturalistic monologue. Not encouraged for the Music Department.
Admissions criteria: Courses and grades in school, standardized test scores, personal profile, essay, recommendations. In general, admission to Middlebury is highly competitive. Applicants must be admitted to the College, not to the department.
Musical instruments taught: Violin, Viola, Violoncello, Flute, Clarinet, Trumpet, French Horn, Piano, Saxophone, Composition. Also Electronic Music program and Voice.
Exchange program: Drama students have the opportunity to work with an Equity company: The Potomac Theater Project, in Washington, D.C.
Facilities: Brand new multimillion-dollar performing arts center, including proscenium stage and student center.
Financial aid: Submit the FAF.
International students: 5% from abroad. Countries most represented: Great Britain, France, Germany, Brazil, India. Very limited financial aid available for students from abroad and an application for aid may influence the admissions decision.
Prominent alumni include: Drama—Charles Frank, Mel Gussow, Amanda Plummer, Jake Weber. Music—Andy Wentzel.

AUTHOR'S COMMENT: Recommended as a strong Drama program within the context of a competitive, bucolic liberal arts college.

Mills College

5000 MacArthur Boulevard
Oakland, CA 94613-1301

Admissions: 415-430-2135

Enrollment. College: 1,000 (women only).
Application deadlines. Early Decision: November 1. Regular Decision: February 1.
Audition. Not required.
Costs. Tuition and fees: $13,005. Room and board: $5,100.

• • • • • • • • • • • • • • • • • • •

Standardized tests: SAT or ACT required. Achievement tests recommended.
Interview: Recommended.
Tapes: Cassettes or videotapes may be sent to the Office of Admissions to be referred them to the department for evaluation.
Financial aid: Submit the FAF.

AUTHOR'S COMMENT: Recommended for Dance. Ethnomusicology also is strong in the Music Department. The composer John Cage was once on this faculty.

Montclair State College

Upper Montclair, NJ 07456

Admissions: 201-893-4444
Music Dept.: 201-893-5228

Enrollment. College: 8,000 undergraduates, 4,000 graduate students. Music majors: 120 undergraduates, 60 graduate students.
Music faculty. 18 full time, 35 part time.
Application deadlines. March 1 for fall semester, November 15 for spring semester.
Audition. Required.
Degrees offered. BA, BM, MM in Music.
Costs. Tuition and fees: In-state—$2,255; out-of-state—$3,185. Room and board: $4,132.

. . . .

Interview: Required for composers.
Tapes: Cassettes and videotapes accepted.
Musical instruments taught: All. Also has Jazz and Electronic Music programs.
Financial aid: Submit FAF. Departmental merit awards available.
International students: 5% from abroad. Korea, China (PRC), United Kingdom most represented. TOEFL required.
Prominent alumni include: Melba Moore, Paul Plishka, George Rochberg.

AUTHOR'S COMMENT: Montclair's Music Department has many fine teachers and it is a good bargain for New Jersey residents.

Mount Holyoke College

College Street
South Hadley, MA 01075

Admissions: 413-538-2023

Enrollment. 1,880 (women only).
Application deadlines. Early Decision: November 15 and January 15. Regular Decision: February 1.
Audition. Not required.
Costs. Tuition and fees: $15,150. Room and board: $4,600.

. . . .

Standardized tests: SAT required. Achievement tests: English Composition and 2 others required.
Interview: Required.
Tapes: Cassettes or videotapes may be sent to the Office of Admissions to be referred to the department for evaluation.
Financial aid: Submit FAF by February 1.

AUTHOR'S COMMENT: Recommended for Dance (Part of Five College Department) and Guitar.

Muhlenberg College

Allentown, PA 18104

Admissions: 215-821-3200
Dept. of Drama and Speech: 215-821-3330

Enrollment. College: 1,500. Drama majors: 28 (10 males, 18 females).
Drama faculty. 5 full time, 3 part time.
Application deadlines. January 15 for Early Decision, February 15 for fall semester, September 15 for spring semester.
Audition. Required for scholarship in Drama and recommended for admissions purposes. Held by appointment with the Drama Department.
Degrees offered. BA in Drama.
Costs. Tuition: $15,115. Fees: $65. Room and board: $4,260.

. . . .

Standardized tests: SAT or ACT required. Achievement tests: English Composition, Math I or II, and 1 other required.
Interview: Recommended.
Videotapes: Accepted; should include a 3-minute monologue and song, if desired.
Admissions criteria: Admission to the college, quality of audition, grades in school, standardized test scores, application essays, recommendations, previous knowledge of student through a summer or pre-college program.
Drama facilities: 392-seat theater, black box theater.
Financial aid: Available. Must submit the FAF and Muhlenberg form. The Drama Department offers 2 merit scholarships, determined by the audition and interview.
Housing: 95% of new students receive on-campus housing.
International students: 3% from abroad. Australia and Greece most represented. TOEFL required. Financial aid available for foreign students, but applying for it may affect the admissions decision.
Prominent drama alumna: Kam Chang.

AUTHOR'S COMMENT: Muhlenberg has a fine Drama Department. The Muhlenberg London Theatre Studies program affords students time to study with British theater professionals. There is also a noteworthy Summer Music Theater Festival company.

National Shakespeare Conservatory

591 Broadway
New York, NY 10012

212-219-9874

Enrollment. 135.
Drama faculty. 12 full time, 1 part time.
Application deadline. Rolling.
Audition. Required. Held in February and by arrangement.
Degrees offered. Certificate in Acting.
Costs. $5,300 per year.

. . . .

Interview: Required as part of audition.
Drama facilities: 70-seat theater, dance studio, rehearsal space.
Financial aid: FAF required. Some merit scholarships available, based primarily on the audition and interview.

AUTHOR'S COMMENT: Recommended for non-degree Drama.

National Theater Conservatory

1050 13th Street
Denver, CO 80204

303-893-4000, ext. 473

Enrollment. 49 students.
Drama faculty. 10 full time, 4 part time.
Application deadline. January 15.
Audition. Required.
Degrees offered. MFA in Acting.
Costs. $7,750, first year; $4,650 second year; stipend for third year. No housing.

. . . .

Interview: Required as part of audition.
Drama facilities: 550-seat theater, 450-seat theater, 155-seat theater, 199-seat theater, scene shop, costume shop, prop shop, welding shop, dance studio, rehearsal space, classrooms.

AUTHOR'S COMMENT: The Conservatory is affiliated with the Denver Center Theater Company, an Equity company. Recommended for graduate Drama.

National Theater Institute

Eugene O'Neill Theater Center
305 Great Neck Road
Waterford, CT 06385

203-443-7139

Enrollment. 40 students from colleges and universities all over the world.
Application deadline. Rolling: Before November 15 for spring semester; before April 15 for fall semester.
Audition. Not required.
Costs. Tuition, room, and board: $9,500.

· · · · · · · · · · · · · · · · · ·

Interview: Required.
Videotape: Not encouraged.
Admissions criteria: Application, personal essays, recommendations, transcript of college work all considered.

AUTHOR'S COMMENT: This is a highly intensive, selective, one-semester program (offered twice a year). It is affiliated with Connecticut College, so college credit is possible. Many serious acting students at small liberal arts colleges apply to spend a semester here. Highly recommended for non-degree Drama.

New England Conservatory

290 Huntington Avenue
Boston, MA 02115-5018

Admissions: 617-262-1120

Enrollment. 370 undergraduates, 371 graduate students.
Music faculty. 55 full time, 123 part time.
Application deadlines. January 15 for fall semester; November 15 for spring semester.
Auditions. Required and held in Boston and regionally January–March. Call for exact dates and locations.
Degrees offered. BM, MM. Nondegree programs: Diploma, Graduate Diploma, and Artist Diploma.
Costs. Tuition: $12,000. Room and board: $5,850.

· · · · · · · · · · · · · · · · · ·

Standardized tests: SAT or ACT required.
Cross-registration: Available with Simmons College, Northeastern University, and Tufts University.
Tapes: Cassette or videotapes accepted.
Musical instruments taught: All Orchestral Instruments, Piano. Also Accompanying, Composition, Voice, Jazz Studies, Historical Performance, and Third Stream Studies.
Financial aid: Submit FAF and Conservatory's own form. All financial aid is need- and merit-based.
International students: 27% from abroad. Japan, Korea, Taiwan, Canada, and Brazil most represented.
Prominent alumni include: Sarah Caldwell, Rosalind Elias, Coretta Scott King, Jean Kraft, John Oliver, Lisa Saffer, Lucy Shelton, Eleanor Steber.

AUTHOR'S COMMENT: Recommended for Accompanying, Double Bass, Early Music, Flute, Guitar, Harp, Jazz, Orchestral Conducting, Piano, Trombone, Trumpet, Tuba, Viola, Violoncello, Voice.

New School for Social Research

Eugene Lang College
65 West 11th Street
New York, NY 10011

212-741-5617

Enrollment. 6,250; 400 undergraduates.
Application deadlines. Early Decision: November 15.
Regular Decision: February 1.
Audition. Required. Call for appointment.
Costs. Tuition and fees: $10,980. Room and board: $6,848.

· · · · · · · · · · · · · · · · ·

Standardized tests: SAT or ACT required. Achievement tests optional.
Cross-registration: With Mannes College of Music.
Interview: Required.
Financial aid: Submit the FAF by March 1.

AUTHOR'S COMMENT: Located in Greenwich Village, the New School is recommended for Jazz.

New World School of the Arts

300 NE 2nd Avenue
Miami, FL 33132

Admissions: 305-347-3472
Dance Dept.: 305-347-3341
Music Dept.: 305-237-3609

Enrollment. 300. Dance majors: 20 males, 65 females. Music majors: 47 undergraduates.
Faculty. Dance: 5 full time, 14 part time. Music: 7 full time, 29 part time.
Application deadline. Rolling.
Audition. Required and held on the campus in January and February. National auditions advertised. Call department for exact dates and locations.
Degrees offered. AA, BFA in Dance. 3-year Dance Certificate. BM in Music.
Costs. In-state: $30.65 per credit; out-of-state: $109.15 per credit.

· · · · · · · · · · · · · · · · ·

Interview: Required.
Videotape: Accepted only if impossible to appear at audition. In Dance, should be at least 2 minutes and no more than 5 minutes of full-shot of applicant in a solo with wide range of technical ability demonstrated.
Cross-registration: With Miami-Dade Community College and Florida International University.
Musical instruments taught: All Orchestral Instruments, Harpsichord, Piano, Classical Guitar. Also has Electronic Music program, Voice.
Dance facilities: 4 dance studios with sprung floors and covered with marley. Access to 3 theaters.
Financial aid: File FAF and School's own form. Merit award available.
International students: 25% from abroad. Costa Rica, Colombia, Argentina, China (PRC), Japan most represented. TOEFL required—550 minimum. International students must file applications at least 3 months before the beginning of a semester.

AUTHOR'S COMMENT: Recommended for Dance. The Music Department graduated its first class in 1992.

New York University

Tisch School of the Arts
721 Broadway, 7th floor
New York, NY 10003

212-998-1900

As of this writing, a new Dean was just hired at NYU. They were unable to complete my questionnaire, but did provide the following information: The graduate acting program provides conservatory actor-training leading to the MFA degree. Artistic Director: Zelda Fichandler. Chair: Ron Van Lieu. The Dance Department provides professional dance training in performance and choreography, leading to a BFA, MFA, or Certificate. Chair: Lawrence Rhodes. Associate Chair: Kay Cummings.
Contact: Roberta Cooper, Director of Alumni Affairs and Recruiting.

AUTHOR'S COMMENT: *Highly recommended for graduate Drama; recommended for Dance and graduate Composition.*

New York University

School of Education, Health, Nursing, and Arts Professions
35 West 4th Street, Suite 777
New York, NY 10003

Undergraduate Admissions: 212-998-4500
Graduate Admissions: 212-998-5030
Music program: 212-998-5420

Enrollment. Music majors: 220 undergraduates; 200 graduate students.
Music faculty. 12 full time, 130 part time.
Application deadlines. February 1 for fall semester, April 1 for transfers.
Audition. Required. Music theory and ear training placement exams and English essay exams required also. Call for specific dates and locations.
Music degrees. BM, BS, MA, MM, Certificate of Advanced Study, DMA, Ph.D.
Costs. Tuition: $14,420. Room and board: $6,650.

. . . .

Standardized tests: SAT required. GRE for graduate students.
Videotapes: Accepted.
Musical instruments taught: All Instruments including Bagpipes. Also has Contemporary, Electronic, Jazz, and Musical Theater programs.
Housing: Approximately 30% of new students receive on-campus housing.
International students: 20% from abroad. Korea, Japan, China (PRC), Taiwan most represented. TOEFL required—500 to 550 minimum.
Prominent alumni include: Cy Coleman, Enoch Light, Jerrold Ross, Wayne Shorter.

AUTHOR'S COMMENT: *Recommended for Bagpipes, Jazz, and Musical Theater.*

North Carolina School of the Arts

200 Waughtown Street
Winston-Salem, NC 27117-2189

919-770-3291 or 1-800-282 ARTS

Enrollment. 460 undergraduates. Dance: 135. Drama: 138. Music: 187.
Audition. Required.
Degrees offered. BM, MM, BFA.
Costs. Tuition: In-state—$1,158; out-of-state—$7,617. Fees: $627. Room: $1,488. Board: $1,675.

• • • • • • • • • • • • • • •

Standardized tests: ACT or SAT required. (ACT minimum: 19; SAT minimum: 800 combined).
Interview: Required.
Tapes: Videotapes accepted in Dance. Cassette tapes accepted in Music, but personal audition preferred.
Admissions criteria: Must have a high school diploma or its equivalent and submit standardized test scores. For high school graduates from the Class of 1990 and beyond, the following courses are required: 4 course units in English, emphasizing grammar, composition, and literature; 3 course units in math, including Algebra I, II, and Geometry; 3 course units in science; 2 course units in social studies; at least 2 course units in 1 foreign language also recommended.

AUTHOR'S COMMENT: Recommended for undergraduate Drama; highly recommended for Dance; also recommended for Clarinet and Guitar.

Northern Illinois University

101 Williston Hall
Dekalb, IL 60115

Admissions: 815-753-0446
School of Music: 815-753-1551
Dept. of Theater Arts: 815-753-1334

Enrollment. University: 20,000 undergraduates, 5,000 graduate students. Drama majors: 140. Music majors: 300 undergraduates, 75 graduate students.
Faculty. Drama: 20 full time, 3 part time. Music: 43 full time, 8 part time.
Audition. Required for Theater program and for consideration for merit scholarships. Required for all Music applicants; held in November–March on campus.
Degrees offered. BA in Dance Performance. BA in Theater. BFA, MFA in Acting. BA, BM, MM, Performer's Certificate in Music.
Costs. Tuition and fees: In-state—$2,431; out-of-state—$5,859. Room and board: $2,706.

• • • • • • • • • • • • • • • • •

Standardized tests: SAT or ACT required. GRE for graduate students.
Interview: Required as part of audition.
Tapes: Accepted in Music only if applicant lives outside of the region.
Admissions criteria: Grades and courses, standardized tests scores, letters of recommendation, but audition most important.
Musical instruments taught: All Orchestral Instruments, Keyboards. Also has Jazz studies, Voice.
Drama facilities: 450-seat theater, 150-seat theater, 125-seat theater, costume shop, scene shop, props shop, welding shop, 2 dance studios, rehearsal spaces, classrooms.
Financial aid: Submit FAF and University's own form. Merit awards available.
International students: 10% from abroad. Taiwan, England, Germany, Brazil, many European countries represented. TOEFL required—550 minimum. Applicants are advised to apply early in March.
Prominent music alumni include: Amanda Halgrimson, Shanghai String Quartet, numerous performers in orchestras throughout the world.

AUTHOR'S COMMENT: Recommended for Drama, Dance, and solid training in Music.

Northwestern University

Evanston, IL 60201

Admissions: 708-491-7271
School of Music Admissions: 708-491-3141
School of Music, general: 708-491-7575

School of Music Address:
711 Elgin Road

School of Speech, Dept. of Theater Address:
1979 Sheridan Road

Enrollment. University: 7,500 undergraduates, 6,000 graduate students. Department of Theater: 360 undergraduates, 80 graduate students. School of Music: 350 undergraduates, 175 graduate students.
Faculty. Drama: 20 full time, 3 part time. Dance: 4 full time, 2 part time. Music: 53 full time, 19 part time.
Application Deadlines. Early Decision: November 1. Regular Decision: January 1.
Audition. Required in Music. Held in 30 cities throughout the United States, January–March. Call School of Music for exact dates and locations. Not required for undergraduate Drama.
Degrees offered. BS, MA in Theater. BA, BM, MM, DMA, Ph.D, Certificate in Music.
Costs. Tuition: $14,370. Room and board: $4,827 (average).

. . . .

Standardized tests: SAT or ACT required. Achievement tests recommended. GRE required for Ph.D applicants.
Tapes: School of Music will accept cassettes and videotapes.
Musical instruments taught: All.
Drama facilities: Theater complex which includes 4 different theaters.
Financial aid: Available. Must file FAF by November 15 (Early Decision) or February 15. Graduate students submit GAPSFAS. Some merit awards available.
Housing: 100% of freshmen receive housing. Lottery system thereafter.
International students: 3% undergraduates, 25% graduate students from abroad. China (PRC), Taiwan, India, Pakistan, United Kingdom most represented. TOEFL required. No financial aid for foreign students. Some merit aid at graduate level in Music.

Prominent alumni include: Drama—Charlton Heston, Ann-Margret, Dermott Mulroney, Peter Strauss. Music—Nancy Gufstafson, Howard Hanson, Cynthia Haymon, Joseph Schwantner, Ralph Votapek, Robert Werner.

AUTHOR'S COMMENT: Highly recommended for Drama; also recommended for Church Music, Clarinet, graduate Electronic Music, Flute, Orchestral Conducting, Piano, Trombone, Trumpet, Violoncello, and Voice. Many of the faculty in the School of Music are members of the Chicago Symphony.

Oberlin College and Oberlin Conservatory

Oberlin, OH 44074-1092

Admissions: 216-775-8411

Enrollment. College and Conservatory: 2,820.
Application deadlines. Early Decision: November 15 or January 2. Regular Decision: February 1.
Audition. Required. Held on the campus and regionally. Call the Conservatory for exact dates and locations. Music theory and ear training exams also required.
Costs. Tuition and fees: $15,645. Room and board: $4,890.

. . . .

Standardized tests: SAT or ACT required. Achievement tests recommended.
Interview: Recommended.
Financial aid: Submit the FAF by February 1.

AUTHOR'S COMMENT: Recommended for Clarinet, Composition, Early Music, Electronic Music, Flute, Harpsichord, Oboe, Organ, Percussion, Tuba, and Viola.

Occidental College

1600 Campus Road
Los Angeles, CA 90041-3393

Admissions: 213-259-2700

Enrollment. 1,680.
Application deadlines. Early Decision: November 15. Regular Decision: January 15.
Audition. Not required.
Costs. Tuition and fees: $13,965. Room and board: $4,859.

. . . .

Standardized tests: SAT or ACT required. Achievement tests recommended.
Interview: Optional.
Facilities: New theater complex.
Financial aid: Submit the FAF or SAAC (California residents) by February 1.

AUTHOR'S COMMENT: Recommended for undergraduate Drama.

Ohio State University

310 Lincoln Tower
1800 Cannon Drive
Columbus, OH 43210

Admissions: 614-292-3980
School of Music: 614-292-5995 or 2870
Dept. of Theater: 614-292-5821
Dance: 614-292-7977

Enrollment. University: 40,120 undergraduates, 14,000 graduate students. Drama majors: 121. Music majors: 375 undergraduates, 190 graduate students.
Faculty. Drama: 19 full time, 4 part time. Music: 59 full time, 9 part time.
Application deadlines. Rolling admissions, but recommended by February 15.

Audition. Required for graduate admissions in Drama and for all Music applicants. Music auditons held in January and February; Music applicants must also take a music theory placement exam.
Degrees offered. BA in General Theater. (Note that the BFA in acting was discontinued in 1989.) MFA in Acting. BA, BM, MM, Ph.D in Music.
Costs. Tuition: In-state—$2,588 per year; out-of-state—$7,608. Room and board: $3,636.

. . . .

Standardized tests: SAT or ACT required. Achievement tests optional. GRE required for graduate students.
Interview: Required for graduate students as part of audition.
Tapes: Cassettes or videotapes accepted but any admission is contingent upon live on-campus audition.
Admissions criteria: GPA, standardized test scores, and audition.
Musical instruments taught: All Instruments except Organ. Has Jazz Studies, Contemporary Music and Electronic Music programs.
Drama facilities: 600-seat theater, 250-seat theater, 70-seat theater, scene shop, costume shop, prop shop, welding shop, dance studio, rehearsal studios, classrooms.
Financial aid: Submit FAF. Some merit awards available.
Housing: All freshmen required to live on campus or at home.
International students: 5% to 7% in Music from abroad. Taiwan, Korea, China (PRC) most represented. TOEFL required—500 minimum. Music talent scholarships available for students from abroad.
Prominent alumni include: Cavani String Quartet, Barbara Daniels, Richard Stoltzman.

AUTHOR'S COMMENT: Recommended for undergraduate Drama; highly recommended for Dance. Has a solid Music program.

Ohio University

120 Chubb Hall
Athens, OH 45701

Admissions: 614-593-4100
School of Dance: 614-593-1826
School of Theater: 614-593-4814

School of Dance Address:
Putnam Hall, 222.

Enrollment. University: 18,000; 14,270 undergraduates. Dance majors: 2 male, 40 female undergraduates.
Faculty. Drama: 19 full time. Dance: 6 full time, 1 part time.
Application deadlines. Rolling admissions to March 1, but earlier recommended.
Audition. Required for Drama, both undergraduate and graduate, and for merit scholarships. Required for Dance.
Degrees offered. BFA, MFA in Acting. BFA in Dance.
Costs. In-state tuition: $907 per quarter; out-of-state tuition: $1,935. Room: $569 per quarter, double room. Board: $589 per quarter, 20 meals per week.

. . . .

Standardized tests: SAT or ACT required. Achievement tests optional.
Interview: Required for Drama.
Videotapes: Accepted from those who live too far away to attend audition on campus or regional auditions.
Admissions criteria: Rank in class, GPA, standardized tests.
Facilities: 3 main theaters seating 300, 302, and 55 respectively, scene shop, costume shop, props shop, rehearsal spaces. 5 dance studios.
Financial aid: Submit FAF. Some merit awards available.
International students: TOEFL required.
Prominent dance alumni include: Bessie Award, Susan Blankensop, Bill Cratty, Tom Evert, and members of Limón and Taylor companies.

AUTHOR'S COMMENT: The Drama program has internship and professional opportunities with many Equity and summer stock companies. Recommended for Drama and Dance.

Ohio Wesleyan University

Delaware, OH 43015-2398

Admissions: 614-368-3020
Dept. of Theater and Dance: 614-368-3845

Enrollment. University: 2,000. Theater and Dance majors: 12 male, 18 female undergraduates.
Theater and dance faculty. 4 full time, 3 part time.
Application deadlines. Early Action: December 31. Regular Decision: March 15.
Audition. Not required.
Degrees offered. BA in Theater or Theater Dance.
Costs. Tuition, room, and board: $19,774.

. . . .

Standardized tests: SAT or ACT required. Achievements tests optional.
Interview: Recommended.
Facilities: Main Theater and Studio Theater of the Chappalear Drama Center.
Financial aid: Submit FAF. Some merit scholarships available.
Housing: 100% of new students receive on-campus housing.
International students: 5% to 10% from abroad. England, Italy, France, Spain, Germany most represented. TOEFL required.
Special program: All majors are urged to acquire an off-campus apprenticeship or study experience during junior or first semester senior year.
Prominent alumni include: Robert E. Lee, Ron Leibman, Ron Phrady, Bob Pine, Dwight Weist.

AUTHOR'S COMMENT: Recommended for Musical Theater.

Paris Conservatoire

(Also listed as: Conservatoire National Supérieur de Musique et de Danse)

209 Avenue Jean Jaurès
75019 Paris, FRANCE

011-33-1.40.40.45.45
FAX: 011-33-1-40.40.45.00

Audition. Required.
Degrees offered. Diploma.

. . . .

AUTHOR'S COMMENT: This world-renowned Conservatory has had among its directors Amboise Thomas, Theodore Dubois, Gabriel Fauré, and Henri Rabaud. It is recommended for Early Music, Guitar, Harp, and Harpsichord.

Peabody Conservatory of Music of Johns Hopkins University

1 East Mount Vernon Place
Baltimore, MD 21202

Admissions: 301-659-8110 or 1-800-368-2521

Enrollment. Conservatory: 245 undergraduates, 310 graduate students.
Music faculty. 71 full time, 59 part time.
Application deadlines. January 1. April 15 (for limited scholarship consideration).
Audition. Required. Music theory and ear training exams also required. Auditions held in February and in May on campus. Traveling auditions held in January in Seoul, Hong Kong, Tokyo, and Taipei.
Degrees offered. BM, MM, DMA. Diploma programs: Peformer's Certificate, Graduate Performance Diploma, Artist Diploma.
Costs. Tuition and fees: $13,000. Room and board: $5,450.

. . . .

Interview: Required of doctoral applicants.
Tapes: Accepted for undergraduates living over 300 miles from Baltimore. Accepted for MM students from abroad only. Live audition preferred.
Musical instruments taught: All Orchestral Instruments, Piano, Organ, Harpsichord, Guitar. Also Voice, Composition, Conducting, Electronic and Computer Music, Early Music, and Jazz Ensemble.
Facilities: 705-seat Miriam A. Friedberg Concert Hall, 200-seat Leakin Recital Hall, 150-seat North Hall.
Financial aid: Available. Submit FAF and institutional form. Some merit scholarships available.
International students: 22% from abroad. Korea, Taiwan, China (PRC), Japan, Canada, Eastern Europe most represented. TOEFL required—500 minimum. Must also file foreign student financial aid form.
Prominent alumni include: Dominick Argento, James Morris, Tommy Newsom, André Watts.

AUTHOR'S COMMENT: Recommended for Piano.

Princeton Ballet School

262 Alexander Street
Princeton, NJ 08540

609-921-7758

Enrollment. 1,200—including summer program. Career Track program—12 to 15.
Dance faculty. 3 full time; 22 part time.
Application deadlines. Varies.
Audition. Required for summer session and Career Track; highly competitive. Audition involves barre and center work, including pointe. Auditions held January–March, various locations, including Boston, Baltimore, Washington, D.C., Philadelphia, Tulsa, Princeton, New York, eastern Pennsylvania. Contact School for exact information.
Degrees offered. Nondegree granting.
Costs. Tuition: summer—$975; fees—$150. Room and board: $1,500.

. . . .

Videotapes: Accepted.
Areas of Dance: Classical ballet (mainly Maggie Black–type); Limón-based technique—Muller style: early Humphrey, Repertory, Jazz, Spanish. Choreography—Tharp-style.
Facilities: 3 dance studios: 50 x 40; 30 x 25; 30 x 20; bounce deck and Marley floors. Performances done in 1,200-seat houses in McCarter Theater in Princeton, State Theater in New Brunswick, and State Theater in Easton, PA.
Financial aid: Scholarships available.
Housing: Summer session housing available at Princeton University.
Prominent alumni include: Jason Jones, Kraig Patterson, Charles Pope.

AUTHOR'S COMMENT: Princeton Ballet School is affiliated with American Repertory Ballet Company (formerly Princeton Ballet). The School offers performing opportunities for younger dancers through the pre-professional training company Princeton Ballet II. It holds an intensive summer program each year plus an intensive Career Track program for local students.

Princeton University

Box 430
Princeton, NJ 08544

Admissions: 609-258-3060

Enrollment. 6,290 students; 4,520 undergraduates.
Application deadlines. Early Action: November 1. Regular Decision: January 2.
Audition. Not required.
Costs. Tuition and fees: $15,440. Room and board: $5,058.

. . . .

Standardized tests: SAT and 3 achievement tests required.
Interview: Recommended.
Tapes: Cassettes or videotapes may be sent to the Office of Admissions to be referred to the department for evaluation.
Financial aid: Submit the FAF by February 1.

AUTHOR'S COMMENT: Recommended for undergraduate Drama and Composition.

Queens College of the City College of New York

Flushing, NY 11367

Admissions: 718-520-7385

Enrollment. 18,093; 14,530 undergraduates.
Admissions deadlines. Rolling admissions, but recommended by January 1.
Audition. Required.
Costs. Tuition: In-state—$1,432; out-of-state—$4,232.

· · · · · · · · · · · · · · · · ·

Standardized tests: SAT and achievement tests recommended for honors and merit scholarships.
Interview: Not required.
Tapes: Personal audition preferred.
Financial aid: Submit the FAF and the College's form.
Housing: No housing available.

AUTHOR'S COMMENT: The view of the Manhattan skyline is pretty spectacular from this fine college of the City University system. The Music Department in general is strong, but especially recommended for Double Bass, Flute.

Rice University Shepard School of Music

P.O. Box 1892
Houston, TX 77251-1892

University Admissions: 713-527-4036
Shepard School of Music: 713-527-4854

Enrollment. 4,230; 2,750 undergraduates.
Application deadlines. Early Decision: November 1. Regular Decision: January 2.
Audition. Required and held January–March or by arrangement. Call the school for exact dates.
Costs. Tuition: $7,700. Room and board: $4,900.

· · · · · · · · · · · · · · · · ·

Standardized tests: SAT required. 3 achievement tests required: English and 2 others.
Interview: Required.
Tapes: Cassettes or videotapes accepted but personal audition preferred.
Financial aid: Submit the FAF. Some merit awards also available.

AUTHOR'S COMMENT: Recommended for Flute, French Horn, Piano, and Violoncello.

Rollins College

Campus Box 2720
Winter Park, FL 32789

Admissions: 407-646-2161
Theater Dept.: 407-646-2501

Enrollment. College: 1,450 undergraduates; Drama: 11 male, 31 female undergraduates.
Application deadlines. Early Decision: November 15 and January 15. Regular Decision: February 15. Transfer admissions: April 15.
Audition. Generally not required, but if you are applying for a number of talent scholarships which are offered through the Theater Department, an audition and interview are required. Auditions are held in February in New York City, Orlando, Dallas, Miami.
Degrees offered. BA in Theater Arts.
Costs. Tuition: $13,500. Fees: $400. Room: $2,320. Board: $1,975.

. . . .

Standardized tests: SAT or ACT required.
Interview: Recommended.
Videotapes: For Priscilla Parker Scholarship but not for admission to the College.
Admissions criteria: Applicants are evaluated by the depth and quality of academic preparation, SAT or ACT score, extracurricular achievements, special talents, and character. Admission is to the College, not the department.
Facilities: Most noteworthy is the Annie Russell Theater. Also 11-seat open stage.
Financial aid: 92% of students receive some form of aid. File FAF by March 1. If applying for special Theater talent scholarships, apply by January 1 for preliminary auditions in February in New York City, Orlando, Dallas, Miami.
International students: Very few enrolled. England and Australia most represented. Limited financial aid available for foreign students .
Prominent alumni include: Freddie Carangelo, Demaris Clement, Buddy Ebsen, Georgia Hovdesven, Dana Ivey, Beth Lincks, Spike McClure, William McNulty, Anthony Perkins, Fred Rogers, Jeff Storer, Robert Warfield.

AUTHOR'S COMMENT: Rollins is a serious liberal arts college in a beautiful setting with a strong and active Theater Department. Recommended for undergraduate Drama.

Royal Academy of Music

Marylebone Road
London, NW1 5HT, ENGLAND

01-935-5461

Degrees offered. Diploma, Professional Certificate, Performer's Course, BM and MM (with University of London).
Costs. £1,500—domestic students; £6,000—international students.

. . . .

Facilities: Theater, Lecture Hall, Library, Sir Jack Lyons Theatre, Sir Henry Wood Library of Orchestral Music, G.D. Cunningham Collection of Organ Music.
Exchange program: With Juilliard.
Musical instruments taught: All Orchestral, Harpsichord, Organ, Piano, Voice, Composition, Conducting, Early Music.

AUTHOR'S COMMENT: Recommended for Early Music, Harpsichord, Guitar, Harp, and Viola.

Royal College of Music

Prince Consort Road
London, SW7 2BS, ENGLAND

01-589-3643

Enrollment. 600.
Music faculty. 170.
Application deadlines. October 1, U.K. applicants. November 1 for applicants from abroad.
Music degrees offered. Performers' Course, Diplomas, BM (with University of London), Advanced Study Course, MM for Composers, Special Course.
Costs. £1,500—domestic students; £6,000—international students.

• • • • • • • • • • • • • • •

Facilities: Practice rooms, teaching studio, concert hall, recital hall, Parry Opera Theatre, Britten Opera Theatre, electronic studio, music library, Museum of Historical Instruments, Department of Musical Portraits, College archives.
Musical instruments taught: All Orchestral, Piano, Composition, Harpsichord, Conducting, Voice. Also has programs in Early Music, Electronic Music, and Repetiteurs' Course.

AUTHOR'S COMMENT: Recommended for Early Music, Composition, Guitar, Harpsichord, Violin, and Voice.

Royal Conservatory of Music

276 Bloor Street, West
Toronto, Ontario, CANADA M5S 1W2

416-978-3756
FAX: 416-978-3793

• • • • • • • • • • • • • • •

AUTHOR'S COMMENT: The former president of the Manhattan School of Music is now the president at the Royal Conservatory in Toronto. The Conservatory is in transition, having separated from the University of Toronto, but shows tremendous promise. Recommended for Piano.

Royal Northern College of Music

124 Oxford Road
Manchester, M13 9RD, ENGLAND

061-273-6283

Enrollment. 500.
Music faculty. 48 full time, 77 part time.
Audition. Required.
Degrees offered. Diploma, BM (with University of Manchester).

• • • • • • • • • • • • • • •

Musical instruments taught: All Orchestral, Piano, Voice. Also has programs in Baroque and Renaissance Music, Composition, and Opera.
Facilities: Practice rooms, Main Concert Hall, Opera Theatre, Music Library, Listening Library.
Financial aid: Available for both domestic and foreign students. Merit-based.
International students: Denmark, Norway, France, Germany, Hong Kong, Iceland, India, Ireland, Japan, Korea, Netherlands, Poland, South Africa, United States all represented.

AUTHOR'S COMMENT: Recommended for Orchestral Conducting, Organ, and Voice.

Rutgers University

Mason Gross School of the Arts
New Brunswick, NJ 08903-2101

Undergraduate Admissions: 908-932-3770
Graduate Admissions: 908-932-7711
Dance Dept.: 908-932-8497
Drama Dept.: 908-932-9891
Music Dept.: 908-932-9302

Enrollment. University: 47,850; 35,200 undergraduates. Mason Gross School of the Arts: 428 undergraduates, 200 graduate students. Drama majors: 52 male, 74 female undergraduates; 50 male, 41 female graduate students. Dance majors: 42 undergraduate females. Music majors: 160 undergraduates, 140 graduate students.

(continued on next page)

Faculty. Drama: 13 full time, 30 part time. Dance: 6 full time, 4 part time. Music: 34 full time, 26 part time.

Application deadlines. Rolling, but no later than March 15 for undergraduates; April 1 for graduate students.

Audition. Required. For all BFA and MFA students in Drama, held in New York, Chicago, Los Angeles, and at Rutgers in January and February. Specific requirements for the auditions are sent to applicants once the Office of Admissions receives the application. Dance auditions in January around the country and in December–May on campus. In Music, held in November, January–April on campus.

Degrees offered. BA, BFA, MFA in Acting. BA, BM, MA, MM, DMA, Ph.D, Artist Diploma in Music.

Costs. Tuition: In-state undergraduates—$3,114; out-of-state undergraduates—$6,338. Undergraduate fees: $732. Tuition: In-state graduate students—$4,432; out-of-state graduate students—$6,496. Graduate fees: $560. Room: $2,344. Board: $1,674.

. . . .

Standardized tests: SAT required.

Tapes: Music will accept cassettes for out-of-state students.

Videotapes: Not accepted in Drama. Accepted in Dance only if the student lives so far from New Brunswick that the cost of travel is prohibitive.

Musical instruments taught: All Orchestral Instruments, Saxophone, Classical Guitar, Piano, Organ, Harpsichord. Also Voice, Composition, Jazz Studies, Conducting.

Facilities: 350-seat black box; 80-seat studio theater; 133-seat studio proscenium theater; 350-seat proscenium theater; scene shops, prop-building and costume design shops, 800-seat concert hall, electronic studio based on the Synclavier II, recital halls, and 4 large dance studios.

Scholarships: Mason Gross School of the Arts, Graduate—20% receive scholarship aid; 50% receive teaching assistantships.

Financial aid: Available. Must submit FAF or GAPSFAS (graduate students).

International students: 2% to 3% undergraduates, 15% graduate students from abroad. TOEFL required—550 to 600 minimum. Financial aid available for foreign students.

AUTHOR'S COMMENT: Recommended for Drama, Dance (modern), Jazz, and Viola.

Saint Olaf College

Northfield, MN 55057

Admissions: 507-663-3025
Dance Dept.: 507-646-3070
Music Dept.: 507-646-3180

Enrollment. 3,000.

Application deadlines. Early Decision: November 15. Regular Decision: February 1.

Audition. Required. Held October–February. Call for exact dates.

Costs. Tuition, room, and board: $16,250.

. . . .

Standardized tests: SAT or ACT required. Achievement tests optional.

Interview: Recommended.

Tapes: Cassettes or videotapes accepted for those who live more than 500 miles from the campus.

AUTHOR'S COMMENT: St. Olaf is affiliated with the Lutheran Church. Recommended for Dance, Choral Conducting, Church Music, and Early Music. The choir at St. Olaf is world renowned.

San Diego State University

San Diego, CA 92182-0219

General information: 619-594-6363
Admissions: 619-594-6871
Dept. of Music: 619-594-6031

Enrollment. University: 35,147. Drama majors: 245. Music majors: 200 undergraduates, 30 graduate students.
Faculty. Drama: 15 full time, 8 part time. Music: 25 full time, 40 part time.
Application deadline. November 1–30.
Audition. Required for graduate school admission in Drama, for certain merit scholarships, and for all Music applicants who must also take music theory, history, ear training, and piano proficiency exams.
Degrees offered. BA in Drama. MFA in Musical Theater, BA, BM, MA, MM in Music.

• • • • • • • • • • • • • • • • • • •

Standardized tests: SAT or ACT required. GRE for graduate students.
Tapes: Cassettes or videotapes accepted in Music.
Admissions criteria: GPA, standardized tests, audition all considered.
Musical instruments taught: All Orchestral, Band, Keyboard Instruments. Also Voice, Composition, Conducting, World Music program.
International students: 2% from abroad. Indonesia, India, China (PRC) most represented. TOEFL required—550 minimum.

AUTHOR'S COMMENT: Recommended for undergraduate Drama; the Music program in general is strong.

San Francisco Conservatory

1201 Ortega Street
San Francisco, CA 94122

Admissions: 415-759-3431

Enrollment. 155 undergraduates; 100 graduate students.
Music faculty. 23 full time, 35 part time.
Application deadline. July 1, but some instruments may have an earlier deadline.
Audition. Required. Held in February and March in San Francisco and regionally. Call the Office of Student Services at the Conservatory for the exact dates and locations.
Degrees offered. BM, MM. Nondegree: Music Diploma, Artist Certificate, Postgraduate Diploma in Vocal Performance.
Costs. Tuition: $9,200. Fees: $200.

• • • • • • • • • • • • • • • • • • •

Standardized tests: SAT or ACT required.
Musical instruments taught: All Orchestral Instruments, all Keyboard Instruments, Classical Guitar. Also Composition, Orchestral Conducting (graduate level only), Chamber Music program, Early Music, Contemporary Music, Electronic Music, Voice.
Facilities: 300-seat Hellman Hall, 75-seat Albert Hall.
Financial aid: Available. Submit FAF and Conservatory's own form. Financial aid decisions are based on merit, financial need, and the musical needs of the Conservatory.
Housing: No on-campus housing.
International students: 28% from abroad. Taiwan, Japan, Korea, Australia, China (PRC) most represented. TOEFL required—450 minimum. Applications should be received well in advance of deadlines. Should also submit the foreign student financial aid application.
Prominent alumni include: Warren Jones, Jeff Kahane, Aaron Kernis, Joel Rosenbaum, David Tanenbaum, members of Ridge Quartet, Franciscan Quartet, Peabody Trio, Philadelphia String Quartet.

AUTHOR'S COMMENT: Recommended for Flute, French Horn, Guitar, Harp, Orchestral Conducting, Percussion, Trombone, Trumpet, and Violin; highly recommended for Violoncello.

San Francisco State University

1600 Holloway Avenue
San Francisco, CA 94132

Admissions: 415-338-2411
Music Dept.: 415-338-1341
Dance Dept.: 415-338-2062
Theater Dept.: 415-338-1341

Enrollment. University: 27,800. Music majors: 250 undergraduates, 55 graduate students. Dance majors: 70. Drama majors: 425.
Faculty. Music: 18 full time, 32 part time. Dance: 5 full time, 5 part time. Drama: 15 full time.
Application deadline. February 1.
Audition. Required. Also music theory placement exam and keyboard proficiency test.
Degrees offered. BA, MA in Drama. BA, BM, MA, MM in Music.
Costs. Tuition: In-state—$870; out-of state—$6,670. Room and board: $3,600.

. . . .

Musical instruments taught: All Orchestral, Piano, Harpsichord, Harp, Organ, Guitar. Also has programs in Electronic Music, Jazz, and Popular Styles.
Facilities: 2 auditoriums seating 750 and 225 respectively.
Financial aid: Submit FAF and departmental form for merit scholarships.
International students: 15% from abroad. Japan, Korea, and Taiwan most represented. TOEFL required—550 minimum. Apply in November for fall entrance. No financial aid for foreign students.
Prominent alumni include: Music—Lou Harrison, Johnny Mathis, Donna Peterson.

AUTHOR'S COMMENT: *Highly recommended for Dance. Recommended for Drama and Music in general.*

Sarah Lawrence College

One The Meadway
Bronxville, NY 10708

Admissions: 914-395-2510 or 1-800-888-2858

Enrollment. College: 1,050 undergraduates, 150 graduate students. Drama majors: 170 undergraduates; 5 male, 6 female graduate students. Music majors: 100. Dance majors: 5 males, 35 females.
Faculty. Drama: 2 full time, 18 part time. Music: 9 full time, 11 part time. Dance: 3 full time, 4 part time.
Application deadlines. Early Decision I: November 15; Early Decision II: January 1. Regular Decision: February 1.
Audition. Not required.
Degrees offered. BA, MA, MFA.
Costs. Tuition: $16,400 Fees: $350. Room: $4,320. Board: $2,080.

. . . .

Standardized tests: SAT or ACT required but achievement tests may be substituted for SAT or ACT.
Interview: Graduate students must interview with the department. Strongly recommended for undergraduates with both an admissions counselor and the department.
Videotapes: Accepted. Send to Admissions which will refer the videotapes to department for evaluation.
Musical instruments taught: All Instruments. Also programs in Early Music, Contemporary Music, Electronic Music, Jazz, Voice.
Facilities: Drama—main proscenium stage, one main stage based on the Globe, two large studio theaters, one large concert hall, Marshall Field House. Dance—4 dance studios, 1 dance theater, 1 traditional theater.
Financial aid: Available. Must submit the FAF and supplementary materials by February 1. All scholarships are need-based.
Housing: 100% of new students receive on-campus housing.
International students: 8% from abroad. Great Britain, Mexico, France, Japan, and Switzerland most represented. Must take the TOEFL—550 minimum. No financial aid for foreign students.

(continued on next page)

Prominent alumni include: Drama—Jane Alexander, Jill Clayburgh, Tovah Feldshuh, Robin Givens, Lauren Holly, Holly Robinson, Joanne Woodward. Dance—Carolyn Adams, Lucinda Childs. Music—Eleanor Cory, Marilyn Dubow, Yoko Ono. Other alumni, including Carol Hall and Meredith Monk, worked in mixed programs in music-theater and dance.

AUTHOR'S COMMENT: *Sarah Lawrence is only about a half hour outside New York City. It is an eclectic college community, which is also a nurturing environment for performing artists. Recommended for undergraduate Drama, Dance, and Musical Theater; the Music Department in general is strong.*

Schola Cantorum Basiliensis

(Also known as Musik Akademie der Stadt Basel)
Schola Cantorum Basiliensis
Leonhardsstrasse, 4
CH-4051 Basel, SWITZERLAND

011-41-61-261-5722
FAX: 011-41-61-261-4913

Enrollment. 200.
Music faculty. 30 full time, 40 part time.
Application deadline. March 15.
Audition. Required. Also tests in music theory, ear training and dictation, improvisation, piano and harpsichord proficiency.
Audition dates. May/June.
Degrees offered. Diploma. (Diploma für alte musik.)
Costs. 1,500 Swiss francs per annum.

• • • • • • • • • • • • • • • •

Facilities: Practice rooms with harpsichords, clavichord or early forte pianos available, 2 concert halls seating 350 and 100 respectively, music library, listening facilities.

International students: Welcome. Enrolled from Germany, France, Sweden, Japan, Australia, United States. Scholarships are available. Apply by November 1.
Financial aid: Few scholarships available. Apply by November 1.

AUTHOR'S COMMENT: *The Schola Cantorum, located in downtown Basel, is internationally renowned for the study of Early Music and Harpsichord. Its facilities for Harpsichord are superb.*

Scripps College

1030 Columbia Avenue
Claremont, CA 91711-3948

Admissions: 714-621-8149

Enrollment. 650 (women only).
Application deadlines. Early Decision: November 15. Regular Decision: February 1.
Audition. Not required.
Costs. Tuition and fees: $13,824. Room and board: $6,000.

• • • • • • • • • • • • • • • •

Standardized tests: SAT or ACT required. Achievement tests recommended.
Interview: Recommended.
Tapes: Cassettes or videotapes may be sent to the Office of Admissions to be referred to the department for evaluation.

AUTHOR'S COMMENT: *Scripps is one of the Claremont colleges. The atmosphere is somewhat like that of a southern California version of Smith. Recommended for undergraduate Drama and Dance.*

Shenandoah College and Conservatory

1460 University Drive
Winchester, VA 22601

Admissions: 1-800-432-2266
Dance Dept.: 703-665-4565
Music Dept.: 703-665-4600
Theater Dept.: 703-665-4545

Enrollment. University: 1,181. Conservatory: 369 undergraduates, 15 graduates. Drama majors: 25 male, 45 female undergraduates. Music majors: 279 undergraduates, 15 graduate students. Dance majors: 1 male, 20 females.

Faculty. Drama: 4 full time, 3 part time. Music: 27 full time, 14 part time. Dance: 2 full time, 4 part time.

Application deadlines. Rolling, but must be submitted prior to audition dates.

Audition. Required. Scheduled January–April. Held on campus and regionally in Atlanta, Tampa, Spartanburg, Boston, Hartford, New York City, Philadelphia.

Degrees offered. BA, BS in Acting. BFA in Dance. BFA in Musical Theater, BM, MM in Music. Certificates in Piano Technology, Pedagogy, and Church Music.

Costs. Tuition: $7,900. Fees: $200 (plus $175 per credit applied music fee). Room and board: $3,900.

• • • • • • • • • • • • • • • • •

Standardized tests: SAT or ACT required.

Videotapes: Accepted only for students who find it absolutely impossible to audition in person.

Admissions criteria: Quality of the audition, grades in school, standardized test scores.

Musical instruments taught: Piano, Harpsichord, Organ, All Orchestral Instruments. Also has programs in Accompanying, Commercial Music, Composition, Jazz, Church Music, Voice.

Drama facilities: 700-seat proscenium main stage, 200-seat black box.

Financial aid: Available. Must submit the FAF.

Housing: 100% of new students receive on-campus housing.

International students: 4% enrolled from Japan, Pacific Rim, and Europe. TOEFL required—450 minimum. Transcripts must be translated. No financial aid available for foreign students, and any application for aid will negatively affect an admissions decision.

AUTHOR'S COMMENT: *Recommended for undergraduate Drama, Dance, and Musical Theater. The Music program in general has strengths.*

Sibelius Academy of Music

Toolonkatu, 28
SF-00260 Helsinki, 26, FINLAND

011-358-90-408-166

Enrollment. 900.

Music faculty. 163 full time.

Degrees offered. Candidate of Music, Licentiate, Doctor of Music.

• • • • • • • • • • • • • • • • •

Facilities: Music library, listening library, practice rooms, concert halls.

Musical instruments taught: All Orchestral, Organ, Piano. Also has programs in Composition, Orchestral and Choral Conducting, Church Music, Jazz Studies, Folk Music, Opera Training.

Language of instruction: Officially bilingual, providing instruction in both Finnish and Swedish.

International students: Welcome. The Academy also has exchange programs with several European music schools.

AUTHOR'S COMMENT: *Recommended for Orchestral Conducting and Voice.*

Skidmore College

North Broadway
Saratoga Springs, NY 12866

Admissions: 518-587-7569

Enrollment. 2,150.
Application deadlines. Early Decision: December 15 and January 15. Regular Decision: February 1.
Audition. Not required.
Costs. Tuition and fees: $14,676. Room and board: $4,915.

• • • • • • • • • • • • • • •

Standardized tests: SAT or ACT required. Achievement tests recommended.
Interview: Recommended.
Tapes: Cassettes or videotapes may be sent to the Office of Admissions to be referred to the department for evaluation.
Facilities: 350-seat theater, set design studio, dance studios.
Financial aid: Submit the FAF by February 1.

AUTHOR'S COMMENT: Recommended for undergraduate Drama and Dance. The Music Department in general has strengths for a small liberal arts college.

Smith College

Garrison Hall
West Street
Northampton, MA 01063

Admissions: 413-585-2500
Theater Dept.: 413-584-2700, ext. 3201

Enrollment. 2,770 (women only); Drama majors: 45. Dance majors: 4. Music majors: 20.
Faculty. Drama: 9 full time, 1 part time. Dance: 18. Music: 23.
Application deadlines. Early Decision: November 15. Regular Decision: January 15.
Audition. Not required for entrance to the College.
Degrees offered. BA.
Costs. Tuition and fees: $14,605. Room and board: $5,650.

• • • • • • • • • • • • • • • • • • •

Standardized tests: SAT or ACT and 3 achievement tests required (English and 2 others).
Interview: Required.
Tapes: Cassettes and videotapes may be sent to the Office of Admissions to be referred to the department for evaluation.
Facilities: 3 theaters seating 461, 220, and 80 respectively, scene shop, costume shop, props shop, 2 dance studios, rehearsal spaces.
International students: 8% from abroad. India, China, Japan most represented. TOEFL required. An application for financial aid may negatively influence an admissions decision for foreign students.
Financial aid: Submit the FAF by January 15.

AUTHOR'S COMMENT: Recommended for undergraduate Drama, Dance (part of Five College Department), Early Music, Guitar, and Voice.

Southern Methodist University

Meadows School of the Arts
Dallas, TX 75275

Admissions: 1-800-323-0672
Division of Music: 214-692-2058 or 2643
Theater Chair: 214-692-2558
Associate Dean for Recruiting and
Admissions: 214-692-3217

Enrollment. University: 5,500 undergraduates, 1,500 graduate students. Theater program: 58 male, 40 female undergraduates; 12 male, 17 female graduate students. Dance majors: 50 undergraduates. Music majors: 175 undergraduates, 75 graduate students.
Faculty. Drama: 15 full time, 6 part time. Dance: 7 full time, 1 adjunct. Music: 30 full time, 30 part time.
Application deadlines. January 15 or prior to audition date.
Audition. Required. Held throughout the United States from mid-October through February for Drama. Drama auditions are 30 minutes long. Applicants prepare contrasting contemporary pieces that show different aspects of themselves. The school strongly recommends against classical audition pieces, dialect pieces, and extreme age characterizations. Auditions required for all Music applicants are held in December–April in Dallas and in 20 cities regionally throughout the United States.
Degrees offered. BFA in Acting, BFA in Theater Studies, MFA in Acting (a 3-year program with a summer at Fort Burgwin Research Center, Taos, New Mexico after second year). BFA in Dance Performance. BM, MM, and Artist Certificate in Music.
Costs. Tuition: $10,440. Fees: $1,328. Room: $2,308. Board: $2,524.

. . . .

Standardized tests: SAT or ACT required. Achievement tests recommended.
Interview: Recommended.
Videotapes: Not accepted in Drama. Videos required for graduate conducting and cassettes accepted with at least 3 contrasting selections for all other Music applicants.
Admissions criteria: Review of SMU application, standardized tests scores, and high school and college transcripts. Quality of audition, grades in school, and a sense of SMU programs being appropriate to the student auditioning also considered.
Musical instruments taught: All.

Drama facilities: 3 theaters—proscenium, black box, classical thrust stage—plus 3 classroom/performance spaces, Bob Hope Theater.
Financial aid: FAF and SMU financial aid application required. Many merit-based scholarships available. Approximately 45% receive scholarships from the school.
Housing: 100% of new students receive on-campus housing.
International students: 10% from abroad. Latvia, China (PRC), Russia, France, and Spain most represented. TOEFL required—550 minimum.
Prominent alumni include: Drama—Dylan Baker, Kathy Bates, Powers Boothe, Bill Fagerbaake, Jack Heifner, Beth Henley, James McClure, Saundra Santiago, Steve Tobolowski, Garland Wright. Dance—Nasha Thomas. Music—Donnie Ray Albert, Robert Floyd.

AUTHOR'S COMMENT: Highly recommended for Drama, Dance, Choral Conducting, Church Music, Flute, Organ, and Piano.

Spelman College

350 Spelman Lane, SW
Box 979
Atlanta, GA

404-681-3543

Enrollment. 1,800. Music majors: 27.
Music faculty. 6 full time, 3 part time.
Application deadline. February 1.
Audition. Required. Also Pre-Assessment Theory exam.
Degrees offered. BA in Music.
Costs. Tuition and fees: $6,326. Room and board: $4,720.

. . . .

Tapes: Accepted.
Musical instruments taught: Piano, Organ, Violin, Harp, Wind Instruments. Also Voice.
Financial aid: Submit FAF.
International students: Less than 1% from abroad. East African countries and South Africa represented. No financial aid for international students.
Prominent music alumni include: Mattiwilda Dobbs, Alpha Floyd, Betty Lane.

AUTHOR'S COMMENT: Spelman is a historically black women's college with a good Music Department.

Stanford University

Stanford, CA 94305

Admissions: 415-732-2091 or 2300
Dance Dept.: 415-723-1234
Drama Dept.: 415-723-2576

Enrollment. University: 13,400. Drama majors: 10 male, 15 female undergraduates; 7 male, 7 female graduate students. Dance Department: 1 male, 3 female graduate students.
Faculty. Drama: 12 full time, 1 part time. Dance: 2 full time, 5 part time.
Application deadline. December 15.
Audition. Not required but held in November at the campus in Drama. Dance holds auditions.
Degrees offered. BA, MA, Ph.D, BA, Dance emphasis, MA in Education with Dance specialization, MFA in Dance.
Costs. Tuition and fees: $14,280. Room and board: $5,930.

. . . .

Standardized tests: SAT required. Achievement tests strongly recommended. GRE required for graduate students.
Interview: Required for graduate students. Not available for undergraduates.
Videotapes: Not encouraged in Drama. Dance will accept videotapes.
Admissions criteria: Stanford is highly selective in admission and you must be admitted to the University. Grades in school, application essays, recommendations, previous training, standardized test scores, quality of audition all important.
Drama facilities: 3 theater spaces, several studios, well-equipped shops. Dance has 2 dance studios.
Financial aid: Available. Must submit FAF and Stanford Supplement, or GAPSFAS, due by April 25. All financial aid awards based on need.
Housing: 100% of new students receive on-campus housing.
International students: 4% enrolled from Canada, Singapore, India, Germany. Must also submit TOEFL—600 minimum. Limited aid is available for international students, and it is easier to be admitted without need. Must also submit the foreign student financial aid form.

Prominent drama alumnus: Andre Brauglier.
AUTHOR'S COMMENT: *Recommended for Dance (modern), Early Music, and graduate studies in Electronic Music. The Drama program is also recommended.*

State University of New York (SUNY) at Brockport

Brockport, NY 14420

Admissions: 716-395-2751
Dance Dept.: 716-395-2153

Enrollment. University: 7,501 undergraduates; 2,161 graduate students. Dance majors: 5 male, 45 female undergraduates; 12 female graduate students.
Dance faculty. 11 full time, 5 part time; 3 graduate assistants.
Application deadline. January 1 for fall semester.
Audition. Required. Held on the campus in fall, February, and April. Call the Dance Department for exact dates.
Degrees offered. BA, BS, MA in Dance.
Costs. Tuition: In-state—$2,150; out-of-state—$5,750. Room and board: $3,865.

. . . .

Standardized tests: SAT or ACT required.
Videotapes: Not generally accepted but an exception may be made for those who live at a great distance.
Dance facilities: 5 dance studios and a renovated theater.
Financial aid: Submit the FAF. Some merit scholarships also available.
International students: 10% from abroad. Taiwan, Hong Kong, England, and Jamaica most represented. TOEFL required. No financial aid for foreign students.
Prominent dance alumni include: Irene Bunis, Wayne Cilento, Elizabeth Streo, Nancy Umanoff, Joseph Wyatt.

AUTHOR'S COMMENT: *Recommended for Dance.*

State University of New York (SUNY) at Buffalo

1300 Elmwood Avenue
Buffalo, NY 14222-1095

Admissions: 716-878-4017 or 716-831-2111
Dept. of Music: 716-636-2758
Dept. of Theater and Dance: 716-831-3933

Dept. of Music Address:
Baird Hall, Room 226
Dept. of Theater and Dance Address:
201 Harriman Hall

Enrollment. University: 27,640; 18,830 undergraduates. Music majors: 168 undergraduates, 98 graduate students. Drama majors: 35.
Faculty. Music: 28 full time, 35 part time. Drama: 13 full time, 1 part time.
Application deadline. Regular Decision: January 1.
Audition. Required for graduate students in Drama, for some merit scholarships, and for all Music applicants, who must also take a music theory placement exam.
Degrees offered. BA, MFA in Acting. BA, BM, MA, MM, Ph.D in Music.
Costs. Tuition and fees: In-state—$1,497; out-of-state—$4,847. Room and board: $3,790.

. . . .

Standardized tests: SAT or ACT required. Achievement tests optional.
Interview: Required as part of the audition for graduate students.
Tapes: Music applicants may submit cassette tapes.
Admissions criteria: GPA, rank in class, standardized tests scores all considered.
Musical instruments taught: All Orchestral, Piano, Organ, Harpsichord, Classical Guitar. Also Voice.
Financial aid: Submit the FAF and Music Department financial aid application for any merit scholarships.
International students: 15% from abroad. China (PRC), Thailand, Korea, Canada most represented. TOEFL required—550 minimum. Must submit application by January 1.
Prominent music alumni include: Anthony deMare, Nils Vigeland.

AUTHOR'S COMMENT: Recommended for Drama and Guitar. The Music Department in general has strengths.

State University of New York (SUNY) at Fredonia

Fredonia, NY 14063

Admissions: 716-673-3251
Rockefeller Arts Center: 716-673-3596

Enrollment. University: 5,000. Drama majors: 93.
Drama faculty. 6 full time, 1 part time.
Audition. Required for Musical Theater and BFA applicants.
Degrees offered. BA in General Theater. BFA in Music Performance, BFA in Musical Theater.
Costs. Tuition: In-state—$1,529; out-of-state—$4,879. Room and board: $3,580.

. . . .

Standardized tests: SAT required.
Admissions criteria: GPA, rank in class, SAT, extracurricular activities, recommendations.
Drama facilities: 2 theaters seating 401 and 150 respectively.
Financial aid: Submit the FAF.

AUTHOR'S COMMENT: Recommended for undergraduate Drama and Musical Theater.

State University of New York (SUNY) at New Paltz

New Paltz, NY 12561

Admissions: 914-257-2414

Enrollment. 5,665.
Application deadline. Rolling.
Audition. Required.
Costs. Tuition and fees: In-state—$1,485; out-of-state—$4,979.

. . . .

Standardized tests: SAT or ACT required.
Interview: Not required.

AUTHOR'S COMMENT: Recommended for Musical Theater.

State University of New York (SUNY) at Potsdam

Pierrepont Avenue
Potsdam, NY 13676

Admissions: 315-267-2180

Enrollment. 3,775.
Audition. Required.
Costs. Tuition and fees: In-state—$1,490; out-of-state—$4,979. Room and board: $3,550.

. . . .

Standardized tests: SAT or ACT required.
Interview: Not required.

AUTHOR'S COMMENT: Recommended for Dance. Also, the Crane School of Music has some fine faculty members.

State University of New York (SUNY) at Purchase

735 Anderson Hill Road
Purchase, NY 10577-1400

Admissions: 914-251-6300
Dance Division: 914-251-6800

Enrollment. University: 4,580. Dance majors: 20 males, 110 females.
Application deadline. Rolling admissions to July 15.
Audition. Required. Dance auditions held on campus December–June. Regional Dance auditions also held. Call for exact dates and locations.
Degrees offered. BFA.
Costs. Tuition: In-state—$2,150; out-of-state—$5,750. Fees: $235. Room: $2,456 to $2,818. Board: $1,358 to $1,608.

. . . .

Standardized tests: SAT or ACT required.
Interview: Required for acting. Recommended for other areas.
Videotapes: Accepted in Dance for international students only.
Dance facilities: 8 studios with marley and wood flooring. Access to Performing Arts Center with 4 theaters.
Financial aid: Submit FAF. Some merit awards available.
International students: 10% from abroad. Taiwan, Korea, Japan, Europe, and South America most represented. TOEFL required—550 minimum. Application must be submitted before June 1. No financial aid available for foreign students.
Prominent dance alumni include: Helen Barrow, Terese Capucilli, Hernando Cortez, George Thompson.

AUTHOR'S COMMENT: Recommended for undergraduate Drama; highly recommended for Dance and Guitar.

State University of New York (SUNY) at Stony Brook

Stony Brook, NY 11794-1901

Admissions: 516-632-6868
Music Dept.: 516-632-7352 (undergraduates)
Music Dept.: 516-632-7042 (graduates)

Enrollment. 17,630; 14,676 undergraduates.
Drama faculty. 13 full time.
Application deadline. Rolling admissions.
Audition. Required.
Degrees offered. BA, MA in Theater. BA, BM, MM, DMA, Ph.D in Music.
Costs. Tuition and fees: In-state—$1,495; out-of-state—$4,845. Room and board: $3,894.

. . . .

Standardized tests: SAT or ACT required. Achievement tests optional. GRE required for graduate students.
Interview: Not required.
Admissions criteria: GPA, standardized tests scores, audition.
Drama facilities: 3 theaters seating 225, 225, and 75 respectively, scene, costume, props shops, dance studio, rehearsal and classroom spaces.

AUTHOR'S COMMENT: Recommended for undergraduate Drama; graduate Clarinet, Flute, Piano.

Swarthmore College

500 College Avenue
Swarthmore, PA 19081

Admissions: 215-328-8300
Drama: 215-328-8149

Enrollment. 1,300 undergraduate men and women; Drama Department: 8 male, 10 female students.
Drama faculty. 3 full time, 3 part time.
Audition. Not required.
Degrees offered. BA.
Costs. Tuition, room, board, and fees: $22,160.

• • • • • • • • • • • • • • • • • •

Standardized tests: SAT and 3 achievement tests (English composition and 2 others) required.
Interview: Recommended.
Videotapes: Not accepted.
Admissions criteria: You must be admitted to the College, not the department. Swarthmore is one of the most highly selective liberal arts colleges in admissions standards. Criteria considered are academic preparation, standardized tests, personal profile, essay questions, character, and intellectual curiosity. Students are advised to see a Theater professor when they visit the campus, and this should be arranged in advance. Otherwise, write or telephone. Admission to the major depends on performance in course work.
Facilities: New performing arts center. Black box 45 x 45, thrust/proscenium with 350 seats.
Financial aid: FAF and Swarthmore form required. 100% based on need. 50% receive scholarship from Swarthmore.
Housing: 100% of applicants are offered on-campus housing.
International students: 10% from abroad, mainly from England, France, Canada, China, Japan. TOEFL for international students—600 minimum. Very limited amount of financial aid available for foreign students.

AUTHOR'S COMMENT: Swarthmore is renowned for the strengths of its academic programs and intellectual challenges. The good Theater program is unusual for such a serious liberal arts college.

Syracuse University

201 Administration Building
Syracuse, NY 13244

Admissions: 315-443-3611

Enrollment. 19,700; 12,250 undergraduates.
Application deadlines. Early Decision: December 1. Regular Decision: February 1.
Audition. Required. Call for exact dates and locations.
Costs. Tuition and fees: $12,120. Room and board: $5,535.

• • • • • • • • • • • • • • • • • •

Standardized tests: SAT or ACT required. Achievement tests optional.
Interview: Recommended.

AUTHOR'S COMMENT: Recommended for undergraduate Drama, Musical Theater, and Organ.

Temple University

Broad and Norris Streets
Philadelphia, PA 19122

Admissions: 215-787-7200
Esther Boyer School of Music: 215-787-8328
MFA program in Drama: 215-787-8748

Enrollment. University: 31,181. Drama Department: 45 male, 60 female undergraduates; 19 male, 10 female graduate students.

Drama faculty. 13 full time, 8 part time.

Application deadline. January 15, undergraduates.

Audition. Required for BFA and MFA in Drama. Scheduled for January–February regionally and on the campus. Confirm Drama audition appointment by calling Eda Manrodt at 215-787-8748. Required for Music. Contact the School of Music for exact dates and locations.

Degrees offered. BA, Theater major, BFA, MFA in Theater. Note that the MFA is 3 years—2 years of course work and last year of professional experience. BM, MM, DMA, Ph.D in Music. Nondegree in Music: Undergraduate diploma, Graduate Professional Studies in Performance.

Costs. Tuition and fees: $7,308. Room and board: $4,056.

Videotapes: Accepted only when personal audition is absolutely impossible. For Drama must contain two 3- to 5-minute monologues; song or dance is optional.

Admissions criteria: Quality of audition, grades in school, application essay, recommendations.

Musical instruments taught: All Orchestral Instruments, Keyboard, Classical Guitar. Also Voice, Choral Music, Composition, Accompanying, Jazz Studies.

Facilities: 3 theaters: Tomlinson, Randall, and Stage Three. Rehearsal hall and classrooms.

Financial aid: Submit FAF or GAPSFAS for graduate students. 10% receive scholarships from the school.

Housing: 30% of new students receive on-campus housing.

International students: About 2%, mainly from Italy, Norway. TOEFL required. No financial aid available for students from abroad. Some merit scholarships in Music may be awarded.

Prominent alumni include: Drama—John Connoly, Charles Hallahan, Thomas Sizemore, Anne Twomey. Music—Nico Castel.

AUTHOR'S COMMENT: Recommended for under-graduate Drama, Dance, Bassoon, Harp, and Percussion. Many of the Music faculty are members of the Philadelphia Orchestra.

Texas Christian University

P.O. Box 32889
Fort Worth, TX 76129

Admissions: 817-921-7490
Music Dept.: 817-921-7602

Enrollment. University: 7,000. Dance majors: 10 male, 40 female undergraduates; 3 male, 7 female graduate students. Music majors: 105 undergraduates, 35 graduate students.

Faculty. Dance: 5 full time, 2 part time. Music: 20 full time, 12 adjunct.

Application deadlines. November 15 for Early Notification; January 15 for scholarship deadline; February 15, final posted deadline.

Audition. In Dance, placement audition required for undergraduates. All students are on 1-year probation. Audition is required for entrance to MFA program. Auditions required in Music. Theory, ear training, and keyboard skills will also be tested. Music auditions held January–March. Call the department for specific dates and locations.

Degrees offered. BFA, MFA in Dance. BA, BM, MA, MM, Graduate Artist Diploma, Undergraduate Performers Certificate all offered in Music.

Costs. Tuition: $240 per credit hour. Fees: $350. Room: $750 per semester. Board: $375 per semester.

. . . .

Videotapes: Not generally accepted.

Musical instruments taught: All Orchestral Instruments, Piano, Organ, Saxophone, Guitar. Also has Jazz, Electronic Music, Choral, Opera/Musical Theater, Sacred Music programs.

Facilities: 3 studios: 35 x 80. Sprung, wooden floors; fully-teched proscenium theater 35 x 30 and another 25 x 30.

Financial aid: 60% of TCU students receive aid. Must submit FAF and IRS forms.

Housing: All students who request it receive on-campus housing.

International students: 2% to 3% in school. China (PRC), Japan, Panama, El Salvador, Germany most represented. Must take TOEFL—500 undergraduate; 550 graduate. Some financial aid available for foreign students.

Prominent alumni include: Dance—Donna Faye Burchfield, Amy Ernst, Carolyn Heilman. Music—Betty Buckley, Ryan Edwards, Don Gillis, John Giordano, William Walker.

AUTHOR'S COMMENT: Recommended for Dance, Church Music, and Piano.

Toho Gakuen School of Music

1-41-1 Wakaba-cho
Chofu-shi
Tokyo 182, JAPAN

81-03-307-4101
FAX: 81-03-3326-8844

Enrollment. 880 College level (has a high school of about 350 students).

Music faculty. 94 full time, 283 part time.

Application deadline. February 1.

Audition. Required. Must also take examinations in music theory, ear training, piano proficiency, essay. Auditions held in February and March.

Degrees offered. BA in Music.

Costs. Tuition and fees: 1,200,000 yen; Entrance fees: 840,000 yen (only for freshmen); Management fees: 1,150,000 yen (only for freshmen); Foreign student course: 288,000 yen.

. . . .

Tapes: Accepted only for foreign student course.

Interview: Required as part of audition.

Facilities: Practice rooms, electronic music studio, concert halls, music library, listening library, dormitory.

Financial aid: Scholarships are available. File application by February 1.

International students: Accepted; Germany, Canada, Brazil, China, Korea, Taiwan, and United States represented in foreign student course.

Prominent alumnus: Seiji Ozawa.

AUTHOR'S COMMENT: Recommended for Piano, Violin and Viola.

Towson State University

Towson, MD 21204-7097

Admissions: 301-830-2112 or 2143
Dance Dept.: 301-830-2760

Enrollment. University: 14,180. Dance majors: 3 males, 57 females. Music majors: 225 undergraduates, 120 graduate students.

Faculty. Dance: 4 full time, 4 part time. Music: 31 full time, 30 part time.

Application deadlines. March 1 for fall semester, December 1 for spring semester.

Audition. Required. Held in February and March on the campus. Call for exact dates.

Degrees offered. BFA in Dance. BFA in Drama. BA, BM, MM in Music.

Costs. Tuition: In-state—$1,608; out-of-state—$3,530. Fees: $886. Room and board: $2,155.

• • • • • • • • • • • • • • • •

Standardized tests: SAT required.

Videotapes: Not accepted.

Musical instruments taught: All Orchestral, Saxophone, Jazz. Also Voice.

Dance facilities: 2 dance studios with sprung floors and Stephens Hall Theater.

Financial aid: Submit FAF and University's own form. Based on need.

International students: 5% from abroad. Korea, Indonesia, Japan, China (PRC), Iran most represented. TOEFL required—500 minimum. Special application forms may be required. No financial aid available for foreign students.

Exchange program: Leningrad State Conservatory.

Prominent alumni: Dance—Mino Nicholas. Music—Spiro Malas.

AUTHOR'S COMMENT: Recommended for undergraduate Drama and Dance. The Music Department in general has strengths.

Trinity College

300 Summit Street
Hartford, CT 06106-3186

Admissions: 203-297-2180

Enrollment. 1,800.

Application deadlines. Early Decision: December 1 and January 15. Regular Decision: January 15.

Audition. Not required.

Costs. Tuition and fees: $15,830. Room and board: $4,470.

• • • • • • • • • • • • • • • • • •

Standardized tests: SAT or ACT and 3 achievement tests required, including English, preferably with essay.

Interview: Recommended.

Tapes: Not encouraged.

Financial aid: Submit the FAF by February 1.

AUTHOR'S COMMENT: Recommended for undergraduate Drama and Dance (an integrated department). Music has cross-registration with Hartt School of Music.

Tulane University

6823 St. Charles Avenue
New Orleans, LA 70118-5698

Admissions: 504-865-5731
Theater Dept.: 504-865-5360

Enrollment. University: 11,516; 7,503 undergraduates. Drama majors: 61.
Drama faculty. 8 full time, 1 part time.
Application deadlines. Early Notification: November 1. Regular Decision: January 15.
Audition. Required.
Degrees offered. BA in general theater, BFA in Acting.
Costs. Tuition and fees: $15,580. Room and board: $5,420.

· · · · · · · · · · · · · · · · · ·

Standardized tests: SAT or ACT required. Achievement tests recommended.
Admissions criteria: GPA, standardized tests, audition, extracurricular activities.
Facilities: 2 theaters seating 200 and 100 respectively, scene shop, costume shop.

AUTHOR'S COMMENT: Recommended for undergraduate Drama.

University of Akron

381 Buchtel Common
Akron, OH 44325-2001

Admissions: 216-972-6416

Enrollment. 28,800.
Audition. Not required.
Costs. Tuition: In-state—$2,277; out-of-state—$5,592. Room and board: $3,200.

· · · · · · · · · · · · · · · · · ·

Standardized tests: SAT or ACT required.
Interview: Not required.
Tapes: Not encouraged.

AUTHOR'S COMMENT: Recommended for Dance.

University of Alabama

P.O. Box 870132
Tuscaloosa, AL 35487-0132

Admissions: 205-348-5666
Dept. of Theater and Dance: 205-348-5283
Dept. of Music: 205-348-7110

Enrollment. University: 19,828; 18,150 undergraduates. Drama majors: 100 (75 undergraduate, 25 graduate students). Dance majors: 40. Music majors: 250.
Faculty. Drama: 9 full time. Dance: 3. Music: 36 full time and part time.
Application deadline. Rolling admissions to April 15.
Audition. Required.
Degrees offered. MFA in Acting. BA in Dance. BM, MM, DMA in Music, BFA in Music Performance.
Costs. Tuition: In-state—$1,810; out-of-state—$5,486.

· · · · · · · · · · · · · · · · · ·

Standardized tests: SAT or ACT required. Achievement tests optional.
Facilities: 1,000-seat Concert Hall, 338-seat theater, 150-seat theater.
Financial aid: Submit the FAF or FFS by March 1.

AUTHOR'S COMMENT: Recommended for Dance, Drama, and Organ.

University of Arizona

Robert L. Nugent Building
Tucson, AZ 85721

Admissions: 602-621-3939 or 3237
Dept. of Drama: 602-621-7007
School of Music: 602-621-5929
School of Dance: 602-621-4698

Enrollment. University: 35,569; 27,170 undergraduates. Music majors: 234 undergraduates; 128 graduate students. Drama majors: 275. Dance majors: 30 undergraduates, 50 graduates.
Faculty. Music: 52 full time. Drama: 15 full time, 2 part time. Dance: 7 full time.
Application deadlines. Early Notification: November 1, December 1. Regular Decision: March 1.
Audition. Required. Music auditions held in January–March on the campus. Call for exact dates.
Degrees offered. BFA, MFA in Acting. BFA in Musical Theater. BFA, MA, MFA in Dance. BA, BM, MM, DMA, Ph.D in Music.
Costs. Tuition: In-state—$1,540; out-of-state—$6,546. Room and board: $3,436.

. . . .

Standardized tests: SAT required.
Interview: Required as part of audition.
Musical instruments taught: All Orchestral Instruments, Piano, Organ, Guitar, Harpsichord, Composition, Saxophone. Also has programs in Accompanying, Early Music, Contemporary Music, Electronic Music, Hispanic Music, Jazz Studies.
Facilities: 2 theaters seating 338 and 150 respectively, scene shop, costume shop, 2 dance studios, rehearsal spaces, classrooms. New building to be completed in fall 1992 with rehearsal space, expanded music library, recital and concert hall.
Financial aid: Submit FAF. Merit scholarships also available.
International students: Approximately 10% from abroad. TOEFL required—500 minimum. Some financial aid available for foreign students.

AUTHOR'S COMMENT: *Recommended for Drama, especially because the school has an affiliation with the Arizona Theater Company, an Equity company; highly recommended for Dance; also recommended for Guitar, Jazz, and Saxophone.*

University of California, Berkeley

110 Sproul Hall
Berkeley, CA 94720

Admissions: 510-642-3175
Dance and Drama Dept.: 510-642-1677
Music Dept.: 510-841-9433

Music Dept. Address:
104 Morrison Hall

Enrollment. School: 21,590 undergraduates; 9,048 graduate students. Dance majors: 4 male, 14 female undergraduates. Music majors: 67 undergraduate, 61 graduate students. Drama majors: 29 male, 42 female undergraduates; 20 male, 8 female graduate students.
Faculty. Dance: 4 full time, 4 part time. Drama: 6 full time, 4 part time.
Application deadline. November 1–30.
Audition. At the departmental level, all auditions must be conducted in person and take place the first day of each semester.
Degrees offered. BA, Dance major. BA, Music major. Ph.D, Composition, BA, Dramatic Arts major.
Costs. California resident tuition: $2,679. Nonresident tuition: $10,437. Room and board: $6,050.

. . . .

Standardized tests: SAT or ACT and 3 achievement tests required (English composition, math, and third of choice).
Videotapes: Applicants may submit videotapes directly to the Admissions Office.

(continued on next page)

Admissions criteria: Admission is based on academic standing and is governed by central Admissions Office.

Facilities: 2 dance studios which are 30 x 50 and 20 x 14 with tongue-and-groove hardwood floors. Durham Studio Theater and Zellerbach Playhouse for performances.

Financial aid: Available. Some merit scholarships available. Submit SAAC (Student Aid Application for California).

International students: 3% of undergraduates and 16% of graduate students from abroad. Taiwan, China (PRC), Korea, Hong Kong, India, Canada, Japan, Germany, United Kingdom, and Iran most represented. TOEFL required—550 minimum. Very limited financial aid available for foreign students.

Prominent dance alumni include: Dancers in the following companies—Martha Graham, Paul Taylor, Merce Cunningham, Twyla Tharp.

AUTHOR'S COMMENT: Recommended for Dance (modern), Composition, and Violoncello.

University of California, Davis

Davis, CA 95616

Admissions: 916-752-2971
Dept. of Dramatic Arts: 916-752-0888
Dept. of Music: 916-752-0666

Enrollment. School: 18,395 undergraduates; 5,503 graduate students. Drama majors: 72 undergraduates; 26 graduate students. Music majors: 54 undergraduates; 9 graduate students.

Faculty. Drama: 11. Music: 12.

Application deadline. Rolling admissions but November 30 recommended.

Audition. Required for MFA program and held in January. Not required in Music.

Degrees offered. BA, MA, MFA, Ph.D.

Costs. Tuition for out-of-state: $7,699. Fees: $2,430. Room and board: $5,121.

• • • • • • • • • • • • • • • • • •

Standardized tests: SAT or ACT required. Achievement tests required: English composition, Math I or Math II, and 1 other. Graduate students in Drama must also take a "background test" to determine the range and depth of the student's knowledge of theater, history, dramatic literature, and various aspects of theatrical production.

Videotapes: Accepted.

Musical instruments taught: All Orchestral Instruments, Piano, Harpsichord, Organ, Lute, Viola da gamba. Also Early Music.

Drama facilities: 500-seat proscenium theater, 200-seat thrust stage, 100-seat area theater, 2 lab theaters.

Financial aid: Available. Must submit FAF or SAAC (Student Aid Application for California).

Housing: 100% of new students receive on-campus housing.

International students: 1% of undergraduates, 4% of graduate students who come from China (PRC), Taiwan, Japan, Korea, Hong Kong. TOEFL required—450 minimum. No financial aid available for foreign students.

Special program: Granada Artists-in-Residence Program, a working relationship with a professional production company in England.

Prominent music alumnus: Steven Mackey.

AUTHOR'S COMMENT: Recommended for Drama and Music in general.

University of California, Irvine

Irvine, CA 92717

Admissions: 714-856-6703
School of Fine Arts–Drama: 714-856-7282
School of Dance: 714-856-7284

Enrollment. University: 16,760; 13,680 undergraduates. Drama majors: 150. Dance majors: 130 undergraduates, 30 graduates.
Faculty. Drama: 15 full time, 10 part time. Dance: 9 full time, 15 part time.
Application deadline. November 1–30.
Audition. Required for graduate students in Drama and for all Dance.
Degrees offered. BA in Drama, MFA in Acting. MFA in Musical Theater. BFA in Dance.
Costs. Tuition: In-state—$1,796; out-of-state—$7,712. Room and board: $4,969.

• • • • • • • • • • • • • • • •

Standardized tests: SAT or ACT required. 3 achievement tests required (English Composition, Math, and 1 other).
Interview: Required as part of audition.
Admissions criteria: GPA, standardized tests, talent.
Facilities: 3 theaters seating 420, 231, and 165 respectively, scene shop, costume shop, 3 dance studios, rehearsal spaces.
Financial aid: Submit the FAF or SAAC.

AUTHOR'S COMMENT: Recommended for Drama, especially in light of the program's affiliation with the South Coast Repertory, an Equity company. Highly recommended for Dance.

University of California, Los Angeles

405 Hilgard Avenue
Los Angeles, CA 90024-1502

Admissions: 213-206-8331

Enrollment. University: 35,290; 23,540 undergraduates.
Application deadline. Regular Decision: November 1–30.
Audition. Required. Call for exact dates.
Costs. Tuition: In-state—$1,602; out-of-state—$7,518. Room and board: $4,850.

• • • • • • • • • • • • • • • •

Standardized tests: SAT or ACT required. 3 achievement tests required (English Composition, Math, and 1 other).
Interview: Not required.
Financial aid: Submit the FAF or SAAC.

AUTHOR'S COMMENT: Recommended for undergraduate Dance, Saxophone. Highly recommended for undergraduate Drama.

University of California, Riverside

2108 Admissions Building
Riverside, CA 92521

Admissions: 714-787-5045

Enrollment. University: 8,720; 7,170 undergraduates.
Application deadline. Regular Decision: November 1–30.
Costs. Tuition: In-state—$1,644; out-of-state—$7,560. Room and board: $4,850.

• • • • • • • • • • • • • • • •

Standardized tests: SAT or ACT required. 3 achievement tests required (English Composition, Math, and 1 other).
Financial aid: Submit the FAF or SAAC.

AUTHOR'S COMMENT: Recommended for Dance.

University of California, San Diego

Student Outreach, B-037
La Jolla, CA 92093

Admissions: 619-534-3160
Dept. of Theater and Dance: 619-534-3791
Dept. of Music: 619-534-3230

Drama Address:
Dept. of Theater, B-044

Enrollment. University: 17,800; 14,295 undergraduates. Drama majors: 103. Dance majors: 300.
Faculty. Drama: 20 full time, 6 part time. Dance: 2 full time, 6 part time.
Application deadline. November 1–30.
Audition. Required.
Degrees offered. BFA in Dance. BFA in Drama, MFA in Acting.
Costs. Tuition: In-state—$1,734; out-of-state—$7,715. Room and board: $5,530.

. . . .

Standardized tests: SAT or ACT required. 3 achievement tests required (English Composition, Math, and 1 other).
Interview: Required as part of audition.
Admissions criteria: GPA, standardized tests scores, recommendations.
Facilities: 3 theaters seating 500, 250, and 99 respectively, scene shop, costume shop, props shop, dance studios, rehearsal spaces, classrooms.
Financial aid: Submit the FAF or SAAC.

AUTHOR'S COMMENT: Recommended for Dance, graduate Drama (the program has an affiliation with La Jolla Playhouse) and graduate Electronic Music.

University of California, Santa Barbara

Santa Barbara, CA 93106

Admissions: 805-893-2881
Dept. of Dramatic Arts: 805-961-3241
Dept. of Dance: 805-893-3241

Enrollment. University: 18,400; 16,935 undergraduates. Drama majors: 172. Dance majors: 64.
Faculty. Drama: 13 full time, 2 part time. Dance: 7.
Application deadline. November 1–30.
Audition. Required.
Degrees offered. BFA in Acting. BFA in Dance.
Costs. Tuition: In-state—$1,651; out-of-state—$7,550. Room and board: $4,732.

. . . .

Standardized tests: SAT or ACT required. 3 achievement tests required (English Composition, Math, and 1 other).
Facilities: 3 theaters seating 340, 118, and 110 respectively, scene shop, costume shop, dance studios.
Financial aid: Submit the FAF or SAAC.

AUTHOR'S COMMENT: Recommended for undergraduate Drama and Dance.

University of Chicago

1116 East 59th Street
Chicago, IL 60637-1513

Admissions: 312-702-8650

Enrollment. University: 10,600; 3,350 undergraduates.
Application deadlines. Early Notification: November 15. Regular Decision: January 15.
Audition. Not required.
Costs. Tuition and fees: $15,135. Room and board: $5,390.

. . . .

Standardized tests: SAT or ACT required. Achievement tests optional.
Interview: Recommended.
Financial aid: Submit the FAF by February 1.
Prominent alumni include: Mike Nichols, Joel Smirnoff.

AUTHOR'S COMMENT: Recommended for undergraduate Composition.

University of Cincinnati

Cincinnati College-Conservatory of Music
Cincinnati, OH 45221

Admissions: 513-556-1100 or 5462
Dept. of Drama and Musical Theater:
513-475-5803
Music Dept.: 513-556-9470
Dance Dept.: 513-556-2700

Drama and Musical Theater Address:
Mail Location 3.

Enrollment. University: 36,000; 30,000 undergraduates. Drama majors: 117. Dance majors: 25. Music majors: 400 undergraduates, 400 graduate students.
Faculty. Drama: 13 full time, 7 part time. Dance: 5 full time, 6 part time. Music: 77 full time, 39 part time.
Application deadlines. Rolling admissions but by December 15 recommended. Voice no later than February 1.

Audition. Required. Music majors will also take a music theory exam. Auditions are held in Cincinnati and regionally from January–March. Call Admissions for exact dates and locations.
Degrees offered. BFA, MFA in Acting. BFA in Musical Theater, BA, BM, MA, MM, DMA, Ph.D and Artist Diploma in Music.
Costs. Ohio resident tuition and fees: $2,838 undergraduate; $4,416 graduate students. Nonresident tuition and fees: $6,774 undergraduates; $8,688 graduate students. Room and board: $4,100.

. . . .

Standardized tests: SAT or ACT required. ACT preferred. GRE required for graduate students.
Interview: Required as part of audition.
Musical instruments taught: All Orchestral Instruments, Piano, Harpsichord, Guitar. Also has a Jazz/Studio Music program, Voice, Composition, Musical Theater.
Facilities: 2 theaters, scene shop, costume shop, 3 dance studios.
Financial aid: Available. Submit FAF. Some merit scholarships available.
International students: 10% from abroad. Germany, China (PRC), Japan, Korea, Canada most represented. TOEFL required—520 minimum. Must be sure to submit application well in advance. Nothing received after April 1 will be processed.
Prominent music alumni include: Ron Barron, Kathleen Battle, Barbara Daniels, Steve Flaherty, Tennessee "Ernie" Ford, Al Hirt, Faith Prince, LeRoy Reams, Ward Swingle, Jim Walton.

AUTHOR'S COMMENT: Recommended for Drama, Dance, Accompanying, Bassoon, Guitar, Saxophone, Viola, and Violoncello. Highly recommended for Musical Theater and Violin.

University of Colorado, Boulder

Campus Box 7
Boulder, CO 80309

Admissions: 303-492-6301
College of Music: 303-492-6352
Dept. of Theater and Dance: 303-492-5037

College of Music Address:
Campus Box 301

Enrollment. University: 21,476 undergraduates; 3,700 graduate students. Dance majors: 3 male, 30 female undergraduates; 1 male, 9 female graduate students. Music majors: 350 undergraduates, 200 graduate students.

Faculty. Dance: 6 full time, 2 part time. Music: 50 full time, 10 part time.

Application deadlines. Rolling admissions to February 1 for fall, November 1 for spring.

Audition. Not required for undergraduate admission in Dance. 2-day audition required for MFA in Dance; held in February. Audition required in Music; held on campus in February and early March.

Degrees offered. BA, BFA, MFA, in Modern Dance. BA, BM, MM, DMA, Ph.D in Music.

Costs. Tuition: In-state—$1,842; out-of-state—$6,000. Fees: $200. Room and board: $3,340.

. . . .

Standardized tests: SAT or ACT required. Achievement tests optional.

Interview: Recommended.

Videotapes: Accepted for foreign applicants to MFA in Dance. Undergraduate applicants in Dance who are denied admission to the University due to GPA or low test scores may submit a videotape to the Dance Department for review and subsequent appeal to the Office of Admissions. Videotapes or cassettes accepted in Music for applicants who cannot appear in person.

Musical instruments taught: All Orchestral, Piano, Organ, Guitar. Also programs in Composition, Voice, Early Music, Jazz Studies, Electronic Music, American Music.

Financial aid: FAF, FFS, and FAAC. Merit-based awards available.

International students: 5% from abroad. Germany, Denmark, Israel, Korea, Canada most represented. TOEFL required.

Prominent alumni include: Dance—Ford Evas, Sandra Fleitell, Therese Freedman, Gerald Otte, Shelly Senter, Mary Staton, Gael Stepanek. Music—Dave Grusin.

AUTHOR'S COMMENT: *Recommended for Dance (modern), Church Music, and Saxophone.*

University of Connecticut, Storrs

28 North Eagleville Road
Storrs, CT 06269-3088

Admissions: 203-486-3137
Theater Dept.: 203-486-4026

Theater Dept. Address:
U-127, 802 Bolton Road

Enrollment. University: 25,630; 15,980 undergraduates.

Drama faculty. 17 full time.

Application deadlines. Rolling admissions to April 1. Transfers to March 1.

Audition. Required.

Degrees offered. BFA, MFA in Acting.

Costs. Tuition: In-state—$2,975; out-of-state—$7,775. Room and board: $4,258.

. . . .

Interview: Required as part of audition.

Drama courses: An unusual course in Puppetry.

Facilities: 2 theaters seating 500 and 100 respectively, scene shop, costume shop, dance studio.

Financial aid: Submit FAF by March 1.

AUTHOR'S COMMENT: *Recommended for Drama.*

University of Delaware, Newark

116 Hullihen Hall
Newark, DE 19711

Admissions: 302-451-8123
Professional Theater Training Program:
302-451-2201

PTTP Address:
Dept. of Theater
Mitchell Hall, Room 110

Enrollment. University: 20,820; 16,700 undergraduates. Drama majors: 73.
Drama faculty. 13 full time.
Application deadline. January 1. (Note that the Professional Theater Training Program enrolls only 1 class at a time, so auditions are held once every 3 years.)
Audition. Required.
Degrees offered. MFA in Acting.
Costs. MFA has tuition waived and students receive a stipend.

. . . .

Standardized tests: GRE required for graduate students.
Interview: Required as part of audition.
Facilities: Theater seating 500, scene shop, costume shop, props shops, welding shop, dance studio, rehearsal spaces.
Financial aid: Awarded on the basis of merit and need.

AUTHOR'S COMMENT: Recommended for graduate Drama. The Music Department has some fine areas, too.   .

University of Denver

Mary Reed Building #107
2199 South University
Denver, CO 80208

Admissions: 303-871-3377 or 1-800-525-9495

Enrollment. University: 7,610; 2,850 undergraduates.
Application deadlines. Early Action: December 1. Regular Decision: March 1.
Audition. Required.
Costs. Tuition and fees: $12,072. Room and board: $4,005.

. . . .

Standardized tests: SAT or ACT required. Achievement tests optional.
Interview: Recommended.
Financial aid: Submit the FAF or FFS by March 1.

AUTHOR'S COMMENT: Recommended for Accordian. Other areas of Music are also noteworthy.

University of Evansville

1800 Lincoln Avenue
Evansville, IN 47722

Admissions: 812-479-2468

Enrollment. University: 2,080.
Costs. Tuition and fees: $9,150. Room and board: $3,560.

. . . .

Financial aid: Submit the FAF by March 1.

AUTHOR'S COMMENT: Highly recommended for undergraduate Drama.

University of Georgia, Athens

114 Academic Boulevard
Athens, GA 30602

Admissions: 404-542-8776
Dept. of Drama: 404-542-2836
School of Music: 404-542-3737

Enrollment. University: 20,000 undergraduates; 7,500 graduate students. Drama majors: 250. Music majors: 285 undergraduates, 80 graduate students.
Faculty. Drama: 15 full time, 26 part time. Music: 50 full time, 5 part time.
Application deadline. Rolling admissions to February 1.
Audition. Required for graduate program in Drama and for all in Music.
Degrees offered. BA in General Drama, BFA in Performance, MFA in Acting. BA, BM, MA, MM, DMA, Ph.D in Music.
Costs. Tuition: In-state—$2,001; out-of-state—$5,313. Room and board: $2,940. Fees: $1,254.

• • • • • • • • • • • • • • • • • •

Standardized tests: SAT or ACT required. Achievement tests optional. GRE may be required of graduate students.
Interview: Required as part of audition.
Tapes: Videotapes or cassettes accepted in music.
Musical instruments taught: All. Also has programs in Early Music, Contemporary Music, Electronic Music, Jazz, Sacred Music, African Music, World Musics.
Facilities: 4 theaters seating 700, 500, 125, and 65 respectively, scene shop, costume shop, props shop, welding shop, dance studios, rehearsal spaces.
Financial aid: Submit FAF. Some merit awards available.
International students: 5% from abroad. Brazil, China (PRC), Japan most represented. TOEFL required.
Prominent music alumni include: Robert Edge, Warren Little, Charles Wadsworth.

AUTHOR'S COMMENT: Recommended for Drama; the Music program in general has strengths.

University of Hawaii at Manoa

Honolulu, HI 96822

Undergraduate Admissions: 808-956-8975
Graduate Admissions: 808-956-8544
Dept. of Theater and Dance: 808-956-7677

Dept. of Theater and Dance Address:
1770 East-West Road, Honolulu, HI 96822

Enrollment. University: 18,550. Drama majors: 23 male, 38 female undergraduates; 17 male, 30 female graduate students.
Drama faculty. 17 full time.
Application deadlines. Early Decision: November 1. Regular Decision: February 1 for graduate students, June 15 for undergraduates.
Audition. Not currently required.
Degrees offered. BA, Drama/Theater major, MA in Theater. BA, Dance Concentration, BFA in Dance Theater.
Costs. Tuition, nonresident undergraduate: $3,680; Tuition, nonresident graduate: $4,380. Fees: $120.

• • • • • • • • • • • • • • • • • •

Standardized tests: SAT required. Achievement tests optional. GRE for graduate programs.
Interview: Not available.
Videotapes: Sometimes helpful.
Admissions criteria: Admission to University, grades in school, previous dance or drama training, recommendations, experience as a performer, interest and commitment to Asian Theater.
Drama facilities: 645-seat theater, 180-seat flexible lab theater.
Financial aid: Available. Must submit FAF. Departmental scholarships also available; must submit form. Scholarships based on merit and need.
Housing: Only 17% of the students live in campus housing.
International students: 6% of entire student body from abroad; 25% of Drama program. Japan, China (PRC), Malaysia, Indonesia, most represented. TOEFL required—600 recommended. Must file application by February 1. Some financial aid, based on merit and need, available for foreign students.

(continued on next page)

Prominent drama alumni include: Beau Bridges, Stan Egi, Carol Honda, Randy Kim, Bette Midler, Sheridan Morley, Stanley Rosenberg.

AUTHOR'S COMMENT: UH is a quality state university in an exquisite setting. The Theater program is nationally and internationally renowned for the special expertise offered in the study and practice of Asian theater forms. An MFA program in World Performance is being planned. Also recommended for Dance, offering not only good training in Ballet and Modern but a broad range of Ethnic Dance.

University of Houston

School of Music
4800 Calhoun
Houston, TX 77004

Admissions: 713-749-2321

Enrollment. University: 33,120; 22,340 undergraduates.
Application deadlines. Early Action and Early Decision: May 1. Regular Decision: Rolling until June 14.
Costs. Tuition and fees: In-state—$1,010; out-of-state—$5,130. Room and board: $3,700.

· · · · · · · · · · · · · · · · · ·

Standardized tests: SAT or ACT required. Achievement tests optional.
Financial aid: Submit the FAF or FFS by April 1.

AUTHOR'S COMMENT: Recommended for French Horn and Piano.

University of Illinois

Urbana-Champaign, Il 61801

Admissions: 217-333-0302
Dept. of Theater: 217-333-2371
Undergraduate Music: 217-244-0551
Graduate Music: 217-333-1712
Music Dept.–General: 217-333-2620

Dept. of Theater Address:
4-122 Krannert Center for the Performing Arts
500 South Goodwin Avenue, Urbana, IL 61801

Enrollment. University: 35,770. Drama majors: 40 male, 36 female undergraduates; 33 male, 31 female graduate students. Music majors: 350 undergraduates, 250 graduates.
Faculty. Drama: 17 full time, 15 part time. Music: 77 full time, 10 part time.
Application deadlines. Priority filing: November 15. Regular Decision: January 1. MFA: April 1; MA and Ph.D: March 1. Music Department: February 1.
Audition. Required. Drama held in conjunction with the University Resident Theater Association (U/RTA) regionally in California, New York, Illinois in January–February. Contact the School for exact dates and locations. Music requires an audition, especially for any merit-based scholarships.
Degrees offered. BFA in Acting, BFA in Applied Theater/Performance Studies, MA in Theater, MFA in Acting. BA, BM, MM, DMA, Ph.D in Music.
Costs. Undergraduate tuition: $2,376. Fees: $736 (in-state).

· · · · · · · · · · · · · · · · · ·

Standardized tests: SAT or ACT required. Achievement tests optional.
Videotapes: Accepted in Drama. Must present two 2-minute contrasting pieces. Music will also accept a videotape.

(continued on next page)

Admissions criteria: Must be admitted to University. Quality of audition, previous training, experience in productions, standardized tests scores, grades in school, recommendations.

Musical instruments taught: Piano, Organ, Harpsichord, All Orchestral Instruments. Also Voice, Accompanying. No Guitar.

Drama facilities: 600-seat proscenium theater, 100-seat experimental theater, 1,200-seat studio theater.

Music facilities: Auditorium, opera theater, concert hall in Krannert Center for the Performing Arts.

Financial aid: Available. Must submit FAF due March 15. Application for graduate school admissions also serves as an application for financial aid within the Drama Department. All decisions are based on merit and need. Music Department has some merit-based scholarships.

Housing: 100% of undergraduates offered on-campus housing.

International students: 5% of student body. China (PRC), Japan, Western Europe most represented. TOEFL required—520 minimum for undergraduates; 590 minimum for graduate students. Applications should be submitted well in advance of the deadlines. Limited financial aid available for international students; all international students must show proof of adequate funding from their own sources in case they do not receive a merit-based award.

Prominent alumni include: Drama— Joan McMurtrey, Fred Rubin, Alan Ruck. Music—Michael Colgrass, Jerry Hadley, Erie Mills.

AUTHOR'S COMMENT: Recommended for Drama; highly recommended for Accompanying; also recommended for graduate Composition, Orchestral Conducting, and graduate Voice.

University of Iowa

107 Calvin Hall
Iowa City, IA 52242

General Admissions: 319-335-3847
Theater Arts Dept.: 319-335-2700
Dance Dept.: 319-335-2228
Music Dept.: 319-335-1603

Enrollment. University: 28,884; 19,260 undergraduates. Dance: 60 undergraduates, 8–12 graduates. Music: 500.

Faculty. Drama: 11 full time, 8 part time. Dance: 8 full time. Music: 50.

Application deadline. Rolling to May 15.

Audition. Required for graduate program.

Degrees offered. BA in Theater Arts, MFA in Acting.

Costs. Tuition: In-state—$1,880; out-of-state—$6,220. Room and board: $2,769.

. . . .

Standardized tests: SAT or ACT required. Achievement tests optional.

Interview: Required as part of audition.

Facilities: 3 theaters seating 477, 150, and 144 respectively, scene shop, costume shop, props shop.

Financial aid: First-come, first-served after January 1.

AUTHOR'S COMMENT: Recommended for Drama, Dance, and Organ.

University of Kansas, Lawrence

126 Strong Hall
Lawrence, KS 66045

Admissions: 913-864-3911
Dept. of Theater: 913-532-6875
Dept. of Dance: 913-864-4264
Dept. of Music: 913-864-3436

Dept. of Theater Address:
Nichols Hall, 129

Enrollment. University: 28,773; 19,480 undergraduates. Drama majors: 60. Dance majors: 30.
Faculty. Drama: 11 full time, 1 part time. Dance: 3 full time, 5 part time.
Application deadlines. Rolling admissions to February 1.
Audition. Call for information.
Degrees offered. BA, BS, MA in Acting. BA in Dance. BM, MM, DMA in Music.
Costs. Tuition: In-state—$1,546; out-of-state—$4,670.

. . . .

Standardized tests: ACT required. Achievement tests optional.
Interview: Recommended.
Facilities: 3 theaters seating 1,800, 280, and 100 respectively and a 400-seat recital hall.
Financial aid: Submit FAF or FES by March 1. Several merit scholarships based on GPA, recommendations.

AUTHOR'S COMMENT: Recommended for undergraduate Drama and Dance. The Music Department in general is strong.

University of Maryland, College Park

College Park, MD 20742

Undergraduate Admissions: 301-314-8385
Graduate Admissions: 301-405-4198
Dept. of Theater: 301-405-6676
Undergraduate Music Dept.: 301-405-5563
Graduate Music Dept.: 301-405-5560

Theater Dept. Address:
Tawes Fine Arts Building

Enrollment. University: 23,561 undergraduates; 8,461 graduates. Drama majors: 150 undergraduates, 30 graduates. Music majors: 160 undergraduates, 200 graduates.
Faculty. Drama: 12 full time, 2 part time. Music: 47 full time, 21 part time.
Application deadline. Before auditions, held in January–March.
Audition. Required. Held on campus in November–March.
Degrees offered. BA in Theater. BA, BM, MM, Ph.D, DMA in Music.
Costs. Tuition: Undergraduate—$1,217.50; graduate—$250 per credit hour. Fees: $120. Room: $1,309. Board: $947 to $1,147.

. . . .

Standardized tests: SAT required. Achievement tests optional. GRE not required for graduate performance majors.
Tapes: Accepted except for graduate Voice students.
Admissions criteria: GPA, SAT, recommendations.
Musical instruments taught: Piano, All Orchestral Instruments, Saxophone. Also Composition, Jazz Studies, Voice.
Facilities: 3 theaters seating 1,340, 100, and 60 respectively, scene shop, costume shop, and new building just being completed. Recital Hall, Tawes Theater, Memorial Chapel.
Financial aid: Submit FAF by February 15. There are also some merit-based scholarships available.
Housing: 25% of all who apply receive on-campus housing.
International students: Special application deadlines: March 1 for undergraduates, February 1 for graduate students. TOEFL required. Financial aid available for foreign students.
Prominent alumni include: Music—Carmen Balthrop, Gordon Hawkins, Alessandra Marc, Emily White. Drama—Kene Holiday, Dianne Wiest.

AUTHOR'S COMMENT: Recommended for undergraduate Drama and Piano.

University of Massachusetts, Amherst

Amherst, MA 01003

Admissions: 413-545-0222
Dance Admissions: 413-545-2413
Dept. of Music and Dance: 413-545-4313
Dept. of Theater: 413-545-3490

Dept. of Theater Address:
Fine Arts Center, Room 112

Enrollment. University: 19,000 undergraduates; 5,000 graduates. Drama majors: 200 undergraduates, 16 graduates. Music majors: 200 undergraduates, 50 graduate students.
Faculty. Drama: 12 full time, 1 part time. Music: 42 full time, 8 part time.
Application deadline. Rolling admissions to February 15.
Audition. Required in Music. Held on the campus in December–April. Call the Department for exact dates. Music history and theory exams also required for graduate students.
Degrees offered. BA, MFA in Theater. BA, BM, MM, Ph.D in Music. BFA in Dance.
Costs. Tuition: In-state—$3,476; out-of-state—$8,329. Room and board: $3,694.

• • • • • • • • • • • • • • • • • •

Standardized tests: SAT or ACT required. Achievement tests recommended.
Interview: Required.
Tapes: Accepted in Music only if distance is an extreme problem.
Musical instruments taught: All Orchestral Instruments, Piano. Also has programs in Accompanying, Voice, Early Music, Composition, Contemporary Music, Electronic Music, and Jazz.
Facilities: 2 theaters seating 565 and 100 respectively, scene shop, costume shop, props shops.
Financial aid: Submit FAF by March 1. Some merit scholarships available.
International students: 10% from abroad. Korea, Japan, Latin America, Europe, South Africa most represented. TOEFL required—550 minimum. Very limited amount of scholarship available for foreign students and based only on merit.
Prominent music alumni include: Bruce MacCombie, Ed Purrington.

AUTHOR'S COMMENT: Although the Massachusetts economy has resulted in funding difficulties for the University, there are some great faculty members here. Recommended for undergraduate Drama, which has an affiliation with Theater in the Works, a summer Equity company; Dance (Part of Five College Department); and Guitar, Jazz, and Voice.

University of Miami

P.O. Box 248025
University Station
Coral Gables, FL 33124-8025

Admissions: 305-284-4323 or 305-284-6439 or 2245
Drama Dept.: 305-284-4474
School of Music: 305-284-2161
School of Dance: 305-284-2521

Drama Dept. Address:
Box 248273

School of Music Address:
Box 248165. Zip: 33124-7610

Enrollment. University: 13,345; Drama majors: 75 male, 50 female undergraduates. Music majors: 500 undergraduates, 200 graduate students.
Faculty. Drama: 15 full time, 5 part time. Dance: 6 full time, 5 part time. Music: 63 full time, 27 part time.
Application deadlines. Early Decision: November 1. Regular Decision: March 1.
Audition. Required. For Drama held in Dallas, Houston, Louisville, Chicago, New York City, Baltimore, Washington, D.C., New Orleans, and Boston. Contact the Drama Department for exact dates. Music auditions held on campus and regionally from December–April. Call the School for exact dates and locations.
Degrees offered. BFA, BA in Drama. BFA, BA in Dance. BA, BM, MM, MS, DMA, Ph.D, Diploma in Performance all available in Music.
Costs. Tuition and fees: $18,000. Room: $3,000. Board: $3,500 (approximate).

• • • • • • • • • • • • • • • • • •

Standardized tests: SAT or ACT required. Achievement tests required for some programs.
Tapes: Videotapes acceptable for Musical Theater and Dance, although live auditions preferred. Cassette tapes for other Music applicants who live outside of South Florida.

(continued on next page)

Musical instruments taught: All Orchestral Instruments, Piano, Guitar, Organ. Also Composition, Voice, Musical Theater, Studio Music and Jazz, Accompanying, Choral and Instrumental Conducting.

Drama facilities: 3 acting studios, 1 movement studio, 1 dance studio, theater.

Financial aid: Available. Must submit the FAF by March 1. Based on merit and need.

Housing: 95% of new students offered on-campus housing. Freshmen must live on campus.

International students: 9% of undergraduates and 12% of graduate students from abroad. China (PRC), Venezuela, Malaysia, India most represented. TOEFL required—550 minimum. Auditions held in the Far East.

Prominent alumni include: Drama—Jerry Herman, Saundra Santiago. Music—Bruce Hornsby, Dawn Lewis, Marvis Martin, Sam Pilafian.

AUTHOR'S COMMENT: Recommended for undergraduate Drama, Dance, undergraduate Composition, Guitar, Jazz, Musical Theater, and Saxophone.

University of Michigan

Ann Arbor, MI 48109

Admissions: 313-764-7433 or 313-764-0593
Dance Dept.: 313-763-5460
Dept. of Theater and Drama: 313-764-5350
School of Music: 313-764-0593

Dept. of Theater and Drama Address:
School of Music, 2550 Frieze Building
University of Michigan
Ann Arbor, MI 48109-1285

School of Music Address:
1100 Baits Drive, Ann Arbor, MI 48109-2085

Dance Dept. Address:
1310 North University, Ann Arbor, MI 48109-2217

Enrollment. University: 23,000 undergraduates: 13,000 graduate students. Drama majors: 30 male, 43 female undergraduates. Graduate Drama students: 6 male, 14 female. Dance majors: 50 undergraduates, 8–10 graduates. Music majors: 460 undergraduates, 296 graduate students.

Faculty. Drama: 13 full time, 2 part time. Dance: 6 full time, 3 part time. Music: 95 full time, 20 part time.

Application deadlines. Rolling admissions to April 1, but be sure to apply early enough to make auditions. Early action and financial aid: February 15.

Audition. Required for BFA . Interview required for Ph.D in Theater Studies. Drama auditions held in Ann Arbor, Chicago, Las Vegas, and New York City, November through February. Contact the School well in advance. Required for Music applicants; held in Ann Arbor and regionally November–April. Audition required for Dance; held January–April on campus and in March in New York City. Call the Dance Department for specific dates and any other locations.

Degrees offered. BA, BFA in Theater. MA, Ph.D in Theater Studies. BM, BMA, BFA, MA, MM, DMA, Ph.D and Specialist in Music all available in Music. BFA, BDA (Bachelor of Dance Arts), MFA available in Dance.

Costs. In-state undergraduate tuition: $3,630; fees: $117.62; out-of-state undergraduate tuition: $12,718. In-state graduate tuition: $6,510; out-of state graduate tuition: $13,626. Room and board on campus: $3,000 to $3,500.

• • • • • • • • • • • • • • • • • •

Standardized tests: SAT or ACT required. Achievement tests optional.

Videotapes: Accepted for BFA in Theater Performance. Send in care of the Head of Drama Performance Training. In Music, special conditions apply to several instrumental or program areas where tapes are strongly discouraged. In Dance, videotapes discouraged and allowed only for international students with extensive recommendations.

Musical instruments taught: All Orchestral Instruments, Carillon, Fortepiano, Harpsichord, Organ, Saxophone. Also programs in Conducting, Church Music, Accompanying, Chamber Music, Musical Theater, Voice.

Financial aid: Must submit the FAF. Some merit-based scholarships available.

International students: About 1%. Must also submit TOEFL—550 minimum—and the Michigan English Language Assessment Battery—82 minimum.

Prominent alumni include: Drama—Christina Canti, James Earl Jones, Arthur Miller, Gilda Radner. Music—George Crumb, Bob James, Bob McGrath, Madonna, Jessye Norman, Ashley Putnam, Roger Reynolds. Dance—Christine Dakin, Carol Teitelbaum.

AUTHOR'S COMMENT: Recommended for Drama, Dance, Church Music, Clarinet, Harp, Musical Theater, Oboe, Orchestral Conducting, Organ, Piano, Saxophone, Trumpet, and Voice. Highly recommended in Accompanying, Composition, and Percussion.

University of Minnesota, Twin Cities

231 Pillsbury Drive
230 Wills Hall
Minneapolis, MN 55455-0294

Admissions: 612-625-5000
Theater Arts Dept.: 612-625-6699
Dance Dept.: 612-624-5060
Music Dept.: 612-624-5093

Theater Arts Dept. Address:
208 Middlebrook Hall, 412 22nd Avenue South

Enrollment. University: 41,000; 30,964 undergraduates. Dance: 48. Music: 250 undergraduates, 170 graduates.
Faculty. Drama: 17 full time, 3 part time. Dance: 3 full time, 9 part time. Music: 45 full time, 40 part time.
Application deadlines. Rolling admissions to December 15.
Audition. Required.
Degrees offered. BA in Theater Arts, MFA in Acting. BFA in Dance. BA, BM, MA, MM, DMA, Ph.D in Music.
Costs. Tuition: In-state—$2,601; out-of-state—$5,703. Room and board: $3,300.

. . . .

Standardized tests: SAT or ACT required. Achievement tests optional.
Interview: Required as part of audition.
Drama facilities: 4 theaters seating 459, 487, 206, and 125 respectively, scene shop, costume shop, props shop, dance studio, rehearsal spaces.
Financial aid: Submit the FFS by April 1.

AUTHOR'S COMMENT: Recommended for Drama, Dance, Church Music, Guitar, Oboe, Orchestral Conducting, Trombone, Viola, and Violin. Highly recommended for Accompanying.

University of Missouri, Columbia

Columbia, MO 65211

Admissions: 314-882-2456
Dept. of Music: 314-882-2604

Dept. of Music Address:
140 Fine Arts

Enrollment. University: 23,000. Music majors: Over 200 undergraduates, 41 graduate students.
Music faculty. 37 full time, 28 part time teaching assistants.
Application deadline. May 15 (freshmen).
Audition. Required. Held in February in St. Louis; Kansas City; Springfield, MO; and on campus by arrangement.
Degrees offered. BM, BA, MM, MA, Ph.D.
Costs. Tuition: $3,577 out-of-state; Fees: $2,187. Room and board: $3,004.

. . . .

Standardized tests: SAT or ACT required.
Admissions criteria: Performance audition, transcript evaluation, standardized tests scores.
Musical instruments taught: All Orchestral Instruments except for Harp; Guitar, Piano, Harpsichord, Organ. Also has a Jazz and Chamber Music program, and Voice.
Music facilities: Recital hall seating 210, auditorium seating 2,500.
Financial aid: FAF and departmental scholarship form must be filed. Merit-based awards available.
Housing: 100% who apply for housing receive on-campus housing.
International students: 8% from abroad. Taiwan, China (PRC), Brazil most represented. Financial aid available to international students.
Prominent music alumnus: Eugene Watts.

AUTHOR'S COMMENT: The University has a solid Music program.

University of Missouri, Kansas City

4825 Troost Avenue
Kansas City, MO 64110-2030

Admissions: 816-235-1111
Dept. of Theater: 816-276-7379
Dept. of Music: 816-235-2959

Conservatory of Music Address:
4949 Cherry
Dept. of Theater Address:
5100 Rockhill Road

Enrollment. 11,500; Drama majors: 110. Music majors: 450.
Faculty. Drama: 15 full time, 1 part time. Music: 47 full time, 10 part time.
Audition. Required for MFA in Acting and for Music.
Degrees offered. BA in General Theater, MFA in Acting. BA, BM in Music.
Costs. Tuition: In-state—$2,012; out-of-state—$5,603. Room and board: $2,942.

. . . .

Interview: Required as part of audition.
Drama facilities: 3 theaters seating 700, 100, and 100 respectively.
Financial aid: Submit the FFS by March 31.

AUTHOR'S COMMENT: Recommended for Drama, which is affiliated with the Missouri Repertory Theater, an Equity company; also Accordian, Flute, and Electronic Music.

University of Nebraska, Lincoln

Lincoln, NE 68588

Admissions: 402-472-2023 or 6320
Dept. of Theater Arts and Dance:
402-472-1606
School of Music: 402-472-2503

Dept. of Theater Arts and Dance Address:
215 Temple Building, 12th and R Streets

School of Music Address:
120 Westbrook Music Building

Enrollment. University: 19,000 undergraduates; 5,000 graduate students. Drama majors: 85. Dance majors: 15. Music majors: 288 undergraduates, 95 graduate students.
Faculty. Drama: 8 full time, 1 part time. Music: 39 full time, 6 part time.
Application deadlines. Rolling admissions for undergraduates. Graduate students: March 15.
Audition. Required. Usually held in February. Call department for exact dates and locations.
Degrees offered. BFA in Dance. BA in General Theater, MFA in Acting. BA in Music, BFA in Musical Theater, BM in Performance, Composition, MM, DMA.
Costs. Tuition: In-state—$1,915; out-of-state—$6,491. Room and board: $2,625.

. . . .

Standardized tests: ACT required. Achievement tests optional. GRE required for DMA applicants.
Tapes: Not accepted for in-state students. Other Music majors may submit a tape or videotape, but live audition preferred. Prescreening tapes required for all DMA applicants.
Musical instruments taught: Piano, Organ, Harpsichord, Saxophone, All Orchestral Instruments; Also Voice. Also has the American String Quartet in residence for lessons, master classes, and chamber music coachings. No Guitar.
Facilities: 2 theaters seating 380 and 180 respectively, scene shop, costume shop, props shop, welding shop, dance studios, rehearsal and classroom spaces, plus new Lied Center for the Performing Arts, (seats 2,300), Westbrook Recital Hall, Kimball Recital Hall (seats 849).
Financial aid: Submit FFS by March 1. Departmental scholarship forms also required for merit-based awards.
Housing: All freshmen under age 20 must live on campus.
International students: 3% from abroad. China (PRC), Korea, France, and Russia most represented. TOEFL required—550 minimum for undergraduates and Master's students; 600 for DMA. Application deadlines for International Students: March 1. Financial aid available for foreign students.

AUTHOR'S COMMENT: Recommended for Drama, Dance, and Musical Theater.

University of New Mexico, Albuquerque

Albuquerque, NM 87131

Admissions: 505-277-5161
Dept. of Music: 505-277-2127
Dept. of Theater Arts: 505-277-4332
Dept. of Dance: 505-277-3660

Enrollment. University: 24,600, 19,986 undergraduates. Drama majors: 76. Dance majors: 15. Music majors: 200 undergraduates, 50 graduate students.
Faculty. Drama: 12 full time. Dance: 5 full time, 11 part time. Music: 28 full time, 12 part time.
Application deadlines. Rolling admissions to July 24 for fall semester, December 15 for spring semester.
Audition. Required in Music; held in March and April. Applicants must also take a Music theory exam. Also required in Dance and Drama. Call for dates and guidelines.
Degrees offered. BA, MA in Theater Arts, BFA in Acting. BA, BFA, MA in Dance. BA, BM, MM in Music.
Costs. Tuition: In-state—$1,453; out-of-state—$5,152. Room and board: $2,990.

• • • • • • • • • • • • • • • • • • • •

Standardized tests: ACT required. Achievement tests optional. GRE required for graduate students.
Tapes: Music Department will accept cassette or videotape but prefers live audition. Videotapes not accepted in Dance or Drama.
Musical instruments taught: All Orchestral, Classical Guitar, Harpsichord, Piano, Organ. Also has Early Music, Voice, Electronic Music, Jazz, and Opera programs.
Financial aid: FAF and University's own form must be submitted by March 1. Merit awards also available.
International students: 2% from abroad. TOEFL required—550 minimum. Financial aid available for foreign students.
Prominent music alumni include: John Chatham, John Lewis.

AUTHOR'S COMMENT: Recommended for Drama, Dance, Flute, and Guitar.

University of North Carolina at Chapel Hill

Graduate School Admisisons
College Box 4010, 200 Bynum Hall
Chapel Hill, NC 27599-4010

Admissions: 919-966-2611
Dept. of Dramatic Art: 919-962-1132

Dept. of Dramatic Art/Professional Actor Training Program Address:
College Box 3230, 105 Graham Memorial
Chapel Hill, NC 27599-3230

Enrollment. University: 15,640 undergraduates; 8,210 graduate students. Professional Actor Training Program (PATP): 9 male, 8 female graduate students.
Drama faculty. 4 full time, 8 part time.
Application deadline. Best to file before the February 1 deadline.
Audition. Required. Held in February in New York City, Chicago, and Chapel Hill.
Degree offered. MFA in Acting. 3-year intensive conservatory program closely affiliated with PlayMakers Repertory Company, the LORT/Equity theater associated with the University and located on the campus.
Costs. Tuition: In-state—$664; out-of-state—$5,106. Fees: $475.

• • • • • • • • • • • • • • • • • • • •

Standardized tests: GRE not required.
Videotape: Accepted in extraordinary circumstances only, but not recommended.
Admissions criteria: Quality of performance at the audition, recommendations, application essay, previous training in Drama, experience in productions, body type, physical, vocal, and articulation equipment that seem potentially responsive to training. Applicants must submit 3 letters of recommendation and an official undergraduate transcript.
Drama facilities: Contemporary thrust stage, small proscenium stage, small black box.
Scholarships: Currently 100% in PATP receive scholarship from the school.

(continued on next page)

Financial aid: FAF must be submitted. Assistantships available for second- and third-year students.
Housing: No on-campus housing available.
International students: 12% from abroad. Canada and South Africa most represented. Very limited scholarship assistance available for foreign students.
Prominent alumni include: Wendy Barrie-Wilson, Michael Cumpsty, Joseph Haj, Latherine Meisle, Demetrios Pappageorge, Matthew Ryan, David Whalen.

AUTHOR'S COMMENT: Highly recommended for graduate studies in Drama. This intensive actor training program, which admits only 8 students a year, has a superb faculty and a demanding curriculum. The opportunity to work within the professional company on this gorgeous campus provides good experience.

University of North Carolina, Greensboro

1000 Spring Garden Street
Greensboro, NC 27412

Admissions: 919-334-5243
Theater Division: 919-334-5562

Theater Division Address:
212 Taylor Building

Enrollment. University: 12,000; 9,000 undergraduates. Drama majors: 140.
Drama faculty. 12 full time.
Application deadlines. Early Decision: October 10. Rolling admissions to August 1.
Audition. Required.
Degrees offered. BA in Drama, BFA, MFA in Acting. BA, BFA in Dance.
Costs. Tuition: In-state—$1,296; out-of-state—$5,792. Room and board: $3,140.

Standardized tests: SAT required. Achievement tests optional.
Interview: Required as part of audition.
Facilities: 4 theaters seating 2,400, 500, 250, and 70 respectively.
Financial aid: Submit FAF by March 1.

AUTHOR'S COMMENT: Recommended for Drama and Dance.

University of Northern Colorado

306 Carter Hall
Greeley, CO 80639

Admissions: 303-351-2881
School of Music: 303-351-2678

Enrollment. Dance: 20. Drama: 120. Music: 440.
Faculty. Dance: 3. Drama: 7. Music: 40.
Application deadlines. Early Decision: February 1. Early Action: March 1. Regular Decision: April 1.
Audition. Required.
Degrees offered. BA in Dance. BA in Drama. BM, MM, DA, DMA in Music.
Costs. Tuition: In-state—$1,819; out-of-state—$4,690. Room and board: $3,200.

Standardized tests: Not required.
Interview: Required.
Videotapes: Accepted.
Musical instruments taught: All Orchestral Instruments, Keyboard Instruments, Band Instruments, and Voice.
Facilities: Frasier Hall, Foundation Hall, Langworthy Theatre, Union Colony Civic Center.
Financial aid: Available. Submit the FAF. Talent scholarships available.
International students: 3% from abroad. Canada, Korea, and China most represented. TOEFL required. 520 minimum.
Prominent alumni include: Members of leading symphonies, opera and musical theater companies, wind and jazz ensembles nationwide.

AUTHOR'S COMMENT: Recommended for Musical Theater and as a strong comprehensive School of Music. Dance and Drama also recommended.

University of North Texas, Denton

P.O. Box 13797
Denton, TX 76203-6797

Admissions: 817-565-2681
Music Dept.: 817-565-2791

AUTHOR'S COMMENT: Highly recommended for Jazz. Recommended for Flute and Tuba.

University of Notre Dame

Notre Dame, IN 46556

Undergraduate Admissions: 219-239-7505
Graduate Admissions: 219-239-7544
Dept. of Music: 219-239-6211

Enrollment. University: 8,000 undergraduates, 2,000 graduate students. Music majors: 14 undergraduates, 25 graduate students.
Music faculty. 17 full time, 5 part time.
Application deadlines. Early Action: November 1. Regular Decision: January 10.
Audition. Required and arranged individually on campus.
Degrees offered. BA, MM, MA.
Costs. Tuition and fees: $12,390. Room and board: $3,475.

. . . .

Standardized tests: SAT required. Achievement tests recommended.
Tapes: Videotapes and cassettes accepted if the applicant is unable to travel to Notre Dame for a personal audition.
Musical instruments taught: All Orchestral Instruments, Saxophone, Piano, Organ, Classical Guitar, Harpsichord. Also Voice.
Financial aid: Submit FAF by February 28. Some merit scholarships available.
International students: China, Canada, Brazil, Argentina most represented. TOEFL required. Financial aid available for foreign graduate students only.
Prominent music alumnus: Thomas Clifton.

AUTHOR'S COMMENT: Recommended for Church Music and Organ.

University of Oregon, Eugene

240 Oregon Hall
Eugene, OR 97403

Admissions: 503-346-3201
School of Music: 503-346-3761
Dance Dept.: 503-346-3386

Enrollment. University: 17,500; 13,790 undergraduates. Music majors: 300 undergraduates, 120 graduate students.
Faculty. Drama: 25 full time, 7 part time. Music: 38 full time, 14 part time.
Application deadlines. Regular Decision: March 1.
Audition. Required. Held on campus and regionally December–early March.
Degrees offered. BA, BM, MM, MA, DMA, Ph.D in Music. BA, BFA in Dance.
Costs. In-state tuition: $2,700; out-of-state tuition: $7,900. Room and board: $3,212.

. . . .

Standardized tests: SAT or ACT required. Achievement tests optional.
Tapes: High-quality cassettes presenting 3 contrasting selections accepted in Music. Videotapes accepted in Dance.
Musical instruments taught: All Orchestral and Band Instruments, Guitar, Piano, Harpsichord, Clavichord, Organ, Recorder. Also Jazz, Electronic and Computer Music programs.
Financial aid: FAF by March 1 and University's own form required. Some merit awards available.
International students: 12% from abroad. Taiwan, Singapore, China (PRC), Korea, Japan most represented. TOEFL required—550 minimum. Some scholarship assistance available for foreign students.
Prominent music alumni include: Robert Culner, Philip Frohnmayer, Jerome Ottley, Dan Sidgel, Ralph Towner.

AUTHOR'S COMMENT: Recommended for Dance. The Music program has strengths, too.

University of Pennsylvania

34th and Spruce Streets
College Hall
Philadelphia, PA 19104-6376

Admissions: 215-898-7507

Enrollment. University: 21,900; 9,500 undergraduates.
Application deadlines. Early Decision: November 1. Regular Decision: January 1.
Audition. Not required.
Costs. Tuition and fees: $14,890. Room and board: $5,700.

. . . .

Standardized tests: SAT required. 3 achievement tests required: English and 2 others.
Interview: Available on campus to children of alumni only. Interviews with alumni recommended.
Tapes: Videotapes or cassettes may be sent to the Office of Admissions to be referred to the department for evaluation.
Financial aid: Submit FAF by January 1. Scholarships based on need.

AUTHOR'S COMMENT: Recommended for Composition.

University of Pittsburgh

Bruce Hall
Pittsburgh, PA 15260

Admissions: 412-624-7488
Dept. of Theater Arts: 412-624-6467

Dept. of Theater Arts Address:
B-39 Cathedral of Learning

Enrollment. University: 24,931; 18,810 undergraduates.
Drama faculty. 12 full time, 1 part time.
Application deadline. Rolling admissions.
Audition. Required for MFA.
Degrees offered. BA in Theater Arts, MFA in Acting.
Costs. Tuition: In-state—$4,086; out-of-state—$8,106. Room and board: $3,314.

. . . .

Standardized tests: SAT required. Achievement tests optional.
Interview: Recommended.
Facilities: 3 theaters seating 580, 120, and 11 respectively, scene shop, costume shop, props shop, rehearsal spaces, classrooms.

AUTHOR'S COMMENT: Recommended for Drama. The program has an affiliation with two Equity theaters: Three Rivers Shakespeare Festival and the City Theater Company.

University of Rhode Island

Kingston, RI 02881

Admissions: 401-792-2872 or 2164
Drama Dept.:401-792-5921 or 5922

Enrollment. University: 16,080. Drama majors: 23 male, 37 female undergraduates.
Drama faculty. 6 full time, 12 part time and about 20 guest artists engaged in all areas of specialization.
Application deadlines. Early Decision: November 1. Regular Decision: Rolling, but submit by March 1.
Audition. Not required.
Degrees offered. BA, BFA in Theater.
Costs. Tuition: In-state—$2,747; out-of-state—$7,251. Room and board: $4,323.

· · · · · · · · · · · · · · · · · · · ·

Standardized tests: SAT or ACT required. Achievement tests optional.
Interview: Recommended.
Videotapes: Accepted for the department to review and give an assessment of talent to the Office of Admissions.
Admissions criteria: Admission to the University, previous drama training, grades in school, commitment, dedication, level of participation in performances all considered.
Facilities: 550-seat proscenium theater, black box, flexible space, lab theater, theater, dance studio seating 100.
Financial aid: Available. Must submit FAF by March 1. Four merit scholarships are available in Drama.
International students: 2% of student body. TOEFL required. Very limited financial aid available for students from abroad.
Prominent drama alumni include: Peter Frechette, J. T. Walsh.

AUTHOR'S COMMENT: Recommended for undergraduate Drama.

University of San Diego/Old Globe Theater

Alcala Park
San Diego, CA 92110

Admissions: 619-231-1941

Enrollment. University: 5,400.
Drama faculty. 20 part time.
Audition. Required.
Degree offered. MFA in Acting.

· · · · · · · · · · · · · · · · · · · ·

Interview: Required as part of audition.
Facilities: 3 theaters seating 614, 580, 225 respectively.
Financial aid: Students are offered full 2-year fellowships with an additional stipend in the second year.

AUTHOR'S COMMENT: This is a young program, but well regarded. All students work and train with members of the Old Globe Theater, an Equity company, and receive an Equity card at the end of training. Recommended for graduate Drama.

University of South Carolina, Columbia

Columbia, SC 29208

Admissions: 803-777-7700
Dept. of Theater and Speech: 803-777-4288

Enrollment. University: 25,610; 16,050 undergraduates. Drama majors: 80.
Drama faculty. 13 full time, 2 part time.
Application deadline. Rolling admissions to August 1.
Audition. Required for MFA.
Degrees offered. BA in Theater, MFA in Acting.
Costs. Tuition: In-state—$2,560; out-of-state—$6,400. Room and board: $2,928.

· · · · · · · · · · · · · · · · · · · ·

Standardized tests: SAT required. Achievement tests optional.
Interview: Required as part of audition.
Facilities: 3 theaters seating 400, 320, and 40 respectively, scene shop, costume shop, props shop, dance studio.
Financial aid: Submit FAF by April 15.

AUTHOR'S COMMENT: Recommended for graduate Drama. The program has developed an affiliation with the Shakespeare Theater at the Folger.

University of South Florida, Tampa

4202 Fowler Avenue
Tampa, FL 33620-6900

Admissions: 813-974-3350
Theater Dept.: 813-974-2701
Dance Dept.: 813-974-2614

Enrollment. University: 31,638; 21,700 undergraduates. Drama majors: 76. Dance majors: 53.
Faculty. Drama: 15 full time. Dance: 9 full time.
Application deadline. Rolling admissions to June 1.
Degrees offered. BA, BFA in Performance.
Costs. Tuition: In-state—$1,322; out-of-state—$4,082.

• • • • • • • • • • • • • • • • • • •

Standardized tests: SAT or ACT required. Achievement tests optional.
Facilities: 2 theaters seating 538 and 300 respectively, scene shop, costume shop, props shop, 3 dance studios, rehearsal spaces.
Financial aid: Submit the FAF or FFS by January 31.

AUTHOR'S COMMENT: Recommended for undergraduate Drama, which has established an affiliation with Tampa Players and Playmakers, Equity companies. Also highly recommended for Dance.

University of Southern California

University Park Campus
Los Angeles, CA 90089-0911

Admissions: 213-740-1111 or 6753
School of Music Admissions: 213-743-2741
or 1-800-872-2213
School of Theater: 213-743-2703

Enrollment. University: 14,555 undergraduates; 11,178 graduate students. School of Music: 333 undergraduates, 376 graduate students. Drama majors: 350.
Faculty. Music: 54 full time, 75 part time. Drama: 12 full time, 24 part time.
Application deadlines. Rolling admissions. Regular admissions: March 1.

Audition. Required for BFA and MFA in Acting programs and for all Music applicants who must also take music theory, ear training and other tests. Music auditions held on campus and regionally throughout the United States in January and February.
Degrees offered. BA in Drama, BFA, MFA in Acting. BA, BM, MM, MA, DMA, Ph.D, Advanced Studies in Performance Certificate, Certificate in Motion Picture and Film Scoring, and Artist Diploma all offered in Music.
Costs. Tuition and fees: $13,446. Room and board: $5,282.

• • • • • • • • • • • • • • • • • • •

Standardized tests: SAT or ACT required. Achievement tests recommended.
Interview: Required for Music applicants.
Tapes: Accepted for Music applicants.
Musical instruments taught: All Orchestral Instruments, Accompanying, Classical Guitar, Studio Guitar, Harpsichord, Piano, Organ. Also Voice, Electronic Music, Jazz Studies, Composition, Choral Music, Early Music, Church Music, Conducting.
Drama facilities: 3 theaters seating 600, 100, and 100 respectively, scene shop, costume shop, props shop, welding shop, 3 dance studios, rehearsal spaces.
Financial aid: Submit the FAF by February 15, and California residents submit the SAAC. Merit awards available.
International students: 40% from abroad. China (PRC), Korea, Taiwan, Japan most represented. TOEFL required—600 minimum.
Prominent music alumni include: Herb Alpert, Jerry Goldsmith, Robert Grayson, Lionel Hampton, Marilyn Horne, Carol Neblett, Christopher Parkening, Nathaniel Rosen, Michael Tilson Thomas.

AUTHOR'S COMMENT: Highly recommended for Accompanying and Voice; recommended for Bassoon, Church Music, Clarinet, Double Bass, Early Music, Flute, French Horn, Guitar, Harp, Jazz, Orchestral Conducting, Organ, Piano, Tuba, Viola, Violin, and Violoncello. Also recommended for Drama.

University of Texas, Austin

Austin, TX 78705-5288

Admissions: 512-471-7601
Undergraduate Music Dept.: 512-471-0504
Graduate Music Dept.: 512-471-1502
Dance Dept.: 512-471-5902

Dept. of Music Address:
MRH, 3.832, 25th and East Campus Drive,
Austin, TX 78712-1208

Enrollment. University: 37,152 undergraduates; 10,867 graduates. Drama majors: 385 undergraduates, 100 graduates. Dance majors: 66 undergraduates. Music majors: 300 undergraduates; 350 graduates.
Faculty. Drama: 29 full time. Dance: 6 full time. Music: 74 full time, 13 part time.
Application deadlines. Rolling admissions to March 1 for undergraduates, June 1 for graduate students.
Audition. Required. Held October through April. Graduate Music students also take diagnostic exams in music history and music theory. Voice and Opera students are required to take a language diction exam.
Degrees offered. BA in Drama, BFA in Acting. BA, BFA in Dance. BA, BM, MM, DMA in Music.
Costs. Tuition: Residents—$916; out-of-state—$3,620. Room and board: $3,300.

. . . .

Standardized tests: SAT or ACT required. Achievement tests recommended (English Composition and Math). All graduate students are required to take the GRE.
Tapes: High-quality cassettes accepted, but live audition preferred for Music.
Musical instruments taught: All Orchestral Instruments, Piano, Organ, Saxophone, Guitar, Composition. Also has programs in Voice, Opera, Choral Conducting, Orchestral Conducting, and Jazz Studies.
Facilities: 3 theaters seating 500, 200 and 150 respectively.
Financial aid: FFS required along with departmental forms for scholarships, fellowships, and assistantships.
International students: 7% of undergraduates, 15% of graduate students. China (PRC), Korea, Japan, Mexico, Canada most represented. TOEFL required—550 minimum. File application by February 1. Some financial aid available for foreign students.

Prominent music alumni include: James Dick, Phillip Moll, Robert Rodriguez, Carl St. Clair, Lawrence Weiner.

AUTHOR'S COMMENT: Recommended for undergraduate Drama, Dance, Guitar, Piano, and Violoncello.

University of the Arts

Broad and Pine Streets
Philadelphia, PA 19102

Admissions: 215-875-4808 or 1-800-272-3790
Dance Dept.: 215-875-2269
Drama Dept.: 215-272-3790
Music Dept.: 215-875-2206

Enrollment. University: 1,245 undergraduates; 65 graduate students. Drama majors: 33 male, 69 female undergraduates. Music majors: 116 undergraduates; 19 graduate students. Dance majors: 12 male, 153 female undergraduates.
Faculty. Drama: 4 full time, 19 part time. Music: 12 full time, 55 part time. Dance: 5 full time, 20 part time.
Application deadline. Rolling.
Audition. Required. Held on campus October through July and regionally at dates and locations to be announced.
Degrees offered. BFA in Theater Arts, Acting emphasis. BFA in Musical Theater, BM, MM, Certificate, Diploma all available in Music. BFA in Dance.
Costs. Tuition: $10,295. Fees: $480. Room: $3,570. Board: Apartment-style housing.

. . . .

Standardized tests: SAT or ACT required; SAT preferred. Recommended SAT minimum: 900 combined.
Interview: Required for scholarship consideration.
Videotapes: Accepted. VHS format. School has strict guidelines about what must be included, so be sure to contact well in advance.
Facilities: School of Theater: 100-seat black box; 200-seat theater; 1,668-seat Shubert Theater; 200-seat Wagman Hall; Great Hall Atrium. 6 dance studios with suspended wood floors.
Financial aid: Pennsylvania residents must submit the APSGFSA. Non-Pennsylvania residents must submit the FAF. All awards are based on need.

(continued on next page)

Housing: 60% of new students receive on-campus housing.

International students: 5% from abroad. Japan, Taiwan, Korea, Canada, and United Kingdom are most represented. TOEFL required—550 recommended minimum score; 450 minimum score for ESL program. Special foreign student application required. Must be filed prior to June 1. School recruits abroad in the United Kingdom, France, Greece, and the Pacific Rim. Very limited number of talent/merit scholarships available for students from abroad.

Prominent alumni include: Music—Michael Ludwig, Florence Quivar, Lew Tabackin, André Watts. Dance—Robert Hill, Judith Jamison, Kathy Rahochik, Carlos Schott.

AUTHOR'S COMMENT: The University of the Arts is the name since 1987 of the union of the Philadelphia College of Art and the Philadelphia College of Performing Arts. While its Theater program is fairly new, it does show promise. Musical Theater as a major was started in 1991. Overall, recommended for undergraduate Drama, Dance, and Musical Theater. The Music program in general has strengths and some of the faculty are members of the Philadelphia Orchestra.

University of Utah

Salt Lake City, UT 84112

Admissions: 801-581-7281 or 801-581-3096
Dept. of Music: 801-581-6762
Dept. of Theater: 801-581-6448
Dept. of Dance: 801-581-8231

Dept. of Theater Address:
206 Performing Arts Building

Enrollment. University: 19,900 undergraduates; 4,500 graduate students. Actor Training Program: 20 male, 10 female undergraduates. Dance majors: 240. Music majors: 290 undergraduates, 50 graduate students.
Faculty. Drama: 15 full time, 21 part time. Dance: 24. Music: 24 full time, 50 part time.
Application deadline. Regular admissions: July 1.
Audition. Required for Dance, Drama, and Music. Drama auditions held at the International Thespian Festival, Muncie, Indiana; Colorado Thespian Festival; Utah Theater Festival, St. George, Utah; and arranged throughout the year at the University of Utah. Music applicants must also take music theory and music history exams.
Degrees offered. BFA in Actor Training, BA in Theater Studies. BFA, MFA in Dance. BM, MM, Ph.D in Music.
Costs. Tuition: $6,000. Fees: $300. Room: $1,400. Board: $1,500.

. . . .

Standardized tests: ACT required. Achievement tests optional.
Interview: Required.
Videotapes: Accepted. In Drama, must include a brief introduction of yourself, your name, residence, background in acting/theater, statement of interest, 2 monologues or 1 monologue and 1 scene (1 contemporary, 1 in verse), and 16 bars of a song.
Admissions criteria: Must be admitted by the University Admissions Office. Quality of audition, recommendations, determination of commitment/desire for training and career gained through the interview and application, grades in school, previous experience.
Musical instruments taught: All Orchestral Instruments, Piano, Jazz Guitar. Also Voice, Composition, Conducting. No Organ.
Drama facilities: Classroom studies, 50-seat Lab Theater; 160-seat Babcock Theater; 1,200-seat Pioneer Theater.
Financial aid: Must submit FAF and departmental scholarship application by February 15. Both need- and merit-based scholarships available.
Housing: 3% of new students receive on-campus housing.
International students: 1% from abroad. England and Australia most represented. TOEFL required—500 minimum. Very limited scholarship help available for students from abroad.
Prominent drama alumni include: Maggie Baird, Julie Boyd, Marilyn Caskey, Keene Curis, Susan Gabriel, Margaret Gibson, Timothy Piggee.

AUTHOR'S COMMENT: The Department of Theater and the Pioneer Theater Company of the University of Utah combine to provide excellent, intensive conservatory training for serious acting students. Highly recommended for the Actor Training Program. Also highly recommended for Dance (modern). The Music program in general has strengths.

University of Virginia, Charlottesville

P.O. Box 9017
Charlottesville, VA 22906-9017

Admissions: 804-924-7751
Dept. of Drama: 804-924-3326

Enrollment. University: 17,910; 11,000 undergraduates. Drama majors: 33.
Drama faculty. 14 full time.
Application deadlines. Early Decision: November 1. Regular Decision: January 2.
Audition. Required for MFA.
Degrees offered. BA in Drama, MFA in Acting.
Costs. Tuition: In-state—$2,966; out-of-state—$8,136. Room and board: $3,150.

• • • • • • • • • • • • • • • • •

Standardized tests: SAT required. Achievement tests: 3 required, including English, Math, and a third of your choice.
Interview: Required as part of audition.
Drama facilities: 2 theaters seating 613 and 170 respectively.

AUTHOR'S COMMENT: Recommended for Drama.

University of Washington

Seattle, WA 98195

Admissions: 206-543-9686
School of Drama: 206-543-5140
School of Dance: 206-543-9843
School of Music: 206-543-1200

Enrollment. University: 33,000. Drama majors: 40 male, 80 female undergraduates; 68 male, 32 female graduate students. Dance majors: 30 undergraduates, 6 graduates. Music majors: 200 undergraduates, 250 graduates.
Application deadlines. January 1 for MFA; February 1 for other programs.
Audition. Required for Dance, Drama, and Music. For MFA in Acting. Auditions are held in Seattle, New York City, Chicago, and Long Beach.
Degrees offered. BA, MFA, Ph.D.
Costs. Tuition: In-state—$1,941; out-of-state—$5,421. Room and board: $3,800.

• • • • • • • • • • • • • • • • •

Standardized tests: SAT or ACT required.
Videotapes: Not accepted.
Admissions criteria: For acting, the audition is primary and everything else is secondary. In general, the University does give preference to state residents.
Drama facilities: 213-seat Glenn Hughes Theater, thrust stage; 171-seat Penthouse Theater, arena in the round; 370-seat Meany Studio, black box; 100-seat Cabaret; 100-seat black box.
Financial aid: Available. Must submit University's form.
Housing: Good availability.
International students: 2% to 3% enrolled, from China (PRC), Israel. No financial aid available for foreign students.
Prominent drama alumni include: Daryl Anderson, Tony Carriero, Patrick Duffy, Pat Finley, Harry Groener, Kyle MacLachlan, Dorothy Provine, Ella Raines, Pam Reed, Marc Singer, Jean Smart, Pam Sterlin, Dawn Wells.

AUTHOR'S COMMENT: Recommended for Drama, Dance, Bassoon, and Guitar.

University of Wisconsin

Madison, WI 53706

Admissions: 608-262-3961
Dept. of Theater and Drama: 608-263-2329
School of Music: 608-263-5986
School of Dance: 608-262-4917

School of Music Address:
455 North Park Street

Enrollment. University: 30,000 undergraduates; 12,000 graduate students. Drama majors: 30 male, 50 female undergraduates; 20 male, 30 female graduate students. Music majors: 270 undergraduates, 120 graduate students.
Faculty. Drama: 14 full time, 1 part time. Dance: 6 full time, 6–8 part time. Music: 62 full time, 5 part time.
Application deadline. Rolling admissions, but by February recommended.
Audition. Required for BA in acting and MFA in acting; held at the time of the U/RTA (University/ Resident Theater Association) auditions. Auditions required of all Music applicants are held on the campus in November, January and February. Ear Training test also required. Dance also requires an audition.
Degrees offered. BA, MA, MFA, Ph.D in Drama. BA, BM, MA, MM, DMA in Music.
Costs. Tuition: In-state—$2,140; out-of-state—$6,530. Room and board: $3,445.

• • • • • • • • • • • • • • • • • •

Standardized tests: ACT required. Achievement tests optional.
Videotapes: Not accepted. Cassette tapes accepted in Music but live audition preferred.
Admissions criteria: Acceptance to the University based on grades, standardized tests scores, recommendations, essays, and the quality of the audition.
Musical instruments taught: All Orchestral Instruments, Piano, Organ, Guitar, Saxophone. Also Composition, Voice, Jazz Studies, Choral Conducting, Instrumental Conducting.
Drama facilities: 4 theaters of differing sizes and shapes.
Financial aid: Available. FAF should be submitted by March 1. Merit scholarships also available.
International students: 1% to 2% of student body. TOEFL required. Limited financial aid available for foreign students.

Prominent drama alumni include: Don Ameche, Jill Eichenberry, Uta Hagen, Jane Kaczmarek, Daniel J. Travanti.

AUTHOR'S COMMENT: *The University of Wisconsin at Madison is a major research institution in a location which allows students access to the cultural activities of Milwaukee, Chicago, and the Twin Cities. The University enrolls a diverse and aware student body and provides a highly selective and rigorous academic environment. Recommended for undergraduate Drama, French Horn, Oboe, and Saxophone.*

University of Wisconsin, Milwaukee

P.O. Box 413
Milwaukee, WI 53201

Admissions: 414-229-3800
Dept. of Theater and Dance: 414-963-4947

Professional Theater Training Program Address:
P.O. Box 413

Enrollment. University: 24,857.
Drama faculty. 12 full time.
Audition. Required.
Degrees offered. BFA, MFA in Acting. BA, BM in Music.
Costs. Tuition: In-state—$2,258; out-of-state—$6,804. Room and board: $3,408.

• • • • • • • • • • • • • • • • • •

Interview: Required as part of audition.
Facilities: 2 theaters seating 550 and 90 respectively, scene shop, costume shop, props shop, 4 dance studios.
Financial aid: Merit and talent scholarships available. Based on audition.

AUTHOR'S COMMENT: *Recommended for Drama and Guitar.*

Vanderbilt University

401 24th Avenue, South
Nashville, TN 37212-2099

Admissions: 615-322-2561
Blair School of Music: 615-322-7651

Blair School of Music Address:
2400 Blakemore Avenue

Enrollment. University: 9,240; 5,000 undergraduates. Music majors: 110 undergraduates.
Music faculty. 28 full time, 38 part time.
Application deadlines. Early Decision: November 1. Regular Decision: January 15.
Audition. Required. Held in Nashville December–March. Call for exact dates.
Degree offered. BM.
Costs. Tuition and fees: $14,474. Room and board: $5,050.

• • • • • • • • • • • • • • • •

Standardized tests: SAT or ACT required. 3 achievement tests required, including English, Math, and one of your choice.
Tapes: Not accepted for percussion. Otherwise accepted for applicants who live outside a 400-mile radius of Nashville.
Musical instruments taught: All Orchestral, Piano, Organ, Guitar, Recorder, Viola da gamba, multiple Woodwinds. Also Voice, Composition.
Financial aid: Submit FAF by February 15 and University's own form. Some merit scholarships available.
International students: Very limited enrollment. TOEFL required. No financial aid available for foreign students.

AUTHOR'S COMMENT: Blair School of Music is just graduating its first class. As a new part of Vanderbilt it can be recommended for Guitar and basic solid musical training.

Vassar College

Poughkeepsie, NY 12601

Admissions: 914-437-7000

Enrollment. 2,350 undergraduates.
Application deadline. January 15.
Degrees offered. BA.
Costs. Tuition: $17,210. Room: $2,930. Board: $2,570.

• • • • • • • • • • • • • • • •

Standardized tests: SAT or ACT required and achievement tests.
Financial aid: Available. Submit the FAF.
International students: 2% of students. Canada, India, Pakistan, Sweden, Great Britain, France most represented. TOEFL required. Very limited financial aid available for foreign students.
Prominent alumna: Meryl Streep.

AUTHOR'S COMMENT: Formerly an all women's college and one of the Seven Sisters, Vassar went co-ed in the late 60's. It is recommended for Music and for Drama within a rigorous liberal arts college.

Virginia Commonwealth University

901 West Franklin Street
Richmond, VA 23284

Admissions: 804-367-1222
Dept. of Theater: 804-367-1514

Dept. of Theater Address:
922 Park Avenue, Box 2524

Enrollment. University: 21,000. Drama majors: 244.
Drama faculty. 13 full time, 3 part time.
Audition. Required for both BFA and MFA.
Degrees offered. BFA, MFA in Acting.
Costs. Tuition: In-state—$2,966; out-of-state—$8,136. Room and board: $3,532.

. . . .

Standardized tests: SAT required.
Drama facilities: 2 theaters seating 255 and 150 respectively, scene shop, costume shop, props shop, welding shop, dance studio, rehearsal and classroom spaces.

AUTHOR'S COMMENT: Recommended for Drama.

Washington University, St. Louis

1 Brookings Drive
St. Louis, MO 63130-4530

Admissions: 314-889-6000
Dance Dept.: 314-889-5858

Enrollment. University: 11,000; 5,000 undergraduates. Dance majors: 5 females.
Dance faculty. 4 full time, 4 part time.
Application deadlines. Early Decision and Early Action: December 1 and January 1. Regular Decision: January 15.
Audition. Required for placement after admission to the University.
Degree offered. BA.
Costs. Tuition and fees: $14,925. Room and board: $4,875.

. . . .

Standardized tests: SAT or ACT required. Achievement recommended.
Videotapes: Accepted. Send to the Office of Admissions which will forward them to the department for evaluation.
Dance facilities: 2 studios with sprung floors. Proscenium theater, studio theater.
Financial aid: Submit FAF by February 15.
International students: TOEFL required.
Prominent dance alumni include: Allison Chase, David Dorfman, Michael Eng, Cathy Lipowitz, Scott Lundius, Georgia Stephens.

AUTHOR'S COMMENT: Recommended for Dance.

Wayne State University

Detroit, MI 48202-3577

Admissions: 313-577-3577
Music Dept.: 313-577-1795
Theater Dept.: 313-577-3508
Dance Dept.:313-577-4273

Music Dept. Address:
5451 Cass Avenue
Theater Dept. Address:
95 West Hancock

Enrollment. University: 25,000 undergraduates; 10,000 graduate students. Drama majors: 215. Dance majors: 15–20 undergraduates. Music majors: 200 undergraduates, 50 graduate students.
Faculty. Drama: 15 full time, 1 part time. Dance: 3 full time, 5 part time. Music: 16 full time, 50 part time.
Application deadlines. Up to July 1 for fall semester; November 1 for spring semester.
Audition. Required.
Degrees offered. BA, BFA, MA, MFA in Acting. BM, MM in Music. Certificate in Church Music, Jazz. BA, BFA in Dance.
Costs. Tuition: In-state—$2,635; out-of-state—$5,853.

. . . .

Musical instruments taught: All Orchestral Instruments, Guitar, Piano, Saxophone. Also Church Music, Composition, Jazz.
Drama facilities: 4 theaters seating 1,173, 532, 245, and 138 respectively, scene shop, costume shop, props shop, welding shop, dance studio, rehearsal spaces.
Financial aid: Submit FAF. Some merit awards also available.
International students: 10% from abroad. Korea, Japan, China (PRC) most represented. TOEFL required—550 minimum.
Prominent music alumni include: Kenny Burrell, William Foster, Robert Harris, Shirley Love, George Shirley, James Tocco.

AUTHOR'S COMMENT: Recommended for graduate Drama. Also Dance, Accordion, Jazz.

Wellesley College

Wellesley, MA 02181

Admissions: 617-235-0320, ext. 2270
Drama Dept.: 617-235-0320, ext. 2029

Enrollment. College: 2,200. Drama majors: 8 women.
Drama faculty. 5 part time.
Application deadlines. Early Decision: November 1. Early Evaluation: January 1. Regular Decision: February 1.
Audition. Not required.
Degree offered. BA in Theater Studies.
Costs. Tuition and fees: $15,145. Room and board: $5,310.

. . . .

Standardized tests: SAT required. 3 achievement tests (English Composition and two others) required.
Interview: Recommended with both the Office of Admissions and Theater Studies faculty.
Videotape: Accepted. Submit to the Office of Admissions which will send it to the Department for evaluation.
Drama facilities: 1 large proscenium house, 1 experimental theater, 1 black-box theater.
Cross-registration: With MIT.

AUTHOR'S COMMENT: Recommended for undergraduate Drama.

Wesleyan University

High and Wyllis Avenues
Middletown, CT 06457-3262

Admissions: 203-344-7900
Theater Dept.: 203-347-9411, ext. 2214
Dance Dept.: 203-347-9411, ext. 2396
Music Dept.: 203-347-9411, ext. 2235

Enrollment. University: 2,700. Drama majors: 45. Dance majors: 8 females. Music majors: 45.
Faculty. Drama: 6 full time, 1 part time. Dance: 3 full time, 6 part time. Music: 15.
Application deadlines. Early Decision: November 15. Regular Decision: January 15.
Audition. Not required. Applicants must be admitted to the University.
Degrees offered. BA in General Theater. BA in Dance. BA in Music.
Costs. Tuition and fees: $15,765. Room and board: $4,845.

· · · · · · · · · · · · · · · · · ·

Standardized tests: SAT or ACT required. 3 achievement tests required, including English Composition.
Interview: Recommended.
Videotapes: Discouraged.
Facilities: 2 theaters seating 400 and 200 respectively.
Financial aid: Submit the FAF by January 15.
International students: 17% from abroad. Germany, Canada, China (PRC), England, South Africa most represented. TOEFL required.

AUTHOR'S COMMENT: Recommended for undergraduate Drama and Early Music. (Music Department is best known for Ethnomusicology.)

Westminster Choir College

Hamilton Avenue and Walnut Lane
Princeton, NJ 08540-3899

Admissions: 609-921-7144
General number: 609-921-7100

Enrollment. College: 230 undergraduates, 87 graduate students.
Music faculty. 46 full time, 22 part time.
Application deadline. Rolling.
Audition. Required and held on the campus October–July. Call for specific dates. All applicants must also take a music theory exam.
Degrees offered. BA, BM, MM.
Costs. Tuition and fees: $11,100. Room and board: $4,780.

· · · · · · · · · · · · · · · · · ·

Tapes: All performance majors must audition in person.
Musical instruments taught: Organ, Piano. Also Church Music, Voice, Choral Conducting, Accompanying.
Financial aid: FAF required. A few merit scholarships available.
International students: 11% from abroad. Korea, China (PRC), Canada, Japan, Taiwan, Trinidad most represented. TOEFL required—535 to 580 minimum. No financial aid for foreign students.
Prominent music alumni include: Adele Addison, David Agler, Daniel Beckwith, David Chalmers, Joan Lippincott.

AUTHOR'S COMMENT: There was a rumor that WCC was going out of business last year, and many who hold this college in high regard for its specialization lamented its demise. It has revived, however, with an affiliation with Rider College. The choir here is the resident chorus for the renowned Spoleto Festival, both in Charleston, SC, and in Spoleto, Italy. Highly recommended for Choral Conducting; also recommended for Church Music, Organ, and Voice.

West Virginia University

P.O. Box 6009
Morgantown, WV 26506

Admissions: 304-293-2124 or
1-800-344 WVU1
Division of Music: 304-293-4091
Division of Theater: 304-293-4022

Enrollment. University: 15,000 undergraduates; 5,000 graduate students. Music majors: 250 undergraduates, 50 graduate students. Drama majors: 104.
Faculty. Music: 39 full time, 10 part time. Drama: 14 full time.
Application deadline. Rolling admissions to July 15 but March 1 preferred.
Audition. Required. Held in Music in February and March. Music majors must also take a music theory exam.
Degrees offered. BFA, MFA in Acting. BA, BM, MM, DMA in Music.
Costs. Tuition: In-state—$1,777; out-of-state—$4,646. Room and board: $3,612.

• • • • • • • • • • • • • • • • • •

Standardized tests: SAT or ACT required.
Interview: Required as part of audition process.
Tapes: Accepted in Music.
Musical instruments taught: All Orchestral, Piano, Organ. Also Voice, Composition, Accompanying, Jazz.
Drama facilities: 3 theaters seating 1,500, 180, and 120 respectively, scene shop, costume shop, props shop, welding shop, rehearsal spaces.
Financial aid: Submit FAF and University's own form.

AUTHOR'S COMMENT: Recommended for Drama; the Music Department provides solid training.

Wheaton College

501 East College
Wheaton, IL 60187-5593

Admissions: 708-752-5005

Enrollment. College: 2,200.
Application deadlines. Early Decision: December 1. Regular Decision: February 15.
Audition. Required.
Costs. Tuition: $10,280. Room: $2,300. Board: $1,670.

• • • • • • • • • • • • • • • • • •

Standardized tests: SAT or ACT required. Achievement tests recommended.
Interview: Required and will even conduct on the telephone.
Tapes: Accepted for those who cannot audition in person.
Financial aid: File FAF by March 15.
Prominent alumni: Billy Graham, Brian Jauhiainen.

AUTHOR'S COMMENT: Wheaton is affiliated with the Evangelical Protestant Church. Recommended for Church Music.

Wichita State University

111 Jardine Hall
Wichita, KS 67208

Admissions: 316-689-3085
Dance Dept.: 316-689-3530
Music Dept.: 316-689-3500

Dance Dept. Address:
1845 N. Fairmount

Enrollment. University: 13,825 undergraduates; 2,843 graduate students. Dance majors: 2 males, 12 females. Music majors: 310 undergraduates.
Faculty. Dance: 3 full time, 3 part time. Music: 60 full time.
Application deadlines. August 1 for fall, December 1 for spring.
Audition. Not required in Dance or Music but held for special scholarships in March.
Degrees offered. BFA in Dance. BA, BM in Music.
Costs. Tuition: In-state—$1,608; out-of-state—$4,732. Room and board: $2,727.

. . . .

Interview: Required in Dance.
Videotapes: Not accepted in Dance.
Dance facilities: 3 dance studios, a main concert and informal studio stage.
Financial aid: Submit the FAF or FFS. Some merit scholarships available.
International students: 10% from abroad. Malaysia, Pakistan, Japan, Taiwan, Indonesia most represented. TOEFL required—550 minimum. No financial aid available for foreign students.

AUTHOR'S COMMENT: *Recommended for Dance (Mid-American Dance Theater), Oboe, and Violin.*

Willamette University

900 State Street
Salem, OR 97301

Admissions: 503-370-6303

Enrollment. University: 2,225; 1,500 undergraduates.
Application deadlines. Early Decision: December 15. Regular Decision: February 15.
Degrees offered. BA in Theater. BA in Music.
Costs. Tuition and fees: $10,730. Room and board: $3,750.

. . . .

Standardized tests: SAT or ACT required. Achievement tests recommended.
Interview: Recommended.
Tapes: Send cassettes or videotapes to the Office of Admissions to be referred to the department for evaluation.
Financial aid: Submit the FAF by February 15.

AUTHOR'S COMMENT: *The Willamette Theater Department has been given a mandate to revise and strengthen its program. It has lofty goals and good direction and can be recommended for undergraduate Drama. The Music Department is also strong.*

William Paterson State College

300 Pompton Road
Wayne, NJ 07470-2152

Admissions: 201-595-2125

Enrollment. College: 7,178.
Costs. Tuition: In-state—$2,466; out-of-state—$3,066.

. . . .

Financial aid: Submit FAF by May 1.

AUTHOR'S COMMENT: *Recommended for Jazz.*

Yale College of Yale University

P.O. Box 1502A, Yale Station
New Haven, CT 06520-7423

Undergraduate Admissions: 203-432-1900
Yale College Dept. of Music: 203-432-2985

Enrollment. University: 11,000; 5,180 undergraduates.
Application deadlines. Early Action: November 1. Regular Decision: December 31.
Costs. Tuition: $17,500. Room and board: $6,200.

. . . .

Standardized tests: SAT or SAT required. 3 achievement tests required.
Financial aid: Available. Based on need. File FAF by January 15.

AUTHOR'S COMMENT: Recommended in general for Music and Drama.

Yale Institute of Sacred Music

409 Prospect Street
New Haven, CT 06510

203-432-5180

Degrees offered. MM, MMA, DMA. Degrees are awarded by the Yale School of Music. Related courses are taken in the Divinity School and graduate departments.

. . . .

Performance concentrations: Organ, Choral Conducting, Composition.

AUTHOR'S COMMENT: See Yale School of Music.

Yale School of Music

Box 2104A, Yale Station
New Haven, CT 06520

Admissions: 203-432-4155

Enrollment. School of Music: 170 graduate students.
Application deadline. January 31, but the School maintains a rolling admissions cycle in several departments until mid-summer.
Audition. Required. Held in February and March on the campus and nationally. Call the Office of Admissions for the exact dates and locations. Musicianship exam also required.
Degrees offered. MM, MMA, DMA. Nondegree programs: Certificate, Artist Diploma.
Costs. Tuition: $12,100. Fees: $2,700. Room: $4,000. Board: $2,500.

. . . .

Standardized tests: GRE required of all composers, organists, conductors, and applicants to the MMA program.
Musical instruments taught: All Orchestral Instruments, all Keyboard. Also has Voice, Composition, Choral and Orchestral Conducting, Contemporary Music program, Institute of Sacred Music in conjunction with the Divinity School, Center of Studies in Music Technology, Electronic Music.
Facilities: 728-seat Sprague Hall, 2,595-seat Woolsey Hall, 200-seat Harkness Recital Hall, 100-seat Whitney Humanities Center, 100-seat Dwight Chapel, 1,600-seat Battell Chapel.
Financial aid: GAPSFAS must be filed. All financial aid packages are based on merit, need of the applicant, and need of the School.
Housing: 50% of new students receive on-campus housing.
International students: 40% to 42% from abroad. Germany, Netherlands, Spain, England, France, Korea, Japan, China, Brazil, Chile, Argentina most represented. TOEFL required—550 minimum. GAPSFAS must be filed for financial aid.

(continued on next page)

Prominent alumni include: Eliot Fisk, Albert Fuller, Ian Hobson, Sharon Isbin, Barbara Kilduff, Mitch Leigh, Joseph Polisi, Willie Ruff, Richard Stoltzman.

AUTHOR'S COMMENT: It is important to differentiate between the Department of Music of Yale and the Yale School of Music. The Yale Department is an arm of Yale College and the Graduate School of Arts and Sciences. The School of Music is a graduate professional school featuring performance and composition. Recommended for Bassoon, Clarinet, French Horn, Guitar, Harp, Harpsichord, Oboe, Percussion, Piano, Trumpet, Trombone, Tuba, and Viola. Highly recommended for Composition and Orchestral Conducting and the Institute of Sacred Music.

Yale University

School of Drama
Yale University 1903-A
New Haven, CT 06520

203-432-1507

Enrollment. School: 197.
Audition. Required.
Degrees offered. MFA in Acting, DFA, Certificate in Drama.
Costs. Tuition: $10,600. Fees: $845. Room and board: $2,670 to $3,030.

• • • • • • • • • • • • • • • • • •

Interview: Required as part of the audition.
Drama facilities: University theater, a 700-seat proscenium theater, experimental theater, scene shops, classrooms, Drama library. Yale Repertory Theater, Vernon Hall, a cabaret theater, Drama School Annex.
Financial aid: Based on need. Submit the GAPSFAS.
Prominent alumni: Paul Newman, Meryl Streep.

AUTHOR'S COMMENT: The Acting Department admits talented and intelligent students who have had some experience as actors. They receive superb conservatory actor training and have the opportunity to participate in productions at the acclaimed Yale Repertory Theater. Highly recommended for graduate Drama.

Yehudi Menuhin School

Stoke D'Abernon
Cobham, Surrey KT11 3QQ, ENGLAND

932-64739
FAX: 932-64633

• •

AUTHOR'S COMMENT: Recommended for Violin, Viola, and Violoncello.

Appendix A:
Index of Schools by State and Country

National Directory of Schools

Recommended Programs

ALABAMA	Alabama Shakespeare Festival/University of Alabama	Drama		
	University of Alabama	Drama,	Dance,	Music
ARIZONA	Arizona State University	Drama,	Dance,	Music
	University of Arizona	Drama,	Dance,	Music
CALIFORNIA	American Academy of Dramatic Arts	Drama		
	American Conservatory Theater	Drama		
	California Institute of the Arts	Drama,	Dance,	Music
	California State University, Fresno	Drama,	Dance	
	California State University, Fullerton	Drama,	Dance,	Music
	California State University, Long Beach	Drama,	Dance,	Music
	California State University, Northridge	Drama,		Music
	Chapman College		Dance	
	Los Angeles City College, Los Angeles Theater Academy	Drama		
	Mills College		Dance	
	Occidental College	Drama		
	San Diego State University	Drama,		Music
	San Francisco Conservatory			Music
	San Francisco State University	Drama,	Dance,	Music
	Scripps College	Drama,	Dance	
	Stanford University	Drama,	Dance,	Music
	University of California, Berkeley		Dance,	Music
	University of California, Davis	Drama,		Music
	University of California, Irvine	Drama,	Dance	
	University of California, Los Angeles	Drama,	Dance,	Music
	University of California, Riverside		Dance	
	University of California, San Diego	Drama,	Dance,	Music
	University of California, Santa Barbara	Drama,	Dance	
	University of San Diego/Old Globe Theater	Drama		
	University of Southern California	Drama,		Music

CONNECTICUT	Connecticut College	Drama,	Dance	
	Hartford School of Ballet		Dance	
	Hartford Conservatory of Music and Dance		Dance	
	Hartt School of Music			Music
	National Theater Institute	Drama		
	Trinity College	Drama,	Dance,	Music
	University of Connecticut, Storrs	Drama		
	Wesleyan University	Drama,		Music
	Yale Institute of Sacred Music			Music
	Yale University	Drama		
	Yale School of Music			Music
	Yale College of Yale University	Drama,		Music
COLORADO	Colorado College		Dance	
	National Theater Conservatory	Drama		
	University of Colorado, Boulder		Dance,	Music
	University of Denver			Music
	University of Northern Colorado	Drama,	Dance,	Music
DISTRICT OF COLUMBIA	American University			Music
	Catholic University	Drama,		Music
	George Washington University	Drama,	Dance	
	Howard University	Drama,		Music
DELAWARE	University of Delaware, Newark	Drama,		Music
FLORIDA	Harid Conservatory		Dance	
	Jacksonville University		Dance	
	New World School of the Arts		Dance	
	Rollins College	Drama		
	University of Miami	Drama,	Dance,	Music
	University of South Florida, Tampa	Drama,	Dance	
GEORGIA	Emory University			Music
	Spelman College			Music
	University of Georgia, Athens	Drama,		Music
HAWAII	University of Hawaii at Manoa	Drama,	Dance	
ILLINOIS	Bradley University			Music
	DePaul University	Drama,		Music
	Illinois State University	Drama,		Music
	Illinois Wesleyan University	Drama,		Music
	Northern Illinois University	Drama,	Dance,	Music
	University of Chicago			Music
	University of Illinois	Drama,		Music
	Wheaton College			Music
INDIANA	Ball State University	Drama,		Music
	Butler University	Drama,	Dance,	Music
	DePauw University			Music
	Indiana University	Drama,	Dance,	Music
	University of Evansville	Drama		
	University of Notre Dame			Music
IOWA	Coe College	Drama,		Music
	Drake University			Music
	Luther College			Music
	University of Iowa	Drama,	Dance,	Music

KANSAS	Kansas State University	Drama,	Dance,	Music
	University of Kansas, Lawrence	Drama,	Dance,	Music
	Wichita State University		Dance,	Music
LOUISIANA	Grambling State University	Drama		
	Louisiana State University			Music
	Loyola University of New Orleans	Drama,		Music
	Tulane University	Drama		
MAINE	Bates College	Drama,	Dance	
	Bowdoin College			Music
MARYLAND	Goucher College	Drama,	Dance	
	Peabody Conservatory of Music of Johns Hopkins University			Music
	Towson State University	Drama,	Dance,	Music
	University of Maryland, College Park	Drama,		Music
MASSACHUSETTS	Amherst College	Drama,	Dance,	Music
	Berklee College of Music			Music
	Boston College	Drama		
	Boston Conservatory		Dance,	Music
	Boston University	Drama,		Music
	Brandeis	Drama,		Music
	Emerson College	Drama,		Music
	Hampshire College		Dance,	Music
	Harvard-Radcliffe College			Music
	Institute for Advanced Theater Training at Harvard	Drama		
	Massachusetts Institute of Technology (MIT)			Music
	Mount Holyoke College		Dance,	Music
	New England Conservatory			Music
	Smith College	Drama,	Dance,	Music
	University of Massachusetts, Amherst	Drama,	Dance,	Music
	Wellesley College	Drama		
MICHIGAN	Central Michigan University			Music
	Michigan State University	Drama,	Dance,	Music
	University of Michigan	Drama,	Dance,	Music
	Wayne State University	Drama,	Dance,	Music
MINNESOTA	Macalester College	Drama,		Music
	Saint Olaf College		Dance,	Music
	University of Minnesota, Twin Cities	Drama,	Dance,	Music
MISSOURI	University of Missouri, Columbia			Music
	University of Missouri, Kansas City	Drama,		Music
	Washington University, St. Louis		Dance	
NEBRASKA	University of Nebraska, Lincoln	Drama,	Dance,	Music
NEW HAMPSHIRE	Dartmouth College	Drama,	Dance	
NEW JERSEY	Drew University	Drama		
	Montclair State College			Music
	Princeton Ballet School		Dance	
	Princeton University	Drama,		Music
	Rutgers University	Drama,	Dance,	Music
	Westminster Choir College			Music
	William Paterson State College			Music

NEW MEXICO	College of Santa Fe	Drama,		Music
	University of New Mexico, Albuquerque	Drama,	Dance,	Music
NEW YORK	American Academy of Dramatic Arts	Drama		
	American Musical and Dramatic Academy	Drama,		Music
	Bard College		Dance	
	Barnard College of Columbia University	Drama,	Dance,	Music
	Brooklyn College of the City University of New York			Music
	Circle in the Square Theater School	Drama		
	City College of the City University of New York		Dance,	Music
	City University of New York-Graduate Center			Music
	Columbia College of Columbia University	Drama,		Music
	Cornell University	Drama,	Dance	
	CSC Rep-The Actors' Conservatory	Drama		
	Eastman School of Music			Music
	Hobart and William Smith Colleges		Dance	
	Hofstra University	Drama,	Dance	
	Hunter College of the City University of New York		Dance	
	Ithaca College	Drama,		Music
	Joffrey II Dancers		Dance	
	Juilliard	Drama,	Dance,	Music
	Long Island University/C. W. Post Campus	Drama,		Music
	Manhattan School of Music			Music
	Manhattanville College			Music
	Mannes College of Music			Music
	Marymount Manhattan College	Drama		
	National Shakespeare Conservatory	Drama		
	New School for Social Research			Music
	New York University			Music
	Queens College of the City College of New York			Music
	Sarah Lawrence College	Drama,	Dance,	Music
	Skidmore College	Drama,	Dance	
	State University of New York at Brockport		Dance	
	State University of New York at Buffalo	Drama,		Music
	State University of New York at Fredonia	Drama,		Music
	State University of New York at New Paltz			Music
	State University of New York at Potsdam		Dance,	Music
	State University of New York at Purchase	Drama,	Dance,	Music
	State University of New York at Stony Brook	Drama,		Music
	Studio of the Actors' Space	Drama		
	Syracuse University	Drama,		Music
	Vassar College	Drama,		Music
NORTH CAROLINA	Duke University	Drama,		Music
	North Carolina School of the Arts	Drama,	Dance,	Music
	University of North Carolina at Chapel Hill	Drama		
	University of North Carolina, Greensboro	Drama,	Dance	
OHIO	Baldwin-Wallace College			Music
	Case Western Reserve University	Drama,	Dance,	Music
	Cleveland Institute of Music			Music
	College of Wooster			Music
	Denison University		Dance	
	Kent State University	Drama,	Dance,	Music
	Kenyon College	Drama		

	Miami University			Music
	Oberlin College and Oberlin Conservatory			Music
	Ohio State University	Drama,	Dance,	Music
	Ohio University	Drama,	Dance	
	Ohio Wesleyan University			Music
	University of Akron		Dance	
	University of Cincinnati	Drama,	Dance,	Music
OREGON	University of Oregon, Eugene		Dance,	Music
	Willamette University	Drama,		Music
PENNSYLVANIA	Carnegie Mellon University	Drama,		Music
	Curtis Institute of Music			Music
	Dickinson College	Drama		
	Muhlenberg College	Drama		
	Swarthmore College	Drama		
	Temple University	Drama,	Dance,	Music
	University of Pennsylvania			Music
	University of Pittsburgh	Drama		
	University of the Arts	Drama,	Dance,	Music
RHODE ISLAND	Brown University	Drama		
	University of Rhode Island	Drama		
SOUTH CAROLINA	College of Charleston	Drama		
	University of South Carolina, Columbia	Drama		
TENNESSEE	Vanderbilt University			Music
TEXAS	Baylor University	Drama,		Music
	Rice University, Shepard School of Music			Music
	Southern Methodist University	Drama,	Dance,	Music
	Texas Christian University		Dance,	Music
	University of Houston			Music
	University of North Texas, Denton			Music
	University of Texas, Austin	Drama,	Dance,	Music
UTAH	Brigham Young University	Drama,	Dance,	Music
	University of Utah	Drama,	Dance,	Music
VERMONT	Bennington College	Drama,	Dance,	Music
	Middlebury College	Drama		
VIRGINIA	George Mason University		Dance	
	James Madison University	Drama		
	Shenandoah College and Conservatory	Drama,	Dance,	Music
	University of Virginia, Charlottesville	Drama		
	Virginia Commonwealth University	Drama		
WASHINGTON	University of Washington	Drama,	Dance,	Music
WEST VIRGINIA	West Virginia University	Drama,		Music
WISCONSIN	Lawrence University Conservatory of Music			Music
	University of Wisconsin	Drama,		Music
	University of Wisconsin, Milwaukee	Drama,		Music

International Directory of Schools

Recommended Programs

AUSTRIA	*Hochschule für Musik und Darstellende Kunst, Wien* . .		Music
BELGIUM	*Brussels Conservatory*		Music
CANADA	*Royal Conservatory of Music*		Music
ENGLAND	*Guildhall School of Music and Drama*	Drama,	Music
	London Academy of Performing Arts	Drama	
	London Contemporary Dance School	Dance	
	Royal Academy of Music		Music
	Royal College of Music		Music
	Royal Northern College of Music		Music
	Yehudi Menuhin School		Music
FINLAND	*Sibelius Academy of Music*		Music
FRANCE	*IRCOM Center*		Music
	Paris Conservatoire		Music
GERMANY	*Hochschule, Cologne*		Music
	Hochschule, Freiburg		Music
	Hochschule für Musik, Berlin		Music
	Hochschule für Musik und Theater, Hannover		Music
	Hochschule, Heidelberg		Music
JAPAN	*Toho Gakuen School of Music*		Music
NETHERLANDS	*Koninklijk Conservatorium voor Musiek en Dans* . . .		Music
NORWAY	*Conservatory in Oslo*		Music
SWITZERLAND	*Schola Cantorum, Basel*		Music

Appendix B:
Alternative Careers for Performing Arts Majors

If you decide that you do not want to pursue being a performer full-time, or if you find yourself needing to supplement your income, there are many related activities in the performing arts which you might want to consider. One recent study reported that only 10 to 15% of all performance majors earn their main income after graduation from performing. The others combine performance activities with other occupations. Following are some examples of alternative career choices for performing arts majors:

For Dancers

Dance majors might also explore any of these career areas:

- □ choreographer
- □ teacher
- □ director
- □ dance or movement therapist
- □ director of a dance school or studio
- □ Labanotation expert
- □ model
- □ cast member at a theme park or in industrial shows

For Drama Majors

Drama students develop observation, communication, analytical, and critical thinking skills which can be transferred to a variety of other career fields.

In addition to the obvious Broadway, film, and television roles, actors should expand their job search to include Off-Off Broadway, dinner theater, children's theater, theme parks, cruise lines, summer stock, industrial shows (sometimes called business theater), cabarets, and improvisation groups.

Many actors find jobs in sales, including telemarketing and commercial voice-overs. Some join the business side of the entertainment industry and become personal managers, casting directors, agents, or publicists. Some work on the "other side" for a time, observe the common mistakes made by other actors, and then go back on the audition mill hoping to benefit from their business experience. Other actors turn to the more technical side of the theater, finding jobs in management, directing, design, teaching, and many other possibilities.

For Music Majors

People trained as musicians may be found in every career from insurance, to medicine, to college administration. With technological advancements, the nature of the music business is constantly changing. Some other related careers include:

- music copyist (Be sure that you know some of the new computer programs such as Finale.)
- arranger/orchestrator
- music critic
- recording engineer
- music therapist
- instrument builder
- music publishing
- piano tuning
- music manager
- music librarian
- music administrator: schools, orchestras, choruses
- radio announcer
- box office manager
- development director
- teacher: elementary, secondary, college, or private instruction

If you decide to teach, be sure that you have piano proficiency for accompanying choruses or other ensembles. If you plan to teach in a public school, you will need certification, so be certain that you take the appropriate courses.

Publications to Explore

There are some very useful publications for help in finding careers in the arts. These include:

ArtSearch. Theatre Communications Group, Inc., 355 Lexington Avenue, New York, NY 10017; 212-697-5230. This listing includes vacancies in administrative positions and other jobs in theater, opera, and other arts.

Back Stage, The Performing Arts Weekly. 330 West 42nd Street, New York, NY 10036; 212-947-0020. In addition to timely articles, this weekly newspaper has valuable information about classes to take, rehearsal space, photographers, and open calls for auditions. It's especially useful for actors, cabaret and other entertainers, music theater people, and some dancers.

Chronicle of Higher Education. Subscription Service, P.O. Box 1955, Marion, OH 43306. A weekly publication listing faculty and administrative positions in all areas of higher education.

College Music Society. Music Faculty Vacancy List. 202 West Spruce Street, Missoula, MT 59802. 406-721-9616. An excellent source for college music teaching positions in the U.S. You must subscribe to receive this.

Dansource. P.O. Box 15038, Dallas, TX 75201. 214-520-7419. A national dance network for dancers, teachers, and choreographers, which also has a computerized information service. They will send out copies of your curriculum vitae, photo, and, if provided, a videotape, to dance companies. You must pay a nominal fee to belong to this service.

Das Orchester. Postfach 3540, Weihergarten, 1-11, D-6500 Mainz, Germany. A listing of vacancies in European orchestras, mainly German.

International Musician. Paramount Building, Suite 600, 1501 Broadway, New York, NY 10036. 212-869-1330. Musicians' Union newspaper. Lists vacancies in orchestras and includes occasional announcements about teaching positions, graduate assistantships, and scholarships.

Musical America. 825 7th Avenue, New York, NY 10019. 800-446-3536. A reliable source of information about competitions, festivals, schools, managers, and much more. Expensive to own, but available at libraries and in most music stores.

National Arts Jobbank. 207 Shelby Street, Suite 200, Santa Fe, NM 87501. A bi-monthly publication listing arts employment, mainly administrative.

Opera America. 633 E Street NW, Washington, DC 20004. 202-347-9262. Publishes a newsletter with mostly administrative job openings.

THEatre JOBLIST: The National Employment Service Billboard for Theater Arts. THEatre SERVICE, P.O. Box 15282, Evansville, IN 47716. 812-479-2281. This listing of jobs is a service affiliated with the Association for Theatre in Higher Education (ATHE).

Theatre Times. The Alliance of Resident Theatres/New York, 131 Varick Street, Room 904, New York, NY 10013. 212-989-5257. Contains interesting articles about New York's Off-Broadway theater scene and also lists current job openings.

(Special thanks to the Juilliard Placement Office for help with this listing.)

If you are looking for internships in New York, *ArtSearch* often has listings, particularly for dance and music. You might also write to the Music Managements listed in *Musical America.* In Drama, you might try contacting the Alliance of Resident Theatres/NY (A.R.T./NY) at 325 Spring Street, #315, New York, NY 10013 or A.I.P. at 311 West 43rd Street, New York, NY 10036.

For any of these and other publications, you should become aware of the specialized book stores, which will usually ship internationally. Some of these include:

Applause Theatre Books
211 West 71st Street
New York, NY 10023
212-496-7511

Drama Bookshop
723 Seventh Avenue (at West 48th Street)
2nd floor
New York, NY 10019
212-944-0595

Juilliard School Bookstore
60 Lincoln Center Plaza
New York, NY 10023
212-799-5000

Patelson's Music Book Shop
West 56th Street and 7th Avenue
New York, NY 10019

Appendix C:
A Checklist for Parents

The college admissions period can be especially stressful in parent-child relations. Here are some pointers for parents of talented young people seeking admission to the best performing arts programs.

Parents should NOT:

☐ call or write an admissions office for the child

☐ fill out the application

☐ write or overly edit the application essay

☐ nag about deadlines

☐ dictate college choices

☐ ask too many questions during the campus tour (Let your child take the lead.)

☐ delay filing Financial Aid information

☐ attend the interview

☐ sit in on the audition

☐ serve as accompanist at the audition

☐ offer too much advice about training

☐ try to bribe or otherwise influence an admissions officer or teacher

Parents SHOULD:

☐ be supportive

☐ help to organize college visits

☐ go along on college visits, but use the time to speak with Financial Aid officers and Placement or Career Counseling Offices

☐ submit all Financial Aid documents promptly

☐ help set up any practice auditions the child may decide to do at home or in a local church or auditorium

☐ arrange to videotape practice auditions

□ rent, buy, or borrow the best instrument within your means for your child to play

□ understand if a child's performing schedule conflicts with family obligations

□ help a child deal with the tension and frustration of trying to excel in both academic and artistic endeavors

Appendix D:
Bibliography

Books for Performing Artists

Anderson, Jack. *Ballet and Modern Dance: A Concise History, 2nd edition.* Princeton, N.J.: Princeton Book Company/Dance Horizons, 1991. An informative and valuable overview of the entire range of Western dance by the *New York Times* dance critic.

Arnheim, Daniel, D. *Dance Injuries: Their Prevention and Care, Third Edition.* Princeton, N.J.: Princeton Book Company/Dance Horizons, 1991. A comprehensive guide to the care and prevention of dance injuries.

Caine, Michael. *Acting in Film.* New York: Applause Theatre Book Publications, 1989.

Charles, Jill, editor; *Directory of Theatre Training Programs II*, 2nd edition. Dorset, VT: Theatre Directories, 1989.

College Music Society. *Directory of Dance Faculties in Colleges and Universities, U.S. and Canada.* Missoula, MT: CMS Publications: (P.O. Box 8208, Missoula, MT 59807—406-728-2002), 1991.

College Music Society. *Directory of Music Faculties in Colleges and Universities, U.S. and Canada.* Missoula, MT: CMS Publications, 1990-1992. Includes 29,663 music faculty listings in 1,745 institutions. An invaluable resource for finding where the teacher with whom you wish to study is on the faculty.

College Music Society. *Directory of Theatre Faculties in Colleges and Universities, U.S. and Canada.* Missoula, MT: CMS Publications, 1990-1992.

Directory of Canadian Orchestras and Youth Orchestras. Toronto: Association of Canadian Orchestras (56 The Esplanade, Suite 311, Toronto, Canada M5E1A7—416-366-8834), 1991. A helpful guide containing everything from listings of orchestras to managers, PR directors, music schools in Canada, government granting departments, etc.

Eaker, Sherry, ed. *The Back Stage Handbook for Performing Artists.* New York: Billboard Publications, Inc., 1990. This is an extremely useful book, particularly for actors. It has a great deal of valuable practical advice and includes advertising for teachers, photographers, agents, etc.

Fleming, Shirley, ed. *Musical America.* New York: Musical America Publications. Annual. Although this publication is expensive, it is the ultimate sourcebook for many people in the music trade and also has a dance section. It has useful listings of everything from managers, to international and national summer festivals, performance halls, competitions, youth symphonies, etc. If you do not buy it, be sure to become acquainted with it at your library or guidance office.

Golovkina, Sophia. *Lessons in Classical Dance for Teachers and Students.* Princeton, N.J.: Princeton Book Company/Dance Horizons, 1991. A syllabus of Russian Classical ballet at the advanced level as taught at the Bolshoi Ballet School. The author was a leading dancer with the Bolshoi Ballet Company for twenty-seven years and has been the director and teacher of the advanced students for thirty years.

Hagen, Uta. *A Challenge for the Actor.* New York: Charles Scribner's Sons, 1991. Uta Hagen, a leading stage actress, is also one of the country's most influential acting teachers. She has taught since 1947 at the HB Studio in Greenwich Village, founded by her husband, the late Herbert Berghof. In this book Ms. Hagen presents her views on performing, her technique, and her exercises.

Handel's National Directory for the Performing Arts. 3626 N. Hall, Suite 404, Dallas, TX 75219. 1-800-423-7215.

Lawson, William James, ed. *Stern's Performing Arts Directory.* New York, DM, Inc. Annual. This publication is similar in some regards to *Musical America* but has a much more extensive listing in dance. Another excellent resource, but also may be used at your local library or guidance office.

Pearl, Kenny. *Dance Life Workbooks.* Toronto: Transition Centre (66 Charles Street East, 2nd floor, Toronto, Ontario M4Y 2R3, Canada), 1990.

Reid, Wendy, and Christopher Wealt. *Auditions Are Just the Beginning: A Career Guide to Orchestras.* Toronto: Association of Canadian Orchestras, 1991. A concise booklet, written by an orchestra administrator and the co-principal bassoonist of the Toronto Symphony and Visiting Associate Professor at Eastman School of Music, about auditioning and keeping a job in an orchestra.

Sidimus, Joysanne. *Exchanges: Life After Dance.* Toronto: Press of Terpsichore, Ltd., 1987. Twenty-one former dancers tell their own stories ranging from training to career transitions.

Uscher, Nancy. *The Schirmer Guide to Schools of Music and Conservatories Throughout the World.* New York: Schirmer Books, 1988. A comprehensive reference of university-level music institutions throughout the world, including conservatories from Beijing to Burma, and New Zealand to New York.

Whitehill, Angela, and William Noble. *The Young Professional's Book of Ballet.* Princeton, N.J.: Princeton Book Company/Dance Horizons, 1990. Valuable advice about how to make the transition from student to professional dancer.

Whitehill, Angela. *The Parents' Book of Ballet.* Colorado Springs: Merriweather Publishing, 1988. A helpful book for parents about the pros and cons of the ballet process.

Selected Periodicals in the Performing Arts

Dance

Dance Magazine, 33 West 60th Street, New York, NY 10023. 212-245-9050.

Dance Notation Journal, 33 West 21st Street, New York, NY 10010. 212-807-7899.

American Dance, American Dance Guild. 31 West 21st Street, 3rd floor, New York, NY 10010.

Ballet International, Readers' Service. P.O. Box 250 125, D-5000, Köln, GERMANY.

Dance and Dancers, 214 Panther House, 38 Mount Pleasant, London Wc1X OAP, ENGLAND.

Dance, Box 2089, Knoxville, IA 50197-2089.

Dance Chronicle, Marcel Dekker, Inc., 270 Madison Avenue, New York, NY 10016.

Drama

American Theater, 355 Lexington Avenue, New York, NY 10017.

Asian Theater Journal, University of Hawaii Press, Journals Dept., 2840 Kolowalu Street, Honolulu, HI 96822.

Back Stage Publications, Inc., BPI Communications, Inc., 330 West 42nd Street, New York, NY 10036. 212-947-0020.

New Theater Quarterly, Journals Department, 40 West 20th Street, New York, NY 10011-4211.

Plays and Players, Subscriptions, Media House, 55 Lower Addiscombe Road, Croydon, Surrey, CRO 6PQ, ENGLAND.

Theater, 222 York Street, New Haven, CT 06520.

Variety, 154 West 46th Street, New York, NY 10036. 212-869-5700.

Music

Brass Players (in general)

The Brass Player, New York Brass Conference for Scholarships, 315 West 53rd Street, New York, NY 10019. 212-581-1480.

Brass Bulletin, P.O. 10-12478-1, SWITZERLAND.

Composition

Computer Music Journal, Journals Department, MIT Press, 28 Carleton Street, Cambridge, MA 02142.

Chamber Music

Chamber Music Magazine, Chamber Music America, 545 8th Avenue, 9th floor, New York, NY 10018. 212-244-2772.

Choral Conducting

American Choral Review, American Choral Foundation, 2111 Sansom Street, Philadelphia, PA 19103.

Double Bass
International Society of Bassists, c/o School of Music, Northwestern University, Evanston, IL 60208.

Flute
Flute Talk, Instrumentalist Publishing Company, 200 Northfield Road, Northfield, IL 60093.

Flutists Quarterly, National Flute Association, Inc., Phyllis Pemberton, P.O. Box 800598, Santa Clara, CA 91380-0597.

French Horn
Horn Call, International Horn Society, c/o Department of Music, Southeastern Oklahoma State University, Durant, OK 74701.

Guitar
Acoustic Guitar, P.O. Box 767, San Anselmo, CA 94979-0767.

Guitar Review, Albert Augustine, LTD., 40 West 25th Street, New York, NY 10010.

Harp
American Harp Journal, American Harp Society, P.O. Box 38334, Los Angeles, CA 90038.

Jazz
Coda (Journal of Jazz and Improvised Music), 33 Winton Lodge, Imperial Ave., Westcliff-on-Sea, Essex, ENGLAND.

Down Beat, 180 West Park Avenue, Elmhurst, IL 60126.

Jazz Journal International, 113-117 Farringdon Road, London EC1R 3BT, UNITED KINGDOM.

Billboard, P.O. Box 2071 Mahopec, NY 10541-2071. 914-628-7771.

Oboe
Double Reed, International Double Reed Society, c/o Lowry Riggins, Executive Secretary-Treasurer, 626 Lakeshore Drive, Munroe, LA 71203-4032.

Orchestral Conductors
American Symphony Orchestra League Bulletin, American Symphony Orchestra League, 777 14th Street, N.W., Washington, DC 20005. 202-628-0099. FAX: 202-783-7228.

Conductors Guild, P.O. Box 3361, West Chester, PA 19381.

Orchestral Instruments (in general)
Das Orchester, Postfach 3540, Weihergarten, 1-11, D-6500, Mainz, GERMANY.

The Instrumentalist, 200 Northfield Road, Northfield, IL 60093.

Orchestra/Orchestres Canada, Association of Canadian Orchestras, 56 The Esplanade, Suite 311, Toronto, Ontario, CANADA M5E 1A7.

Symphony Magazine, American Symphony Orchestra League, 777 14th Street, N.W., Washington, DC 20005. 202-628-0099. FAX: 202-783-7228.

Organ
The American Organist, 475 Riverside Drive, Suite 1260, New York, NY 10025.

Diapason, Scranton Gillette Communications, Inc., 380 East Northwest Highway, Des Plaines, IL 60016-2282.

Organ Yearbook, c/o Vitgerverij Frits, Knuf, B.V. Box 720, 4116, ZJ, Buren, NETHERLANDS.

Tracker, The Organ Historical Society, Inc., P.O. Box 26811, Richmond, VA 23261.

Percussion
Modern Drummer, P.O. Box 480, Mt. Morris, IL 61054-0480.

Percussive Notes Magazine, c/o Percussive Arts Society (PAS), 214 West Main Street, Box 697, Urbana, IL 61801-0697.

IDRS, 4663 Glenway Avenue, Cincinnati, OH 95238. 513-251-1829.

Piano
Clavier, 200 Northfield Road, Northfield, IL 60093. 312-446-5000.

Keyboard Classics, 352 Evelyn Street, Paramus, NJ 07652. 201-967-9495.

Keyboard Magazine, GPI Publications, 20085 Stevens Creek, Cupertino, CA 95014.

Piano Guild Notes, National Guild of Piano Teachers, Box 1807, Austin, TX 78767.

Piano Journal, 28 Emperor's Gate, London SW7 4HS, ENGLAND.

Piano Quarterly, String Letter Press, Publishers, P.O. Box 767, San Anselmo, CA 94979-0767.

Rock
Rolling Stone, 1-800-837-9944.

Strings (in general)
American String Teacher, American String Teacher Association, 4020 McEwen, Suite 10E, Dallas, TX 75244.

The Strad, Hainault Road, Little Heath, Rumford, Essex, RM6 5NP, ENGLAND.

Strings, P.O. Box 767, San Anselmo, CA 94960.

Trombone
International Trombone Association Journal, Box 5336, Denton, TX 76203.

Trumpet
International Trumpet Guild Journal, Box 50183, Columbia, SC 29250.

Viola
Journal of the American Viola Society, c/o BYU Music, Harris Fine Arts Center, Provo, UT 84602.

Violexchange, P.O. Box 6046, Ann Arbor, MI 48106.

Violin
Violin Society of America Journal, c/o Edward C. Campbell, Chimneys Violin Shop, 614 Lerew Road, Boiling Springs, PA.

Voice

Central Opera Service, Metropolitan Opera, Lincoln Center, New York, NY 10023.

The NATS Journal, National Association of Teachers of Singing, 250 West 57th Street, Suite 2129, New York, NY 10107.

Opera, c/o Opera, D5B, 2a Sopwith Crescent, Hurrican Way, Shotgate, Wickford, Essex SS118YU, ENGLAND.

Opera Canada, Foundation for Coast to Coast Opera Publication, 366 Adelaide Street, East, #433, Toronto, Ontario, CANADA, M5A 3X9.

Opera Journal, National Opera Association, c/o Marajean Marvin, Executive Secretary, School of Music, Ohio State University, Columbus, OH 43210.

Opera Monthly, P.O. Box 816, Madison Square Station, New York, NY 10159.

Opera News, Metropolitan Opera Guild, 1865 Broadway, New York, NY 10023. 212-582-7500.

Opera Quarterly, Journals Division, Duke University Press, 6697 College Station, Durham, NC 27708.

Vocals, 142 N. Milpitas Blvd., Suite 280, Milpitas, CA 95035-4400.

Some Helpful Organizations

American Symphony Orchestra League (ASOL)
777 14th Street, N.W.
Washington, DC 20005
202-628-0099. FAX: 202-783-7228

Association for Theatre in Higher Education (ATHE)
c/o THEatre SERVICE
P.O. Box 15282
Evansville, IN 47716

Independent Educational Consultants Association (IECA)
Cove Road
P.O. Box 125
Forestdale, MA 02644
508-477-2127

Miller Institute for the Performing Artist
St. Luke's/Roosevelt Hospital
West 59th Street and 10th Avenue
New York, NY 10019
A specialized clinic for treating health-related problems of performing artists.

Music Educators National Conference (MENC)
1902 Association Drive
Reston, VA 22091

National Arts Medicine Center
National Rehabilitation Hospital
Bethesda, MD
202-877-1623
A clinic devoted to occupation-related medical problems
of performers and visual artists.

National Association of College Admissions Counselors (NACAC)
1800 Diagonal Road, Suite 430
Alexandria, VA 22314
703-836-2222

National Association of Schools of Music (NASM)
11250 Roger Bacon Drive, Suite 21
Reston, VA 22090
703-437-0700

National Association of Schools of Theater (NAST)
11250 Roger Bacon Drive, Suite 21
Reston, VA 22090
703-437-0700

National Foundation for Advancement in the Arts (NFAA) (ARTS)
3915 Biscayne Boulevard
Miami, FL 33137
305-573-0490

Network of Visual and Performing Arts Schools
3421 M Street, #218, N.W.
Washington, DC 20007
202-966-2216. FAX: 202-966-2283

University/Resident Theater Association (U/RTA)
1560 Broadway, Suite 903
New York, NY 10036
212-221-1130